PLATO'S DEFENCE OF POETRY

This is the first full-scale treatment of this topic in English since J. A. Stewart's *The Myths of Plato* in 1905. It advances the highly original thesis that Plato offers a defence of poetry in response to his own famous challenge: The poets, he says, are ignorant, irrational, and irresponsible, and are to be expelled from the Republic unless someone can come forward and defend them. Plato acknowledges that he is not insensible to the charms of poetry, and he is himself a poet of the very first rank, as Shelley says of him in *A Defence of Poetry*.

Earlier commentators have generally agreed that the myths are Plato's poetry, but have interpreted the myths in a number of wildly inconsistent ways. They have been seen as an impoverished primitive philosophy superseded by the clearer insights of later thought – usually Hegelian. Or they are taken to be quasi-Romantic insights looking forward to mystical revelations – usually Christian. Or they may be read literally and abominated (like Popper) or loved (like Findlay). Or, finally, they may be ignored as lacking the rigour of dialectic – which has been their fate in contemporary analytical philosophy.

This study restores them to their proper place in the Platonic corpus by showing their methodological relationship to the dialectic and their substantive connection to Plato's theories of knowledge, ethics, politics, and aesthetics. There is a 'weak' defence: poetry is indispensable because it makes accessible and palatable truths demonstrable by reason where the audience is in no mood to be lectured or preached at – yet poetry must be, as all readers of Plato agree, harnessed to the service of truth and socially desirable values.

The 'strong' defence, however, is the most novel and important feature of this study. It argues that the myths embody the indemonstrable axioms of Plato's system; that Plato was aware that in every system, including mathematics, certain fundamental presuppositions necessarily remain unproven; and that, rather than assert these presuppositions dogmatically, Plato expresses them poetically so as to capture their emotional persuasiveness while confirming their inconclusiveness. The myths themselves are interpreted afresh in light of these claims.

Julius A. Elias is Professor of Philosophy and Dean of the College of Liberal Arts and Sciences at the University of Connecticut. He was born in England and, after some years with the United Nations in Europe after the Second World War, he moved to the USA in 1952. He taught philosophy at the City College of New York from 1960 to 1974.

He is the author of a critical edition of Schiller's *Naive and Sentimental Poetry* and *On the Sublime*, and of numerous articles in professional journals, and was managing editor of the *Journal of the History of Ideas* from 1969 to 1974.

PLATO'S DEFENCE OF POETRY

Julius A. Elias

University of Connecticut

ὡς ξύνισμέν γε ἡμῖν
αὐτοῖς κηλουμένοις ὑπ'αὐτῆς

Rep. X, 607C

State University of New York Press
Albany

First published in the U.S.A. by
State University of New York Press, Albany

For information, address State University
of New York Press, State University Plaza,
Albany, New York 12246

Library of Congress Cataloging in Publication Data
Elias, Julius A.
Plato's defence of poetry.
Bibliography: p.
Includes index
1. Plato. 2. Poetry—History and criticism.
3. Mythology, Greek—History and criticism. I. Title
B398.P6E44   1984   184   83–9137
ISBN 0–87395–806–3

For Wilma, in loving memory

Contents

Preface

One ventures with great diffidence into the vast field of Platonic scholarship, never quite certain that all the debts owed to one's predecessors can ever be fully acknowledged. Wholly original ideas are improbable and must be suspect just to the extent they are original. Still, the myths have been neglected, and it remains my hope that, new or not, what is said here is worth saying. Among my most obvious benefactors has been the Research Foundation of the University of Connecticut for assistance during the writing and toward the publication of this book. I am no less grateful to the Warden and Fellows of St Antony's College for their hospitality during a sabbatical spent in Oxford at their invitation, and for the friendship of the Warden, Mr Raymond Carr and, among the Fellows, Messrs Archie Brown and Malcolm Deas, who went out of their way to make me feel at home in a climate highly stimulating to productive work. The editors of the *Journal of the History of Philosophy* graciously gave permission for the incorporation, in slightly amended form, of an article of mine published in that journal. The commentary of an anonymous reader for the St Antony's/Macmillan editorial board was invaluable, saving me from infelicity of expression, defects of argument, and outright error. The same must be said of some of my colleagues past and present: Professor H. S. Thayer of the City University of New York, and Professors Joel Kupperman and A. S. McGrade of the University of Connecticut. Steve McGrade supplied me with many pages of notes, and no one could have had a more knowledgeable or more sympathetic critic.

I dedicate this book to the memory of my wife Wilma who sustained me throughout its preparation, but who did not live to see it in print.

Storrs, Conn.   J. A. E.

1 The Attack

Lying is a privilege of poets because they have not yet reached the level on which truth and error are discernible. (Santayana)[1]

I

The title of this book is supposed to be provocative. Everybody knows that Plato attacked poetry, or at any rate the poets, and undertook to eject them from the Republic (X, 607C) unless someone could show that they could be defended after all, in which case they might be let in again. The argument apparently rests on a fairly simple-minded version of the imitation theory, but to make poetry Platonically acceptable it would not suffice to demolish this: we shall have to meet the more sophisticated objections to inspiration, intuition, enthusiasm (being filled with the god), ecstasy (being outside or beside oneself) as well.

Any number of Plato's readers and commentators have been bowled over by the severity and, on occasion, the bitterness of the attack,[2] and many of them have taken the denunciations at face value. Most commentators, however, have been even more impressed with the manifest genius of Plato himself as poet, and have tried one way or another to reconcile the apparent contradiction. A common way of approaching the problem is to say that Plato was attacking *bad* poetry[3] and irresponsible poets, but that he left room for good poetry, namely his own.[4] Such an argument is acceptable as far as it goes (I shall make use of it myself), but it is rarely well articulated within the framework of Plato's metaphysical, epistemological, and political/ethical theories.

The challenge to defend poetry has been accepted by many, notably by Aristotle (and not alone in the *Poetics* – the *Politics* and *Rhetoric* include important parts of the defence), by Sir Philip Sydney, and by Shelley. What I will try to show is that Plato's writings contain and imply an acknowledgement of the indispensability of poetry; that his writings contain examples of good poetry – the myths; and that to the extent that we cannot find an explicit defence I will try to show that Plato had

1

sound, if distasteful, reasons for suppressing what must have been perfectly clear to him – that where the logic of discourse is incapable of definitive demonstration, we fall back of necessity on poetry to persuade. However, and I place the greatest stress on this, we need not rely on a dichotomy between reason and emotion, logos and mythos, to make the case. Poetry is going to be as rational as it *can* be, and reason as passionate as it *may*.

I shall first address myself to the attack on the poets and other liars, fakes, and madmen, like the rhetors, sophists, and demagogues. The material is familiar enough, but I want to pick out of it certain features that will be useful as the argument unfolds. We should be able, as we go along, to dismiss the literal-minded acceptance of the imitation theory. Mimesis, as Auerbach, Cassirer, and Verdenius have shown, scarcely meant one-to-one representationalism even to the ordinary Greek, let alone to a mind as subtle as Plato's. We can likewise dispense with those features of argument, like fallacy, amphiboly, or paradox, that were standard elements of an advanced rhetoric as found, for example, in Isocrates and Lysias. It is reasonable to assume that even though the untutored might be gulled by such devices, rival rhetors would keep each other honest, or at least cancel out each other's errors.

While poetry, in the sense generally understood in modern times, is central in the attack, it cannot be separated from the comparable criticisms brought against a whole series of targets by Plato. These include artists in media other than words: musicians, sculptors, and architects, for example. The Greek words *poiesis* and *mousike* bore, as is well known, a much wider application than is currently the case. *Poiesis* simply means 'making', and its connotations ranged over all the productive arts and crafts.[5] The distinction we generally draw between the work of art as a product of imagination, say, and the output of the craftsman as primarily attributable to technical skill in handling materials and tools, was scarcely meaningful to the Greeks, and certainly not in the sense we understand these terms. Similarly, *mousike* included but was not confined to music; it encompassed euphony in poetry and rhythm in gymnastics, and it is not too much to say in any discussion of Plato that the spiritual harmony of a soul in balance is likewise an example of *mousike*.[6] Tredennick quite properly translates *mousiken poiein* as 'practising the arts' in *Phaedo* 61A. Socrates is there telling of a dream in which Apollo bade him make music while in jail, and 'philosophy is the greatest of the arts (*mousikes*).' We need not follow out in greater detail here the history and changing import of these terms, but do need to bear in mind that they must be understood in their widest sense.

Only thus can we see how alien to Plato's mode of thought it would be to separate the attack on the poets from his treatment of artists of every sort. And beyond that we can see the overall coherence of his arguments against the sophists, the rhetoricians, the politicians, demagogues ('people-leaders'); indeed, against all capable of influencing public opinion in the market-place, courts, and legislature, as well as shaping that sensibility which more subtly underlies common beliefs unconsciously held and so produces an ethos, the social bond of ethical and religious convictions that unify a society. For the moment I leave out of account questions which will have to be raised later about the desirability of such uniform beliefs – there are, after all, many possible alternative constellations of belief, including the cherishing of pluralism rather than homogeneity – but we must first make Plato's aims clear if we are to understand them, let alone bring criticism to bear. Thus the attack on poetry takes in his concerns as a religious reformer along with all those already mentioned. It is surely the moral focus that is central in Plato's thought and we should be reversing the natural order of his programme if we took the attack on poetry narrowly conceived as the point of departure. It is with his moral vision that we must primarily engage ourselves, and then it becomes clear why all those, including the poets, who shape and reinforce morality, are the objects of his analysis and criticism.

Plato begins his attack at a deceptively simple level: it is indispensable, given his strategy, that he discredit his opponents for the popular ear. The tyranny of the poets over the culture of his contemporaries can hardly be exaggerated. It has often been remarked that Homer (and to a lesser degree, Hesiod) was a combination of Bible, Shakespeare, and Milton to the Athenians; as the old lady said of Hamlet, they are full of quotations. This popular wisdom enshrined much that Plato needed to make use of himself for reasons spanning the limitations of his readers as well as the unavowed limitations of his own theory. But the inadequacies of that popular wisdom had first to be displayed; this was undertaken by Socrates in the early and middle dialogues, and by Plato in the middle and late ones. Later on I shall hazard a partial solution to the Socratic problem based on two fairly distinct methodologies; for the moment I shall not need to rely on any particular distinction between what might be Socrates' own voice and what Plato is saying on his own.

The passages most frequently cited to document the attack on the arts are those dealing with the misrepresentation of the gods as spiteful, venal, and immoral; pictorial representation as thrice removed from reality; actors and bards depicting effeminate and cowardly personages whom, by dint of repetition, they come to resemble; sad music that makes you sad while martial music fits you for the draft; walls that are curved inward so as to look straight; statues that have large heads and small feet so as to offset foreshortening – they will *look* right, but will not *be* right. The objections to these things are soundly grounded in Plato's metaphysics and epistemology.

The fundamental objection is outlined in the methodology of the *Phaedo* and *Republic*: a limited and conditional reliance on phenomena is perfectly permissible and inductive generalizations from empirical data are not without merit in Plato. He is no mere a priorist, and I will have more to say later on the quite significant role of phenomena in his epistemology. But the probabilistic and hypothetical character of such generalizations certainly is stressed. In particular, their hypothetical character is something to be overcome by showing them to be theorems deduced with logical certainty from 'higher hypotheses'. A series of such hypotheses of increasing generality and comprehensiveness ultimately converges on the One, if Plato's programme is to be realized. The poets (in all artistic media), like the sophists and the rhetors, do not rise from the surface of appearance; they offer reflected images of appearance, not a penetrating illumination of reality – in Yeats' striking phrase, they are a mirror, not a lamp.

The religious objections, still closely related to these, stress the irresponsibility of the poets who represent the gods and the moral order of the universe in an offensive manner. The gods indulge in all seven deadly sins with an enviable immunity to hangovers, guilty consciences, and venereal disease. The only deplorable aspect of human vice, for these poets, is thus made by the poets to seem the inevitable retribution at the hands of jealous gods. To sin without fear of punishment is the concept of divinity beyond which the poets cannot see. Yet no more abominable blasphemy is conceivable to a religious reformer like Socrates, intent on a vision of the conduct of the gods fit to furnish appropriate exemplars for men to imitate. Besides these superficially moral considerations some deeper motives are at work (of which more than a hint is found, for example, in Aeschylus' *Prometheus Bound*). The anarchy of the poets' version of Olympus is intolerable: the gods go their several ways, shifting alliances and allegiances resting on power and opportunity rather than upon reason; their very number reflects the incoherence and fragmentation of the divine order as represented by the poets. Yet behind the gods and their arbitrary powers stand other shadowy figures to whom the gods themselves are subordinate in ways the poets, including Homer, can hardly make out. The mysterious goddesses Nemesis, Moira (Destiny), Anangke (Necessity) redress the imbalance of the justice both of gods and men. A fundamental metaphor runs through Plato's arguments: the gods must be made rational, but that entails their subordination to a unitary principle. While the Hebrew insistence upon monotheism has other origins, in Greek thought it emerges more slowly, but unquestionably in association with the notion of a rational unity, as much embodied in mathematics and science as in morality and teleology.

The poets are also mad. Mere irrationality, the inability to 'give an account' of what they mean, is made an object of ridicule in the *Ion*, *Phaedrus*, *Protagoras*, and *Republic* (and elsewhere). But a deeply-rooted tradition conspires with Plato's own recognition of the power of inspired poetry (and of his own power to write it) to compel a much more ambiguous treatment of divine madness. For Plato something like a divine visitation is indispensable, by all means, but the human science is hermeneutics – deciphering the oracle. Plato's *theoria* demands the ultimate rationality of the world – episteme is knowledge in the sense that its propositions are logically demonstrable and binding on all rational minds. But the poets, who merely transmit the message of the Muse and garble it in transmission, disclaim responsibility for the outcome, and are a mixed blessing. How to discredit them without discrediting the source of their wisdom is a problem Plato has difficulty resolving, as *Phaedrus* 244 shows. This conjunction of the human and the divine is central to his thought – how to sift rational insights, intuitions, inspirations, from their mad simulacra.

II

That the poets themselves cannot be counted on to do it is a theme Plato pursues in several dialogues. The texts are fairly familiar and do not call for very detailed examination here. The principal themes are, as already noted, the ignorance, incoherence, irresponsibility, and madness of the poets.

In the *Ion* Socrates engages in conversation with the newly returned winner of the Asclepius festival at Epidaurus. Ion is a rhapsode, with special expertise, or so he claims, in Homer, though he is simply bored by Hesiod and the other poets. Socrates amuses himself at Ion's expense, compelling him to agree that he must know something about the other poets, despite his disclaimer, if only to know in what respects Homer surpasses them. It soon becomes plain that, apart from a certain flair for declamation, Ion knows very little about anything. He is carried away, as well he might be, by a lyric effusion from Socrates (533D–535A) declaimed in rhapsodic style, much the way Plato elsewhere displays his astonishing capacity for pastiche. (Consider the speeches in the style of Lysias in the *Phaedrus* and of Aristophanes and Eryximachus in the *Symposium*, among other examples.) The image is of poetic power like that of the magnet which not only attracts iron rings, but makes the rings themselves magnetic. So the poets, deriving some magical power by inspiration from the gods, pass it on through their interpreters to the listener. The interpreters are ecstatic (535B), beside themselves as they become what they portray: vengeful Odysseus or pitiful Andromache. And that magnetic force by which emotion is transmitted[7] passes down to the spectators, who are themselves seized by it.

But it derives from the gods by whom the poets are 'possessed' (536B). Socrates suggests that when the gods speak by the mouths of the poets, the latter have no idea what these utterances mean. Ion rejects this, insisting that the poet (and the rhapsode) do know what they are talking about. But bit by bit he is made to concede that he is not a doctor, a pilot, or a fisherman, although Homer writes with apparent authority on all these métiers. At the last he balks, before every claim to specialized knowledge slips away, insisting that he shares Homer's knowledge of generalship, and so is a general. Socrates gives him a final chance: either the artist deceives by speaking from ignorance and so is unjust, or he is touched with divinity and blameless. Ion choose divinity, and on this sweet-natured note the dialogue ends. Almost anybody could better defend poetry than Ion; we must look elsewhere for weightier arguments and worthier opponents.

An interesting interpolation in the *Protagoras* gives the celebrated sophist an opportunity to offer a most unconvincing exegesis of a poem of Simonides. His interpretation rests on an apparent contradiction between being good and becoming so (339BD); since the sophists proclaimed the interpretation of poetry as being among the most important skills they had to teach, Socrates affects to have been sent reeling, as by a punch from a boxer. He sees no contradiction, and recovers from the blow in time to offer a vastly superior interpretation of the poem (342A–347A). There are important hints of the metaphysical import of the difference between being and becoming in Plato's thought, but they scarcely rise to the surface in this dialogue. These passages are notable, however, for an instance of Socrates' conviction that no man willingly does evil (345E), and for the observation with which Socrates returns the dialogue to its principal theme:

No one can interrogate poets about what they say, and most often when they are introduced into the discussion some say the poet's meaning is one thing and some another, for the topic is one on which nobody can produce a conclusive argument. (347E) (trans. Guthrie)

This statement recurs in several places, and so must be given weight as it stands. But Findlay is not far off in suggesting[8] that the discussion is deliberately offhand for the discomfiture of Protagoras; although he surely goes too far in finding Simonides' lines 'asinine'. Thayer[9] is sounder in taking Simonides to be a principal target in the discussion of poetry in the *Republic*, where the poet is as defective an imitator as the painter of a bed. (Cf. *Rep.* X, 600E.)

It is in the *Republic* that Polemarchus falls heir to the defence of Simonides' definition of justice as 'rendering what is due', a definition that Socrates finds 'riddling' as most of the poets' utterances (I, 332B). We shall find many more such references, but there is no point in reciting them all. What is of greater importance is the argument from imitation; when we have looked at this we can turn to problems posed by the adverse moral effects of poetry.

It is Plato's claim that the poets (and the sophists, etc.) are imitators of the appearances of things. Instead of tracing these appearances back to their underlying reality, the artists offer a still more misleading copy of the already sufficiently imperfect appearances. Those appearances may be, as in the most celebrated example – the painting of the bed thrice removed from reality (X, 596B ff.) – physical objects depicted visually by the painter, but no distinction is drawn among the imitations of non-physical objects: traits of character, actions, or motives, nor among the several media through which such imitations can be expressed: words, pictures, music, sculpture, etc. Classical Greek is a language especially rich in visual imagery, as Partee and Thayer[10] have both pointed out, and this tends to reinforce Plato's arguments treating the several arts in the same way as a commonplace of Greek thought. But there is an aspect of Plato's approach touching words in particular that makes the simplest version of the 'thrice removed' argument rather more complex.

As descriptive labels words constitute a kind of veil over objects making them a degree more obscure than even the physical objects to which they are applied. To the extent that language includes descriptive terms, these are derived from common usage and agreement (and as such are suspect) in a manner described in the nominalist tradition in later philosophy. Even when a word denotes a class of fairly simple objects, say 'beds', that denotation is at the mercy of future experience which must change the meaning of the word in accordance with whatever new experience may bring. This is very far removed from even the most elementary understanding of the forms or ideas; by these Plato is seeking to convey an essence, an incorrigible definition from which empirical experience can itself be inferred and, if necessary, corrected. Ordinary language, but especially the language of the poets, if not fixed on that ideal vision, remains rooted in the senses and carries us still further away from the real. Among the implications of this position, to which we shall have to return later, is the foundation of Plato's mistrust of written language and of his deliberate avoidance of a vocabulary of fixed meanings, as opposed, say, to Aristotle who supplies a glossary of his technical terminology in Book Delta of the *Metaphysics*.

But it is the moral defects of poetry that are at the centre of the attack. Not everything is immoral: Adeimantus finds passages from Hesiod and Homer in which justice is praised (*Rep.* II, 363 ff.), but against this must be set the flatly immoral accounts of the gods (II, 377E–III, 392C. Cf. *Laws* II, 672B, X, 886C, XII, 941B; also *Euthyph.* 6A). Some of these hardly call for subtle exegesis: the castration of Cronos by Uranus, Hera bound and Haephestus lamed by Zeus, to say nothing of the innumerable battles and deceits waged on Olympus. Like much of earlier religious belief in most cultures these are anthropomorphic projections such that an earthly battle between warring tribes has its precise heavenly counterpart between patron gods. But Socrates' conception of godhead is far in advance of this, and indeed so far in advance of his day that it is no wonder that a chief accusation at his trial was that he taught of gods other than those of the State.

The offence runs deeper than this crude level. The poets lend credence to the view that the gods can be bribed by sacrifice and swayed by entreaty, and that priests can bring about any desired intervention by spells and incantations (II, 364BC). Men's destinies, moreover, are a result of a random drawing by Zeus from two urns at his side, one filled with blessings, the other with evil gifts (*Iliad* 24, 527 ff., quoted at *Rep.* II, 379D). It is bad enough that evil is ascribed to the gods, but worse surely is the irrationality of the chance draw that makes distributive justice insusceptible of achievement, even in principle. Besides Homer, passages and allusions are found by Socrates in Hesiod, Musaeus, Pindar, and in the utterances ascribed to Orpheus. Aeschylus is held to account (II, 380A) as furnishing an example of the doom visited by the gods on whole dynasties (for which, however, a healing madness spoken of at *Phaedrus* 244DE may supply a purgation[11]), thus nullifying individual merit and responsibility; punishment, therefore, is seen as the exercise of brute and mindless power, not as salutary and redemptive.

From yet another perspective, more important for Plato than its unpromising initial statement suggests, reference is made to the many incidents in which the gods change their shape (*Rep.* II, 380D–381D: Zeus as bull, swan, or shower of gold, for example). These surpass the deceits already noted, but the basis of the objection is not, as Popper[12] repeatedly insists, that Plato is opposed to change of any kind as intrinsically evil. Rather it is to the idea that the gods change. The image to be pursued must be consistent with the status of the unchanging forms: if the ideas are eternal essences, sets of fixed defining properties, then *a fortiori* the gods who create the forms are still less liable to change. Popper has entirely misconstrued these passages. Change in the world of appearances is desirable if in the direction of ever-increasing approximation to the ideal; it is clearly undesirable if the other way, and obviously if change were postulated in the already perfect.

I note in passing here, because we shall have occasion to return to these passages later, Plato's disparagement of immoderate grief and mirth in gods or men. The vice chiefly lies in promotion of a false attitude towards death (III, 386 ff.), false because of the inconsistency with belief in the immortality of the soul, but especially false in this context because an intemperate grief reinforces a craven attachment to staying alive at all costs. And from another but related aspect, exaggerated grief, along with mirth, anger, lust, greed, and other examples of excessive emotion, are condemned because they cloud rational judgement. Yet all these are ascribed to the gods by the poets.

The argument against imitation that follows is of the greatest importance. The context in which it appears rests on an assumption introduced earlier (II, 377B): children are impressionable and likely to be shaped by the stories they are told, and so we cannot be casual about those influences. Now (III, 395B), it is urged, if one is habituated to the imitation of false models, they become second nature and one becomes what one has merely imitated (cf. *Laws* II, 656B). As in the case of change, it is not imitation itself that is condemned, but the imitation of bad example. Nonetheless, certain forms of imitation are at least relatively undesirable: tragedy, as compared with narrative, for example (III, 393C). The reason for this is not particularly convincing: narrative is merely descriptive without that shift into impersonation that entails the risk of excessive empathy with the character represented. Narrative might be said to be a 'cooler' medium with much less chance of emotional entanglement from which one could not easily disengage. So profound is Plato's mistrust of emotion in contrast to reason that he cannot allow for the 'willing suspension of disbelief' as a feature of aesthetic experience; and so carries the argument virtually to the point where he must mistrust the right kinds of emotion and imitation. He seems closer to Hamlet's query of the Player King: 'What's he to Hecuba, or Hecuba to him?' The actors are thus classed with the rhapsodes among those vulnerable to the dangers of aestheticism. Those dangers are only derivative as concerns performing artists, but are primary for the poets and imitators in other media.

The celebrated discussion of the artist at a third remove from reality (*Rep.* X, 595A ff.) more easily fits the painters, if only because of the representation of physical objects, but is certainly intended to fit all artists. If we presuppose a single form of any class of objects (of abstract ideas) of which particular instances are merely the copies, deriving their reality from their relationship to (or 'participation' in) the forms, then we are to take the physical bed, for example, as an instance of the form bed, sometimes referred to as bedness, to indicate that it possesses all the essential properties of a bed. The specific instance of a bed such as we buy in a furniture store will be at best an approximation to 'bedness' possessing some of those properties (many if it is a good bed), but not all, and having other properties irrelevant to bedness. On a functional analysis (to which Plato is sometimes given) one can illustrate this by saying that a bed must be long enough and wide enough to support the sleeper, and rigid enough so that he does not fall through it. But a particular bed is exactly 30 inches by 74 inches and made of brass, say. There is nothing in the essence that demands this, and so in these respects and in many others which could be pursued indefinitely, the physical bed is at best an approximation of bedness, and so at a second remove from the reality that bedness embodies.

Now comes the painter: Van Gogh, say, painting his bedroom at Arles. All sorts of distortions are now added to the defects of the physical bed. Two dimensions instead of three, a play of colour that has other aims than the accurate depiction of the bed; it certainly cannot be slept on, and so forth. It is Plato's contention that the painted bed (as well as the poet's descriptions) is at a third remove from reality (X, 597C). This rests on Glaucon's incautious agreement that the bed copied by the painter is the physical bed made by the craftsman (598A). If that be allowed to stand then the argument has some merit. If the craftsman's bed is already imperfect, then it is not entirely unreasonable to allow that an imperfect copy of that would be even less perfect. It does not, however, follow with the rigour we are entitled to expect from Plato at this point (we are about to expel the artists from the Republic!). The imperfection of the artist's bed relative to the craftsman's might cancel out the imperfections of the latter, for example; but that is playing with words (the status of logical contradictories, to be technical). At the very least the two beds might be equally imperfect, and so share second-class honours.

If this approach misses Plato's real point, Plato is himself in part to blame – he wants the argument to be taken literally at this superficial level: ' . . . if he were a good painter, by exhibiting at a distance his picture of a carpenter he would deceive children and foolish men, and make them believe it to be a real carpenter' (598C). If we are to make sense of this we shall have to dig somewhat deeper. What is at issue is the extent to which the copy of bedness rests on knowledge of the form. In the case of the craftsman that knowledge may develop over some period of time, by a process of trial and error, largely in terms of adequacy of function. Plato ascribes to the craftsman insights we might be more inclined to see as those of the designer who stands to the craftsman as the architect stands to the builder. That is, a theoretical grasp of bedness that goes beyond the mere functioning of a bed as such to encompass the bed as, say, part of a style of living. The painter of the bed is held to be innocent of all this.

The counterclaim on behalf of the artists which does not appear to have occurred to Plato, or perhaps he was merely being disingenuous, is that it is the form itself they attempt to copy, not the physical copy of it. Aristotle's *Poetics*, which may well be considered the first defence of poetry offered in response to Plato's challenge, contains an important argument along these lines. 'Poetry', he says, 'is more universal than history'. Poetry seeks to crystallize the essence of some recurrent situation affecting all human beings, stripping it of the fortuitous circumstances surrounding some particular instance of it. This is close enough to be a response to Plato's view, without committing Aristotle to a theory of forms, to which indeed he does not want to be committed. A rival terminology addressing the same question is found in Plotinus; this stresses the role of nature (*physis*) as contrasted with art (ifice). In the *Enneads* (V, viii, 1)[13] it is nature herself working through the artist as agent by which nature perfects herself. Shakespeare says the same thing, three times over, in a brief passage in *The Winter's Tale*:

Yet nature is made better by no mean
But nature makes that mean; so over that art,
Which you say adds to nature, is an art

That nature makes. . . .
                              This is an art
Which does mend nature – change it rather; but
The art itself is nature. (IV, iv, 89–92, 95–97)

But Plato's objection still stands, even if we make every allowance for those products of art of which it could be claimed persuasively that by these means nature perfects herself. It cannot be claimed of many works of art which are plainly pernicious in their effect; nor of artists who far from investing their works with some ideal content ground them instead on self-indulgence, partisanship, or outright falsehood. Even when they escape these charges, others remain: there is a madness that overtakes them in the form of a possible divine inspiration (*Phaedrus* 245A). That has still to be interpreted, false inspiration (*Laws* IV, 719C) sifted from the true (*Laws* III, 682A), and in this the rhapsodes and poets are entirely unreliable (cf. also *Rep.* X, 600CE; *Apol.* 22C; *Prot.* 347E; *Meno* 99D), as we have seen. To the extent then that the painters, like the poets, are imitators of imitations, they will also have to be banished from the Republic (X, 595A). Indeed, wherever the work of craftsman-artist is rooted in sense, it caters to the lower parts of the soul; this applies to optical illusions (X, 602C), to equal magnitudes that appear unequal if seen at different distances, and to things seeming 'concave or convex'. These latter allusions are rather more obscure, but in all probability refer to foreshortening in monumental sculpture, and to the practice (entasis) of making the sides of large buildings slightly concave to offset the appearance of convexity if they were built precisely straight. *Sophist* 235E–236A[14] explicitly refers to distortions to offset foreshortening in sculpture, but I find no other reference to those in architecture. These rather flatfooted objections are dismaying; they are advanced with no suggestion of irony and are evidently intended to be taken literally as well as seriously.

Even more blunt are passages in the second and seventh books of the *Laws* which repeat the programme of the *Republic*, but take a much more stringent view of the criteria for art, as is indeed true of the *Laws* (the 'second-best Republic') generally, compared with the earlier writings. Most of the references below are to Book II, but several are to the discussion in Book VII of education, and other scattered references to *mousike* in its broad meaning. Thus, while some of the observations are directed to music, or to tragedy in particular, the argument is aimed at the role of the arts in society as a whole. Their task is to do good (661D), to educate taste (659CD), to compel, if necessary (660A) the production of art in accordance with settled canons (656CE; cf. VII, 811BC), as is said to have been the case in Egypt for 10 000 years. Judgments of taste cannot be left to children or mere popularity (658E–659C) but to sound judges of age and experience (this is repeated at VII, 802B). The penalty is to be 'little short of death' (662B) for those representing the wicked as happy: on the contrary, children 'while they are young and tender' are to hear only 'noble doctrines' (664B). What is emphasized throughout is the correctness of judgment based on sound knowledge (669AB); and the obverse of these affirmative criteria is a rigid censorship (VII, 801B, 817D, VIII, 829D) of which there was little mention in the *Republic* (cf. III, 401B). One's depression deepens on advancing into this formidable treatise: 'But the verse of composers who are in their own persons men of worth, held in public honor as authors of noble deeds, may be sung, even though it have no real musical quality' (VIII, 829D).

III

It might be wise now to step back from these texts before moving on to Plato's treatment of music proper. It is too easy to become lost in details of an attack on poetry so apparently extreme as to appear fanatical to the modern reader. One major reason for this is the shift toward lyric poetry in most Western cultures, certainly since the Augustans; what it displaced is a bardic tradition intimately connected with religion: ritual, myth, cosmogony, the divine genealogy of heroes and ruling houses. The Greeks had a significant body of lyric poetry, of course, but Plato had little interest in it (save as it falls under the criticisms of music) because it cannot run foul of his epistemological and moral criteria in the portentous fashion that applies to the poetry that shaped the religious sensibility of his day. Plato wrote his own poetry in the myths – what they say and why they are cast in the form he has chosen is what this book is mainly about – but he drew on a tradition more familiar to his first readers than to us. Some consideration must therefore be given to the meaning of the classical myths to his contemporaries.

The general context is, of course religious and social. The cults of the gods were active, though the old fervour had broken down in the face of weakened political stability and the propagation of a materialistic and relativistic viewpoint. Whether this is to be accounted an advantage or a drawback it is hard to say, but the Athenians were a good deal more sophisticated than their neighbours to the north and southwest.

Religion still played an important role, not merely in the festivals, but also in the everyday life of the citizens; and its status was reflected in the social importance of the priests and attendants in the temples. At least a nominal adherence to the official beliefs was demanded of the citizens, and not the least of the charges against Socrates was that he 'does not believe in the gods of the state, but has other new divinities of his own' (*Apology* 24B).

For this charge to have been possible at all other than as a legal quibble was a result of the changed atmosphere under the restored democracy in regard to religion. In the attempt to bring back old and trusted values there was no discrimination between Socrates' attack on the poets' representation of the gods as immoral, and the very real assault upon the values of religion by the Sophists. Socrates was opposed to both these positions; nonetheless in the then prevailing political atmosphere his rejection of a literal interpretation of popular beliefs in the powers and spheres of influence of the gods was taken as plausible grounds for prosecution. Where religion achieves the status of a formalized institution in the structure of society (one of Plato's own aims), nobody can assault it with impunity.

Now in the Greek world, as we have already noted, the Homeric and other legends of the gods were as current as the Bible is, or was, in our own. References, by means of quotations, to incidents in the legends had the effect of the pointing up analogies with everyday situations in a way that presupposed a common heritage of tradition and belief. The ease with which Socrates quotes from all the standard poets in the course of the dialogues is never remarked on as something extraordinary; nor would the provision, several times repeated in the discussions of education, for children to learn a great deal of poetry by heart have excited any notice as a novelty. This familiarity with the myths, and with their moral significance, where they possessed any, would not, however, be any guide to the degree of acceptance of the myths as historical accounts of the deeds of superhuman beings.

In many cases the association of gods or early heroes with given places, allegedly of their birth, death, or as the location of some great deed, was exploited in the establishment of some local cult, or in the attribution of divine origin in the genealogy of some prominent family. Thus Plato himself came of a family reputedly descended from Apollo. The origins of such attributions would be less obvious than, say, the dedication of a shrine at some rocky and wave-tossed coast to Poseidon. History, geography, genealogy, and politics all played their part in this aspect of the manipulation of quasi-religious myths. Nevertheless, there is no doubt that, as in societies in every age, a great many Athenians were fundamentalists who accepted the myths, together with the accretion of superstition accumulated about them, as facts, not merely not to be questioned, but preferably not to be thought about either.

The reason for this is to be found in the relation of myth to the rituals performed to honour or, more to the point, to appease the gods. Jane Harrison, in *Themis*, points out:

> . . . a *mythos* to the Greeks was primarily just a thing spoken, uttered by the *mouth*. Its antithesis or rather correlative is the thing done, enacted – The primary meaning of myth in religion is just the same as in early literature; it is the spoken correlative of the acted rite. (p. 328)[15]

Most anthropologists and other students of the early myths, like Malinowski, Lord Raglan, and Robert Graves, agree with this analysis, and we may certainly accept it as applying to a stage in Greek history which by the time of the fifth and fourth centuries Athens had already left far behind.

Another view, nominally opposed to this, but not calling for detailed discussion here, is advanced by Nilsson:

> Some modern anthropologists blame classical scholars for not noticing the use of myths as ritual texts or their social importance. This proves only the anthropologists' ignorance of Greek myths and of their characteristic peculiarities. It is no less wrong to judge Greek myths by the standard of certain primitive peoples than it is to judge the myths of primitive peoples by Greek standards, as was done earlier. We have some few scanty remains of Greek ritual texts; myths are hardly referred to in them. At the festivals of the gods myths were chanted; but they were poetical not liturgical, compositions. A myth rarely affected ritual.[16]

But even if we follow Graves' view, taking myth as the relic of decayed ritual, we may say that by Plato's time both ritual and myth had long since lost their peculiar urgency and direct appeal *vis-à-vis* real gods wielding real power and had taken on a symbolic force in a more social framework.

The object of myth 'is not at first to give a reason', Miss Harrison continues, 'that notion is part of the old rationalist fallacy which saw in primitive man the leisured and eager inquirer bent on research.[17] By the time of Plato, philosophy had had leisure for inquiry, and the early power of a correctly executed ritual to allay the wrath of gods and the fears of mortals had waned. What I am suggesting was left was an atrophied and institutionalized state religion capable of commanding the devotion of the fervent as well as the respect of *les gens bien pensants*. The latter would, for example, include the majority, in all probability, of those citizens who were Socrates' judges.

In seeking to evaluate the significance of the classical myths to Plato's contemporaries there are two dangers at least which must be avoided. The first would be to imagine that they would have the same attitude as is attributed by most anthropologists, as we have seen, to primitive societies. Athenian society was not primitive, and its investigations into natural forces, particularly its studies in astronomy and mathematics, make wholly inadmissible the idea that magic and ritual could command the literal acceptance often found in primitive societies as a direct means of influencing natural events. We shall have occasion to note later that besides the predominantly moral reasons Plato had for recasting the classical myths, he did not hesitate to change them in accordance with the latest scientific discoveries. Against this must be weighed the extent, inextricably entangled among political and other motives, to which Socrates' condemnation must be attributed to his offending the religious sensibilities of his judges. We must be cautious about predicating some instant when rational enlightenment suddenly succeeded benighted superstition.

The second danger is to impose our own attitudes toward myth upon the Athenians, taking the view, say, of an enlightened churchman to argue that, however excessively ritual may become overlaid with purely formal elements, at the core of them, implicitly recognized in one degree or another by all, is a mystery and a truth of the kind that finds a profound response in communicants. It is indeed just that formal element that gives an appropriate solemnity to such rituals as the purgation of grief or guilt, as in the wake or confessional. Spirit may call to spirit across the centuries and cultures, but we cannot be certain to what degree we, albeit unconsciously, may distort a remote intention into something idiomatic to our understanding.

Despite the dangers inherent in this second position, it is something like this that I should like to attribute to the Athenians. The historical parallel would not be with our own day, but closer to the strains within the Church of England in the nineteenth century, as described in Butler's novels or in the plays of Bernard Shaw. The analogy is not with the pitched battles between science and religion; rather it is with the attempts within the church to come to terms with the new scientific findings without abandoning the moral ascendancy of doctrine. In support of this view I will adduce the internal evidence of the Platonic myths. Taking these cautions into account, we may assume that Plato's myths were written in such a way as to be recognizable and acceptable to the Athenians as accounts of the acts and motives of the gods, and that they would not affront any current notions of seemly worship in the eyes of the guardians of public morality. On this assumption we may infer something about the significance that the classical myths had for the Athenians.

For Plato's attack upon the poets to have had a meaningful target we must presuppose a rather complex situation. We can simplify it by leaving out of account for the moment Plato's antipathy towards the Sophists, the inheritors of the poets' side in the war with the philosophers. Also we must leave out of the discussion the role played by the Sophists in making the young man with political ambitions fluent in public piety. Finally, we must defer consideration of the somewhat artificial function of state religion in the *Republic* and *Laws*.

What is left, if our previous assumptions are correct, is an attitude towards the classical myths that tolerated some divergence of belief concerning the balance between a literal and a figurative understanding of them. There is a continuum of possible attitudes towards this balance, ranging from scepticism to dogmatic acceptance. Between these, however, we may note that with increased control of the natural environment based on scientific knowledge and critical philosophical theorizing, the value of myth, while still to be appreciated for its special functions (into which we have yet to inquire), is found in an ever-increasing multiplicity of symbolic meanings. The less sophisticated the belief, the more transparent the acceptance of ritual as a direct means of influencing the environment; but as belief becomes more sophisticated the meaning of myth shifts to vacate territory claimed by science, without however surrendering metaphysical, moral, and religious realms. The form of Plato's myths is unmistakably like that of the classical myths, and claims credence on that ground alone; for their content, one need not be aware of the effort self-consciously employed to ensure that nothing in them should be inconsistent with the rest of Plato's teachings in order to see that they fulfil that other criterion of myth, that it be capable of being all things to all men.

It seems to me, then, that from Plato's myths we can infer something about the attitude of his contemporaries towards the classical myths; in particular that there was recognition of their symbolic form and content, and that this was a function of the individual's sophistication. Further, although it was politically safer to affect an unquestioning conformity to the official beliefs, some divergence from them was tolerated.

IV

None of the claims advanced by Plato in the realm of art can be appreciated unless we grasp how central a role the arts played in social life in his day. In *Art as Experience* Dewey speaks of the arts generally, and of the drama in particular as a 'civic commemoration' among the Greeks, and denounces what he calls 'museum art' – art separately shut off from the vital concerns of everyday living and thought; these terms vividly capture the atmosphere we must breathe if we are to see the point of the intensity and high moral purpose of Plato's discussions. Quantitatively at least, it is fair to say that the art of our own day is dominated by criteria considered by Plato, acknowledged to have some limited relevance, but mostly rejected by him as destructive of what is of genuine value to individual and society. Thus while I propose to deal with his treatment of music in this section, there is a context which must be given first.

Among the elements of aesthetic discussion then as now are: the way in which the art work gives pleasure, serves our need of relaxation and recreation, is 'escapist' in its aims and effects, is to be evaluated by autonomous criteria after the manner of 'art for art's sake'. None of these is dismissed out of hand, but is treated in a manner consonant with Plato's wider objectives. He does not deny, for example, that art gives pleasure; on the contrary, he affirms that it should. Some simple pleasures, like children's play, are harmless and, as it were, morally neutral. But pleasure, as he has argued more generally in the *Philebus*, could not be a primary determinant, because evil men take pleasure in evil things, and so, leaving the harmless pleasures to one side (provided they are not overdone!), what must first be considered is the worth and propriety of whatever we take pleasure in. In the *Laws* (II, 655D), which takes a strong view of everything, to treat pleasure as the basis of goodness in music is 'blasphemy'.

What makes the discussion of music difficult is not just the broad meaning of *mousike* already noted. Even where some of its elements, narrowly construed, are considered – melody, rhythm, harmony, counterpoint – the implications are often drawn from and spill over into, the other arts and, indeed, the spiritual realm generally, which is served by the arts as gymnastics serves the body (*Laws* II, 673A). Yet all this is entirely idiomatic, precisely because Plato, as is similarly true of other writers of antiquity, does not make the divisive distinctions between art and life, art and nature, art and society, that we tend to do. Thus, to take another and most important example, it has sometimes been said that Greek drama is a *Gesamtkunstwerk* of which we have only the libretto. The poetry was chanted, not spoken; the choral odes were sung; strophe and antistrophe were accompanied by a dance-like march between and about the pillars on each side of the stage: to say nothing of the lesser-known aspects of setting and scenic design. Homer did not recite his poetry — "e smote 'is bloomin' lyre'; yet the music was subordinate to the word, rather like the stage works of Monteverdi, or pre-Gluck opera generally. Plato insists (*Rep.* III. 398D, 400D, and elsewhere) on this subordination: the cadences of speech, largely determined by meaning, determine the rhythm of music, and so invest music with meaning.

That, of course, is the essence of the problem of music for Plato. If music cannot be attached to words or to numbers (the two principal approaches he takes) it collapses into subjective lyricism of the most undisciplined kind. A third approach, musical forms hallowed by tradition, is chiefly found in the Second and Seventh Books of the *Laws*; we need to consider what he says there before turning to more rational validations of music. If it can be represented that musical forms were fixed, preferably by the gods, in remotest antiquity, then innovations and departures from them would be acts of blasphemy. He offers the historically dubious example of Egypt, where he says the musical forms (and those of the other arts) were laid down 10 000 years ago (*Laws* II, 656E, VII, 799A, E); these ancient melodies were ascribed to Isis (II, 657B). In Book III (700A–701B) he transfers this claim to ancient Attica where, he says, the old music was governed by rules applied to the nature of the gods and their festivals to which those forms were dedicated: hymns, laments, dithyrambs, and the like. Hallowed by tradition and fixity of ritual these forms were unchangeable and beyond all vulnerability to popular acclaim or preference for something different. Innovation was impermissible (II, 656E), an aim earlier addressed at *Republic* IV, 424B, but here conveniently sanctified by the divine origins of the forms. Not much of this is very reliable as history, since the Egyptian dynasties were notorious for erasing the records of their predecessors; however it is true to say that in the rigidly structured society of ancient Egypt the arts were subordinated to religion, were codified and mummified (though certainly not 10 000 years before Plato), and that the priests claimed a divine sanction for all their ritualized doings; it should be added that, while much is known from Egyptian artifacts of religion, writing, and the visual arts, very little is known about their music. Why Plato has argued as he does has very little to do with history, and his target presently appears.

It is that new poets appeared, 'possessed by a frantic and unhallowed lust for pleasure' (*Laws* III, 700D) and mixed up the old forms. The sole criteria governing this anarchy were the self-indulgence of the artists and the applause of the mob, the latter soon coming to dominate the former as the artists saw profit in pandering to the lowest common denominator of popular taste. Thus, far from being edifying, the task of the artists being to educate and improve the people, the rules were overthrown, and the audience educated the artists in their own vulgar preferences (*Laws* II, 659C). But it is 'inevitable that a man should grow like whatever he enjoys, whether good or bad' (II, 656B), yet judgement of what is good in art is now delivered up to children and to popular acclaim, instead of being left to the best judges, those educated in wisdom (II, 658E and *Rep.* III, 402BC), who will of course be very old men (II, 659D), the old Plato (Athenian Stranger) assures his ageing interlocutors. Tradition has failed (unless it can be revived), and so we turn to the rational foundations of art.

It is impossible to overstate the force of Plato's convictions concerning the arts and their importance in the institutions of society, their centrality in education, and their capacity to shape and discipline attitudes. They pose an insoluble dilemma for him: like Love in Diotima's account in the *Symposium* they are midway between heaven and earth, between reason and emotion, between mind and sense. Yet if the majority of people on his view lead lives dominated by appetite and emotion it will be by these means that they can be reached. He is no more opposed to emotion than he is opposed to art; it is bad emotion and bad art he seeks to remove from the republic (*Rep.* III, 401BC, 411B, 424D; *Laws* II, 655B, 656B; *Philebus* 62C) because men come to resemble the models they imitate. Not all the senses are to be treated in the same way; it was a commonplace of Greek and later thought that sight and hearing were privileged above touch, taste, and smell (cf. *Hippias Major* 298B), presumably because the latter require direct contact with the object sensed, while sight and hearing operate at a distance. Thus while the arts are rooted in sense, their appeal is to the higher senses and their effect is on the soul, beginning no doubt at its lowest levels of appetite and emotion, but reaching upward to the higher parts. Similarly there will be baser emotions and nobler ones, and we need assurance in all these areas that appeal will be made to the proper level.

Part of our problem is to identify what kind of music has Plato's approval and which kinds are condemned, and why. The texts tell us something, particularly the account of the modes in Book III of the *Republic*; and some inferences may be drawn from scattered remarks about the flute and cithara. But such reconstructions of early Greek music as have been possible for modern scholarship necessarily leave serious gaps in our knowledge.[18] There was, for example, no reliable system of notation and, even had there been, much by way of popular music and the more ephemeral kinds of ballads and songs might never have been written down. What we do have, while it remains speculative, is fairly monotonous and can hardly account for Plato's agitation. It resembles to some degree plainsong or Gregorian chant, mostly monophonic, that is, only a single line of melody attached to the words of some narrative or liturgical piece, with pitch held within a narrow compass, and with both pitch and rhythm largely determined by the sense of the words. This description is consistent with Plato's brief account of the Dorian mode (*Rep*. III, 399A): it is steadfast, consonant with the brave man's speech (400A) and, along with the Phrygian mode, is endorsed by Plato as evocative of the emotions proper to society. The Phrygian mode is military (399C), probably in four-four time, as may be inferred from his approval of iambic rhythms, while dactyls and trochees are suspect (400BC). While children love to leap about and frolic, these more sober chants and marches, with their accompanying grave dance-steps and words, make plausible the continued activity of old men who will still dance and sing, according to the *Laws* II, 654A ff. Only the simplest instruments – lyre and cithara are approved for this purpose (*Rep*. III, 399D). This depressing account places the greatest strain on those who love both music and Plato.

The other side of the coin is no more cheerful, and Plato is mostly silent on the excesses that offend him most. The worst are the Ionian and some forms of the Lydian modes (convivial drinking songs, soft and effeminate) and the mixed and intense (hypo-) Lydian (including dirges and lamentations) (*Rep*. III. 398E). These have a bad effect (411B) because they are attached to frivolity and disaffect for many pursuits. No doubt it is these that were played or accompanied by the disapproved instruments: harps, flutes, or many-stringed (399D). Plato's hostility to the flute always startles the modern reader, who thinks of the flute as a chaste, long, thin instrument with hardly any protuberances played by a girl of approximately the same description. But it seems to have been the sexophone of antiquity, clearly associated with girls at drinking parties (*Prot*. 347C; *Symp*. 212D)[19] and condemned as seeking to gratify large numbers of people by giving pleasure without regard for what is best (*Gorg.* 501E). A curious technical point arises out of a passage at *Philebus* 56A: the pitch of the flute seems to have depended on the skill of the player (this is hardly the case with the modern Boehm flute), or what Socrates says is a lucky shot with the finger rather than precise measurement. Equally serious is the fact that it was played freely without words (*Laws* II, 669E); the objection is no doubt that the appeal was purely sensuous and emotional without the discipline and order of words. For Plato lyricism and subjective feeling were just as offensive in music as in poetry.

Composers should not be free to produce whatever they please (*Laws* II, 656C); there is an objective standard aiming at number (668A), and everybody should be trained in technical knowledge of scales and rhythms (670A; cf. VII, 812D) if correctness of form is to be maintained. A last word on the modes before we turn to the question of number. We have nothing in Western music that precisely corresponds to them. One near association that conveys some flavour of Plato's argument is found in major and minor keys which set a more or less jolly or sad mood; the black keys on the piano are a mode (exactly which one is not now clear) producing mock-Chinese music; one may also encounter the so-called pentatonic scale of whole notes (C, D, E, F-sharp, G-sharp, A-sharp, C) which produces a mood characteristically different from that of the conventional western diatonic scale. Finally, it must be observed that the tempering of modern instruments, i.e., making the half-steps equal in difference of pitch, has changed the modal impact of the various key signatures, though some modern composers (Rachmaninoff, Hindemith) still insist that differences of tone-colour and meaning attach to each key. The chromaticism of late Romantic music and twentieth-century atonalism carry us still further away from understanding Plato's criticisms. The only thing left to him is the equivalent of Sousa's marches and anybody's national anthem. He reminds one of the man who knew only two tunes: one of them was God save the Queen, and the other one wasn't.

The references to number are tantalizing and tempt us into speculation beyond what is directly verifiable from the text. *Philebus* 17C tells us that musical relationships are numerically determined, though less exact than the use of numbers in, say, carpentry (*Phil.* 56C), and that they are only of value because of number (*Epinomis* 978A). If music reflects our state of mind (*Rep.* III, 400E) then the best music will correspond with 'beautiful reason' (401D). And that will be a vision of the whole vast structure of the mythical universe of the *Timaeus*, its harmonies, its numbers, the mathematical relationships with their adherence of magic, its elements in infinite compound: these all must be viewed as an attempt to render a synoptic vision of the unity of all creation. Poincaré proved mathematically why the regular polyhedra are limited to five (in three dimensions; six in four dimensions); but to the Pythagoreans, whose influence is pervasive throughout Plato's writings, but especially in the *Timaeus*, the mysterious relation of certain numbers to each other was evidence, not of the natural limiting factor that not more than five equilateral triangles can be adjacent to each other in different planes, but evidence rather of a divinely rational plan.

If one plots the steps of the musical scale on a graph one obtains a smooth exponential curve; but this branch of mathematics was fairly primitive in Plato's time, and so starting from the remarkable ratios of the string lengths producing the fifth and the octave to the length producing the tonic, they worked out an elaborate series of ratios for the other tones of the scale. If these values are then plotted on the same graph we find an angular line that zig-zags back and forth across the exponential curve, but is always quite close to it. The logical inference from this is that they relied on their ears for the accuracy of the string lengths producing each tone, and then worked out, by reference to the tetractys and other mystical (and, I fear, *ad hoc*) formulae, the curious mathematical relations which are set out in detail in the *Timaeus*. In time, no doubt, it was forgotten which came first, the string lengths or the formulae, and it became easy to marvel at the accuracy with which the formulae yielded the correct string length! Contemporary mathematics made it impossible for Plato to specify exactly what these numbers were (indeed, a well-tempered scale could be produced only after Descartes and Leibniz laid the groundwork); but he would have been the first to agree that it must be derived mathematically and not empirically.

The celebrated harmony of the spheres furnishes another example of the 'unheard music' that is sweetest. We are given an elaborate account at *Rep.* X, 616C of the Spindle of Necessity along which at specified intervals are yoked the spheres carrying the planets. On each a Siren sings one note, probably corresponding to the string length of the position of each planet, and the whole producing a harmony emblematic of the perfection of all creation. Yet it is also the harmony that in microcosm invests the individual soul, for such is the power of music that it inculcates balance and civilization (*Prot.* 326AB; cf. Eryximachus' speech at *Symp.* 186E–187C, also *Soph.* 253B).

Moreover, so much of music as is adapted to the sound of the voice and to the sense of hearing is granted to us for the sake of harmony. And harmony, which has motions akin to the revolutions of our souls, is not regarded by the intelligent votary of the Muses as given by them with a view to irrational pleasure . . . but as meant to correct any discord which may have arisen in the courses of the soul, and to be our ally in bringing her into harmony and agreement with herself. (*Timaeus* 47CD; cf. *Laches* 188D)

No Sophist tricked out as a musician or other poet (*Prot.* 316E) is fit to undertake the 'sovereign' task (*Rep.* III, 401A) of teaching music, central in education (*Theaet.* 206A; *Tim.* 18A) and critical especially in the early formation of the child (*Laws* II, 653AB). For no one can be a proper judge of an imitation who does not know the true existence of what is imitated (669AB). These matters cannot be left, as already noted, to popular acclaim, to the opinion of children, or to the Sophists who, without principles or convictions of their own, confirm and play to the prejudices of the mob. The composers must be kept within bounds, public standards maintained by submission to the censors of all works to determine their suitability for public performance (*Laws* VII, 801DE, 817D; VIII, 829C–830A). Because of its direct emotional appeal music leaves its hearers especially vulnerable to false and harmful influences, against which Plato warns with an eloquence equal to his indignation. But it is in the discussion of music, even more than in the case of poetry, that we are not concerned with a flat condemnation of the art, but equally with the specification of what would constitute acceptable practice.

V

Rhetoric has been referred to so far rather loosely together with poetry and sophistry, but because of its importance in the overall attack warrants special consideration. The material on rhetoric is rather less familiar than that on poetry but, if anything, it is even more bitter. Moreover, rhetoric plays a special role in my argument, being midway between cold dialectic and hot poetry. It has to convince and it has to sway. Thus I see an intimate relationship between rhetoric, myth, and dialectic – in many respects they overlap or mutually determine one another.

The unity of Plato's thought is such that it is extremely difficult to separate his comments on any one subject without doing damage to the whole. That this is an abundant source of misunderstanding is easily seen from the comments of critics of his political views like Popper, Crossman, and Fite. Whatever he discusses, Plato's prime consideration is a moral one – always it is a question how the subject matter in hand can best serve towards the fulfilment of the highest good.

Nothing illustrates this better than the discussion of rhetoric in the *Gorgias*. Ostensibly we have a familiar attempt to obtain a definition of rhetoric (by a dialectical procedure that foreshadows its fuller development in the *Sophist*), but soon the real implications of the conversation with Gorgias are brought out in a discussion with Callicles. Beginning with rhetoric, we find inevitably that the *sine qua non* for the execution of any art lies in the presupposition that it must not be incompatible with the good life. This means, as always for Plato, knowledge of what is best for man. The same theme is developed in the *Phaedrus* where, as we shall see, the prerequisite for an art of rhetoric is knowledge of men's souls and the nice adjustment of one's presentation to the great differences of understanding among men. I shall later argue that this new approach to rhetoric by Socrates points rather towards myth than towards dialectic: for the present I would observe that the ability of myth to be all things to all men – to be capable of a virtually infinite suggestiveness in the levels of interpretation of which it is susceptible – meets this requirement to perfection.

Let us try with due caution to extract from the discussions in the *Gorgias* and *Phaedrus* what is the basis of Socrates' attack on the art of rhetoric as then practised by the Sophists, and what is the nature of the philosophical rhetoric which he proposes in its stead. I hope to show that dialectic is a necessary but not a sufficient condition for this philosophical rhetoric, and that it is myth conjoined with the knowledge that dialectic yields – or with the error that dialectic avoids – that constitutes the essential element in responsible rhetoric directed towards man's good.

In the *Gorgias* we find Socrates confronted in turn by the Sophist Gorgias, by Polus, a hanger-on with little of honest value to contribute, and by Callicles, whose attack represents a reasoned disagreement with Socrates as to the moral basis underlying the latter's theory. That it is the moral issue which is uppermost in Plato's mind is shown by the fact that both in bulk and substance this conversation outweighs the other two.

The discussion with Gorgias (447E–466A) begins with a form of questioning familiar from the earliest dialogues and designed to secure a definition of the rhetorician. First we proceed by way of analogy: just as

the musician is concerned with the composition of melodies and the
cobbler with the making of shoes, so the rhetorician is concerned with
discourse. But there is a form of discourse connected with every art and
some, like mathematics, depend wholly upon words for their exposition
(450D) and do not even involve some physical action. We must pursue
the classification further so as to distinguish rhetoric from the other arts.
Gorgias replies that the words which rhetoric uses relate 'to the greatest
and best of human things' (451E).

But, Socrates points out (and here we approach the important theme
for him), each man has his own notion of what is the best for man: the
physician will say health, the gymnast strength and beauty, and the
merchant thinks that money is the greatest good. Gorgias' answer is that
rhetoric is greater than these since the rhetorician is able to persuade
men, including the physician and merchant, to act in accordance with
the interest of the rhetor, and this gives him that freedom and power over
men that sets his art apart. Rhetoric, then, is the 'artificer of persuasion'
(453A).

Socrates continues: all the arts persuade us (i.e. give us knowledge or
belief about their subject matter). What does rhetoric persuade us of?
And does it give us knowledge, or belief only? In his reply, Gorgias
concedes the point Socrates has been aiming at:

> Soc: And which sort of persuasion does rhetoric create in courts of law
> and other assemblies about the just and the unjust, the sort of
> persuasion which gives belief without knowledge, or that which
> gives knowledge?
> Gor: Clearly, Socrates, that which gives only belief. (454E–455A)

We have thus established a point which we shall meet again in the
Phaedrus and which is employed, to opposite effect, both by Socrates
and the rhetors he is attacking. The rhetor boasts of his independence of
subject matter: he is better able to state a case than the one who knows.
That knowledge of a thing does not necessarily go hand in hand with the
ability to communicate, it is pointed out at 456B, C. Here the power of
the orator to convince the multitude in matters in which he shares their
ignorance is greater than that of the physician or engineer, or of anyone
commanding some technical knowledge. The rhetor is thus seen as a
kind of executive who makes policy and is able to sway men to his views.
That this is true, Socrates does not attempt to deny. But is it good?

He now brings out the suspicion of Gorgias' claims which he alluded
to before (453B). If the rhetorician's 'independence' of his subject matter
means that he may be perfectly ignorant of medicine and engineering,

then there is no reason to suppose that he needs or will possess any knowledge of the just and the unjust either. Gorgias is not very happy with this, and argues that knowledge of good and evil is a prerequisite for rhetoric. The student who does not already know what is good will have to learn that first, and he is unwilling to deny that he can teach him.

This leads in turn to a fresh difficulty. Earlier (456C ff.), Gorgias had said that one should not blame the teacher for any abuse by the rhetor of his skill, because the teacher intended him to make good use of his instructions. Socrates now shows the inconsistency between these two statements. If the rhetorician must be a good man before he can be a rhetorician, then no such abuse could arise. The key sentence in Socrates' argument is: 'He who has learned what is just, is just' (460B). Gorgias agrees to this, but there is room for disagreement. Socrates is relying on the curiously intense meaning he consistently gives to 'knowing' in such expressions as 'knowing the good', or 'knowledge of the best interests of man'. For him it is impossible for the man who knows the good to act otherwise than in accordance with it. His categorical imperative is based on knowledge.

Gorgias, however, used 'knowing' in a slighter, more everyday, sense. His use of the word is similar to its meaning in law. A man may very well say: 'I know that it is wrong to steal, yet I did it just the same'. Indeed, such knowledge of the nature of an offence is required in law (and in ordinary language) for responsibility for one's acts to be imputed and for punishment to be legitimately imposed. But Socrates would not allow this – his equation of knowledge with good, and of ignorance with evil has the corollary that the man who truly knows what is good *cannot* act otherwise. There is an ideal embedded in this formulation, the truth of which is not to be demonstrated despite the attempts of dialectic to do so. The inconsistency which Socrates lays at Gorgias' door depends on these two different senses of 'knowing' – and, it must be allowed, it is Socrates' meaning which is the more idiosyncratic of the two. We have a similar situation in the discussion between Thrasymachus and Socrates in the *Republic*.

Thus far the discourse has been marked by mutual respect due, as Taylor points out,[20] to the fact that Gorgias is not willing 'to break with conventional views about morality'. But now Polus breaks in rudely (461B) to complain that Socrates has taken advantage of Gorgias' unwillingness to deny that he could teach the good, and has thus brought about the contradiction we have just mentioned. Polus says that now he will put the questions, and let Socrates answer: What is rhetoric? Socrates replies that it is not an art at all, but one of a number of knacks or tricks which, since their chief purpose is to cater to the pleasure of others, he will together call 'flattery' (463A). He proceeds to build up an analogy between four such elements: cookery, rhetoric, cosmetics, and sophistry; and the four real arts of which they are but a parody: medicine, justice, gymnastic, and legislation. In each case the parody seeks to gratify the common desires of men, but without regard to their real welfare.

All that is most hateful to Socrates in the vicious irresponsibility of the Sophists and rhetoricians is brought out in this discussion with Polus. For the latter is willing, as Gorgias was not, to abandon conventional morality and the claim that justice must underlie the orator's pleadings. When Socrates again brings the argument to the point where he shows that one cannot knowingly do evil (468D), Polus taunts him:

> *Pol*: As though you, Socrates, would not like to have the power of doing what seemed good to you in the state, rather than not; you would not be jealous when you saw any one killing or despoiling or imprisoning whom he pleased, oh, no!
> *Soc*: Justly or unjustly, do you mean?
> *Pol*: In either case is he not equally to be envied?
> *Soc*: Forbear, Polus!
> *Pol*: Why 'forbear'?
> *Soc*: Because you ought not to envy wretches who are not to be envied, but only to pity them.

This is a truly dramatic moment, and scarcely any passage in Plato better displays the deep distress the good man must feel when faced by a vulgar opportunist. It shows, too, as well as the example of Pericles' being unable to make good men of his sons, the vanity of Gorgias' claim that he can teach wisdom – for Polus is his student. But Polus is unregenerate, and goes on to display the worst features of the demagogue. It is tedious to continue in detail with this part of the dialogue – Plato has achieved his purpose in exposing the worthlessness of the kind of rhetorician Polus is. If rhetoric is to be of any use, Socrates concludes (480B), it should be not to excuse our own injustice but to heap execration on ourselves in the hope of purgation.

The discussion with Callicles of what makes for the good life which takes up the rest of the dialogue does not bear directly on our subject, although it is of great interest for the study of Plato's teachings generally. Two passages, however, are relevant, and serve to sum up the conclusions of the *Gorgias* on the subject of rhetoric:

Soc: I am contented with the admission that rhetoric is of two sorts; one, which is mere flattery and disgraceful declamation; the other, which is noble and aims at the training and improvement of the souls of the citizens, and strives to say what is best, whether welcome or unwelcome to the audience . . . (503A)

Soc: And will not the true rhetorician who is honest and understands his art have his eyes fixed upon these [temperance and justice] in all the words which he addresses to the souls of men . . . Will not his aim be to implant justice in the souls of his citizens and take away injustice, to implant temperance and take away intemperance, to implant every virtue and take away every vice? (504D)

We turn now to the *Phaedrus* where the discussion of rhetoric is continued and in which we shall find those indications which point toward the relationship between rhetoric, myth, and dialectic. To say merely that all three must be employed in the service of the highest good would be true, but too general: it cannot, indeed, be too often repeated that Plato is nothing if not a moralist, and the whole of his teaching, be it metaphysics, aesthetics, political science, or education, is shot through with high moral purpose. That is all true, but we must still seek some narrower bond among these subjects, and it is in the *Phaedrus* that we shall find it.

Socrates was the first, it seems, to see that rhetoric had a wider application than the somewhat academic and codified technique current in his day:

Is not rhetoric, taken generally, a universal art of leading souls (*psychagogia*) by arguments; which is practised not only in courts and public assemblies, but in private houses as well, having to do with all matters, great as well as small, good and bad alike, . . . (261AB)

The purpose of his analysis in the last part (257B ff.) of the *Phaedrus* is to point up the difference between eristic and sophistic rhetoric on the one hand, and philosophical rhetoric on the other: the distinction being that foreshadowed in the passages quoted from the *Gorgias* above. The first is designed to win the argument at all costs, to play on popular opinion: its approach stresses the etymology of *rhetor*, the flow, the mellifluous stream of eloquence which carries all before it, relying on its appeal to the lowest common denominator of emotion and to the ostensible interest of the audience to conceal its logical flaws and factual errors. Philosophical rhetoric, however, while it shares the function of exhorting and persuading its hearers, is primarily concerned with the truth. This claim is specifically rejected as a function of rhetoric by the Sophists (Gorgias and Thrasymachus, for example), on the grounds that the art of rhetoric is manifested by the ability to persuade anybody of anything. Lysias' speech (*Phaedrus* 230E ff.) was designed to show the total independence of subject matter that characterizes this view of rhetoric. And Gorgias' remark – that mere knowledge of a thing does not make a man the best exponent of it – bears this out once again.

Socrates applies the dialectical method to Lysias' speech, just as he did to show the shortcomings of Gorgias' and Polus' views, but this time so as to illuminate his own theories concerning legitimate rhetoric. Love is not an unequivocal term like silver or gold, but ambiguous like justice and goodness (263A), and in need of prior definition. This Lysias did not do; Phaedrus recalls that Socrates did define love at the outset (Socrates affecting to have been too inspired to remember). On the contrary, Lysias began where his discourse should have ended, and the points he made were assembled anyhow, violating the criterion, given at 264C, that a discourse should have a beginning, middle, and end, and be an organic whole, like a living creature. A further criterion, which was observed even in the myth, despite the reservations to which we must return later, is that of appropriate analysis of subject matter. The passages in question are at 265D–266B which describe the dialectical process of collection and division, similar to that employed by the Eleatic Stranger in the *Sophist*. Collection (265D) is the 'comprehension of scattered particulars in one idea'. Division (265E ff.), as exemplified in Socrates' two discourses, was the analysis of the synthetic definition of love as a form of madness, into a dichotomy of human affliction and divine inspiration, and the further division of the 'right-handed' (divine) madness into four parts, of which love was one (265AB, 266A). Phaedrus agrees that Lysias failed here, too, and cannot be called a dialectician. In the argument that is to follow we shall see that this concession is fatal, because the prerequisite for an art of rhetoric is necessarily based on the art of thinking, dialectic.

But this still leaves us without a positive discussion of rhetoric. What is left to constitute it as an art are certain rules of structure: how a speech should begin, statement of facts, testimony of witnesses, proofs, probabilities, confirmations, and so on. Socrates strikes an even more ironical note in mentioning the rhetorical principles of Tisias, Gorgias, Polus, Protagoras, and Thrasymachus (the 'academic' rhetors) – all this, however, is unimportant – and he carries us back to the important question (268A):

What power does the art of rhetoric possess, and upon what occasions? What Socrates is after is made clear by an analogy with medicine, which recalls the similar argument of the *Gorgias*. If the ability to put people into a passion and out again is a mark of a rhetorician, as suggested of Thrasymachus just before, is a like ability to apply a heating or a cooling drug a mark of a physician? That would be so only if it is accompanied by the knowledge to whom and when the art should be applied. If, as the rhetorician answers, this is not his concern, but that of the audience or patient, he would be laughed out of court. So, too, the writer of tragedies or music must have a knowledge of the intrinsic subject matter of his field, not just a superficial attention to its elementary manifestations. What is required is a natural gift which may be aided by art, knowledge, and practice. The perfection of rhetoric, as of anything else, lies in this formula. In a word, what these theorists of rhetoric give are merely the necessary conditions for the art, not the sufficient ones.

Where the rhetoric of Lysias and Thrasymachus fails is in the most important of these elements, knowledge, and the critical scrutiny of a subject matter which constitutes dialectic. Pericles is Socrates' example of an accomplished orator, combining a subject matter of intrinsic worth, the truths of nature, with the two elements of 'loftiness of thought and completeness of execution' (270A). Since rhetoric is an art of persuading others, a correct account of it must examine the soul in general, and then the differences in individual souls so that the orator can calculate his effect on his audience.

Philosophical rhetoric is thus subject to the conditions laid down so far: the rhetorician must know the truth of what he is to speak about (within human limitations), he must know the nature of the soul, and be able to gauge the impact on a highly diverse audience. Further (273E), he must make his discourse acceptable to the gods, as also his actions. That this is an arduous undertaking is compatible with the end to be achieved. Even if it is not practicable of achievement, it is still honourable to fail in an honourable aim. Here we see again Plato's emphasis, as a moralist, on intentions, as opposed to the Sophists' stress on consequences, as for example in Polus at *Gorgias* 470A.

It is critical to note that the exercise in dialectic carried out on Lysias' speech has served, no doubt, to expose the errors in his argument and style of address. But instead of supplying a dialectical elucidation of the principles of philosophical rhetoric, Socrates first furnishes an example of it (in his second speech on love), and then proceeds into the great myth of the afterlife. Such a transition is both characteristic and surprising;

characteristic, because it is repeatedly the case in the middle dialogues that a myth is supplied following passages of inconclusive dialectic: these have no doubt served the purpose of displaying the errors and confusions of Socrates' interlocutors, and the further purpose perhaps of preserving his claims to ignorance intact. But they are surprising also because one would expect, sooner or later, that as Plato developed his notions of dialectic beyond Socrates' more modest aims, something would emerge by way of dialectical demonstration that realized his own expectations of the method of hypothesis sketched in the *Meno* (86E ff.) and *Phaedo* (101D ff.). But he does not do so, and once more a myth picks up where dialectic ends. Let me here first assert, deferring to the next chapter the more detailed examination of this profoundly important question, a possible interpretation of the reasons for this extraordinary treatment of dialectic and myth in the context of philosophical rhetoric.

The relationship between dialectic and myth, I shall argue, is complementary: to the demonstrable but negative certainty of dialectic is added the indemonstrable truths of myth. But myth for Plato may not be irresponsible, and here the criteria of philosophical rhetoric apply. So self-conscious a method of composition as Plato here establishes does not, he has specifically said, exclude the inspiration of divine madness which is the gift of the poets, but the self-consciousness consists precisely in the critical examination of what has been said, once articulated, and this relieves Plato of the charge he has laid against the poets generally. To this extent at least the foundations have been laid for a defence of poetry.

The philosophical rhetoric about which a theory is thus tentatively constructed points therefore towards myth rather than towards dialectic. This rather hardy statement calls for closer scrutiny if it is to be sustained. There is no doubt, though, that one at least of the elements constituting the rhetoric, namely the method of collection and division, clearly belongs to dialectic: the discussion of this method in the *Sophist* confirms this. Over against this, however, must be set the concept, pointed out in the *Phaedrus*, that dialectic leads to *certain* knowledge, whereas rhetoric is concerned with those things which of necessity remain uncertain and ambiguous:

> *Soc*: Then in some things we agree, but not in others? . . . In which are we more likely to be deceived, and in which has rhetoric the greater power?
> *Phae*: Clearly, in the uncertain class. (263B)

In short, I should want to argue that what Plato primarily has in mind in speaking of dialectic is the kind of knowledge which is certain in the sense that it can be made common property, binding on all rational minds, because it is capable of verification by empirico-logical means such that the denial of it is impossible without self-contradiction. But this kind of knowledge is simply not attainable in those fields in which Plato's principal interest lies. He was fully aware of this and was much more sceptical than is generally believed about the areas, if any, in which certain knowledge can be attained. Unlike the eighteenth-century rationalists who imagined with an optimism still not wholly rebuffed that their mathematical and logical discoveries could be applied in ethics and politics, Plato was never so sanguine.

It seems to me that dialectic is essentially negative in its procedures and serves principally to delimit the area in which it can itself be employed. The myths are the necessarily uncertain attempts at elucidating those truths that can never be demonstrated logically. Thus, while the dialectical method may, on the argument of the *Phaedrus*, in one sense be included as part of the rhetoric, I should want to say that it is the lesser part and, because rhetoric is the art of persuasion, of leading souls, the greater part of rhetoric must be directed towards the myths. I rest the case for this view chiefly on the passage from the *Phaedrus* quoted above (263B), and also on the discussion of the divided line in the *Republic*, of which more later.

Socrates' use of the elenchus is designed to purge of error rather than to persuade. The dialectic which proceeds in this manner is clearly negative in its intent. The respondent is obliged logically, having asserted A, to agree to a series of propositions derived in turn from A and leading to not-A. This merely shows that the original statement A (or some intermediate statement) must be abandoned; sometimes the logic is deliberately faulty and unnecessary concessions are made (as in the *Parmenides*), and in such cases dialectic is being employed to provoke the reader to independent thought on the subject (or, it should not be overlooked, Homer may have nodded!). We shall return to some of the implications of this use of dialectic in the next chapter.

The often noted structure of the early dialogues which merely brings the argument to the point of rejecting the various A's which have been advanced has led to some misunderstandings of Plato's purpose in these dialogues. Taylor,[21] refers to a commentator who takes Socrates to task for not providing a solution to fill the vacuum thus left; he also quotes Grote's reply to this objection: that Socrates refrains from doing so because any possible definition of these terms (piety, courage, virtue, etc.) would be open at the dialectical level to the same or similar objections that Socrates has brought to bear on his deuteragonists. The filling of the vacuum, then, cannot be undertaken by dialectic in a positive sense; it is confined to scrutiny of truths capable of symbolic representation in myth alone, and after having applied every logical test, can then pronounce its most favourable judgment: *nihil obstat*.

This is not to deny that Plato makes a most strenuous effort to set dialectic to positive use. I shall later examine the model of what I call 'Platonic' dialectic (in contrast to the more negative 'Socratic' kind) as a means of securing certain knowledge after the manner of mathematics. But this kind of a priori thinking modelled on mathematics does not and cannot, as the subsequent history of philosophy shows, be made to apply in metaphysics and ethics. It is a major problem of Platonic scholarship to establish whether Plato was aware of this or not, and since most commentators take his claims for dialectic at face value, my burden will be all the heavier. I will have to show that he was aware of the limitations of dialectic as supplying demonstrable and irrefutable knowledge in any area, including mathematics. Certainly the use of myth in the middle dialogues implies that at this period at least he was sceptical of the power of dialectic in the perennially insoluble problems of ethics and metaphysics.

VI

The attack on the artists is very wide-ranging and leads to the various formulations in which Plato proposes to expel them from the republic. I have drawn together in this chapter all the sustained passages from the dialogues that are directed against the poets, musicians, rhetors, both within and outside the Sophist tradition, especially as those attacks bear on religion, politics, ethics, and epistemology. Besides the passages I have paraphrased and quoted there are hundreds of scattered references to the arts; most simply repeat or reinforce arguments sufficiently familiar from the passages reviewed here. But one argument at least reappears within the treatment of each of the arts in a manner that makes it more convenient to deal with it in a summing-up. At *Philebus* 56B, for example, in the discussion of architecture and building he stresses the 'considerable use of measures and instruments, and the remarkable exactness thus attained makes it more scientific than most sorts of knowledge'. He goes on to divide those arts, 'like music', which are less exact from those using numbers. The distinction is approximately that which we draw between the arts and the crafts. Generally speaking, when we speak of the crafts we are emphasizing the role of manual dexterity, the manipulation of tools and materials, and the precision and apt functioning of the product. We associate the arts principally with the exercise of imagination, inventiveness, and the giving of more 'aesthetic' satisfactions ranging from the pleasing to the sublime. The *dulce* of the arts is widely separated from and set hierarchically superior to the *utile* of the crafts.

The distinction is admittedly somewhat fuzzy, since technical skill cannot be divorced from the arts, nor can imagination be denied its place in the crafts. This topic has a lengthy history reaching into our own time, but we must confine ourselves here to Plato's view of it. If anything he reverses the conventional judgment of the relative value of arts and crafts, so as to set the technical competence, thought to be closer to the latter, rather higher than the imaginings of the artists. The reason for this somewhat surprising attitude is clear enough, and of a piece with some of the arguments considered earlier. In its simplest form it is that the craftsmen know something (cf. *Prot.* 319B: the architects; *Statesman* 260A: builders; etc.). At *Prot.* 312D even the painters, like the builders, have knowledge how to make likenesses, 'but what do the sophists know?' A fairly crude version of the imitation theory underlies this preference for the crafts and accounts for the momentary recall of the painter: there is a way of verifying the skills of the craftsman by comparing his copy with the original. Is the portrait a good likeness? Does the brooch fasten? Does the shoe pinch? Is the house snug and four-square? The elements which lend themselves in answering these questions are accuracy, precision, functionalism; there is a high degree of objectivity in furnishing the answers, and a high degree of agreement among the judges.

This is not the case in the arts, where the widest discrepancy may obtain between whatever the artist sought to convey and what the observer perceives. 'When I wrote that, madam, God and I knew what it meant', Browning is reported as saying of some of his more cryptic lines, 'now God only knows.' Where there is no precise correspondence between signified and signifier susceptible of verification (as in the examples from the crafts just given) room is left, all too much room to Plato's taste, for subjectivity, ambiguity, and ignorance masquerading as insight. The names of things are not onomatopoeic or 'musical' as he says at *Crat.* 423A. Hence the reiterated examples of cobblers, shipbuilders, flutemakers, all of whom know something, always favourably contrasted with poets and orators, soldiers and statesmen, whose words have no fixed value. And when, as in the case of the poets, they hide behind the sources of their irrational inspiration and disclaim responsibility for the manifest effect of their words, the evil is compounded. The rhetoricians are worse: they do not have the excuse of a possibly divine source for their utterances: their art is explicitly found in the ability to persuade of any side of any argument – it is this reckless indifference to truth that excites the indignation and bitterness we have seen in the *Gorgias*.

And so Plato's resolution of the ancient quarrel between the philosophers and the poets is to banish the poets, crowning those with fillets of wool (*Rep.* III, 398AB) who may perhaps be inspired by the gods, but those who foster only the lower parts of the soul (X, 605B) and whose works are not edifying (Laws VII, 817D) would presumably have to leave without these marks of respect. We shall deny access to those who sing the praises of tyranny (Rep. VIII, 568B), since we can allow only 'hymns to the gods and the praises of good men' (X, 607A). But at *Rep.* X, 607CD is the celebrated challenge to defend poetry:

> But nevertheless let it be declared that, if the mimetic and dulcet poetry can show any reason for her existence in a well-governed state, we would gladly admit her, since we ourselves are very conscious of her spell . . . . And we would allow her advocates who are not poets but lovers of poetry to plead her cause in prose without meter, and show that she is not only delightful but beneficial to orderly government and all the life of man. And we shall listen benevolently, for it will be clear gain for us if it can be shown that she bestows not only pleasure but a benefit.

The myths are Plato's poetry, designed not only to escape the criticisms levelled at the other poets but in the manner of their telling to supply the defence he has called for. The task is complex: it certainly will not suffice that the myths are told with consummate literary skill, that generations of readers have been ravished by their language and borne to empyrean heights by intimations of immortality that appeal secretly to an inner ear. All that is noblest and most generous in Christianity is anticipated by Plato; and the martyrdom of Socrates, as he has related it, is an emblem of the tragic fate of goodness in an evil world that can nonetheless be redeemed by the hope inspired by that goodness. It is not enough that Plato is a greater artist than all those he cherished or condemned; if Kant is the Bach of philosophy, Plato is the Mozart. All these things are true; I proclaim my adherence to them. But the defence must rest on a sober and even pragmatic examination of the arguments and the methods of the dialogues; and whatever conclusions may be reached must be consistent with Plato's more pedestrian aims in epistemology, ethics, and politics.

In the discussion of rhetoric I stressed its powers of persuasion, and assimilated these to myth rather than to dialectic. Plato's conviction of an absolute truth underlying all attempts to utter it does not alter his equally profound conviction that those attempts are at the mercy of any person who wishes simply to reject whatever conclusions may be reached. That rejection may spring merely from an inability to follow the argument, or from a rival conviction that rests on other presuppositions. From the former I shall develop what I call a 'weak' defence of poetry. This would acknowledge the dogmatic aspects of Plato's system as it is widely understood – there is an absolute knowledge, Plato or his Philosopher-King possesses it, but most people cannot understand it. For them Plato has written myths, compatible with that truth, to render it accessible at least at the emotional level and within the limited understanding of his various hearers. But I shall also advance a 'strong' defence. This will trace in Plato, to the extent that it can be found, an acknowledgement that dialectic cannot attain its goals by demonstrating the truth of first premises. If that is so, then those first premises are myths. The irony of Santayana's remark placed at the beginning of this chapter is that he intended no irony; but Plato does when he calls his myths 'lies'. The axioms of every system of thought are myths in this sense, and if the strong defence can be made plausible the autonomy and integrity of poetry will be vindicated.

2 The Inconclusiveness of Dialectic

> . . . if [the poet] had genuine knowledge of the things he imitates he would far rather devote himself to real things than to the imitation of them (*Rep.* X, 599B)

I

Some rather extravagant promises were made in the preceding chapter on which I must now begin to deliver. Plato, I say, supplies a defence of poetry in response to his own challenge. The defence is not merely implied by the actual use of myth, but can be derived consistently from Plato's methodology and from his epistemology and metaphysics. There is to be a 'weak' defence in which poetry is indeed indispensable for those individuals too emotional, or too dull, lazy, or busy to grasp rationally what is demonstrable by rational means. The 'strong' defence is much more interesting – it will have to show the indispensability of poetry for even the most rational of men.

Plato has attacked the poets – and the sophists, rhetors, and politicians – as liars, madmen, and as unintelligible mantics. Nonetheless he is a great poet himself and makes considerable use of poetic devices in great variety. He does so for two kinds of reasons: either dialectic is able to sustain the claims made for it as a method adequate to the attainment of knowledge, or it is not. Even if it can do so, we fall back on the weak defence of poetry. But dialectic cannot sustain these claims, and if that can be shown the way is open for the strong defence. Thus there are two major tasks to be undertaken: the first, which I shall address in this chapter, is to examine 'Socratic' and 'Platonic' dialectic for what they can achieve and where they fall short; the second, in chapters 4, 5 and 6, is an examination of the myths themselves both as to what they say, and as to what is said or may be inferred about them.

It will not suffice to rely for the failure of dialectic on the Socratic elenchus which is clearly negative. But it is possible to identify, notably in the *Phaedo* and *Republic*, some leading features of a distinctively Platonic dialectic which claims to establish knowledge on a firm foundation. The model is geometry and the aim is to find a set of indisputable axioms reached by a method of successively more general hypotheses (*Phaedo* 102D). Each of these loses its hypothetical character by being deduced as a theorem from a logically prior, and ultimately most general, axiom. In the *Republic* at VII, 531C, Plato attacks the mathematicians for being bad dialecticians because they do not attempt to verify the truth of the axioms of geometry. But the fact is that axioms can never be verified within the system of which they are part – the only alternatives are an infinite regress or, short of this, circularity. Such axioms can only be asserted. I am persuaded that Plato became aware of this, but he never articulated the necessarily nondogmatic inferences that such a discovery entails. Thus, dialectic furnishes necessary conditions for knowledge – a methodology that requires, among other aspects, firstly an intelligible structuring of concepts in hierarchical sequence, and secondly a considerable (though underestimated) reliance on empirical data ('saving the appearances') so that it is impermissible to maintain theoretical explanations at odds with the facts. But dialectic does not, and cannot, furnish the sufficient conditions for knowledge.

Because the weak defence presupposes the attainment and possession of positive knowledge it cannot do very much for poetry. Indeed, on this weak view poetry is not strictly necessary, though it may have vast practical value as we shall see; in fact it is strictly unnecessary, but if this were all my thesis amounted to it would hardly be worth pursuing. The strong defence must prove much more, but not too much more, lest we run foul of those Platonic texts that plainly support the substantial advantages of dialectic. I shall argue that dialectic is inconclusive, that it disposes where poetry proposes, but that Plato's rational methods cannot propose. I shall not argue, like neo-Platonists of the Alexandrian decadence, that dialectic fails, only that it is inconclusive. The danger of overstating the case is that one thereby lapses into the rhapsody, mysticism, primitivism, and know-nothingism that Plato has condemned. The descendants of the rational and beautiful Plotinus were merely beautiful romantics, but their descendants were merely romantic barbarians. It would be inadmissible to move in this direction. On the contrary, it is the evidence for a severe rationalism that must be heeded, like the motto placed at the head of this chapter.

Thus far my strategy has been to display the shortcomings, at least on the surface, of poetry and rhetoric. Plato's attack must be taken seriously, but Plato is himself an important poet; hence the attack must be on bad poetry. Before we can say what good poetry is, there is another direction that we must take. My emphasis in the quotation from the *Republic* is on the '*if*' – a standard answer, apparently offered by Plato in this context, is that the poet (or anybody else) *would* have genuine knowledge of the things he imitates if he were to devote himself to dialectic. This presupposes that the dialectical method will in fact lead to the kind of positive knowledge that would render poetry unnecessary. Thus what I must now attempt to show falls under two heads:

1) that dialectic does not and cannot lead to unequivocal knowledge in the required sense, and that Plato knows this;
2) that the relationship between philosophy and poetry (or the arts generally) will, on analysis, reveal several theories of literature, three in fact compatible in over-all terms with the Platonic text, and a fourth theory that is incompatible.

Under 1) I shall draw a distinction between Socratic and Platonic dialectic; the first manifestly negative, the second ostensibly affirmative, seeking to supply both the necessary and the sufficient conditions for knowledge. However, I will show that it is not and cannot be effective for this purpose, that Plato knew this, and that while he gives many indications of this fatal shortcoming, he is unwilling to state it explicitly or draw the conclusions that follow all too uncomfortably from his awareness. It would not, of course, follow from the inconclusiveness of dialectic (or of rational methods in general) that poetry thereby succeeds (it does not), only that the best that can be done humanly is to combine dialectic with poetry.

That brings me to 2). I shall describe a fourfold relationship between philosophy and literature, and locate Plato somewhat uncertainly within it so as to show the indispensability of both. It will also show the weaknesses of both, but those weaknesses will be relative to the unwarranted extravagance of the claims that have been made by Plato and others for and against poetic and discursive utterance. Then in the following chapters I shall examine the issues on which Plato expresses himself in the form of myths; and also the connection within the dialogues between dialectic and myth. If the *Laws* is the second-best Republic because of the unattainability in principle of the best, so too is philosophical poetry a second-best philosophy because of the necessary inconclusiveness of dialectic, but it is the best that we can attain. Moreover, Plato has attained it.

II

The Socratic problem remains intractable in the sense that, despite innumerable attempts to separate Socrates' and Plato's positions either by contrast with Xenophon and Aristophanes, or on the internal evidence of the Platonic dialogues alone, no consensus has so far been established. Yet the repeated attempts to do so have proven irresistible if only because almost everyone who immerses himself in the Platonic corpus becomes convinced at the very least of substantial modifications in the course of Plato's thought – its alleged unity notwithstanding – from what are now more or less universally taken to be the earliest dialogues to the latest.[1] In the area of Plato's political philosophy, especially, commentators have not hesitated to draw very far-reaching conclusions concerning the Socratic question. Popper,[2] most notably, is at pains to preserve Socrates' reputation as a martyr of democracy, if only to strike the harder at Plato's version of the 'closed society', no matter whether communist or fascist.

I propose to examine the concept of dialectic in the early and middle dialogues in order to show a distinction between the negative approach taken by Socrates and a much more affirmative rationalistic method favoured by Plato, though he may indeed be said to have despaired of it at the last.[3] Most commentators who have addressed themselves to the problem of dialectic in the dialogues have taken a stand against the so-called Burnet-Taylor thesis,[4] which traces all the features of Platonic thought through the middle dialogues, especially the theory of Forms, to their Socratic, if not earlier, origin, allowing Plato little or no originality or independence of philosophical judgement. While giving no support to this view, Stenzel nonetheless sees no issue as to a 'fundamental change in Plato's doctrines' affecting the dialectic until dialogues as late as the *Parmenides, Sophist*, and *Statesman* are reached.[5] And despite his closer analysis of the earlier dialogues, Robinson[6] relies mainly on Stenzel in attributing to Socrates the developments of dialectic in the middle dialogues that belong properly, I think, to Plato. Rogers' main criterion for the distinction between Socrates and Plato is the emphasis on Socrates as a 'moral sage', as opposed to Plato, who is seen as a 'political expert and professional dialectician'.[7]

There seems to be little doubt that the earliest dialogues are 'Socratic' and that the latest are 'Platonic', both in their doctrines and methodology. The issue is at what point in the sequence of the dialogues the appearance of distinctively Platonic features can be detected. To find them side by side with Socratic elements need not lead to the exaggerated conclusions, found in the literature of the Socratic problem, that Plato must have 'betrayed' Socrates, nor that the gravest doubts must be cast on the veracity or reliability of Plato, Aristotle, or of others whose remarks are accepted or rejected according to the exigencies of the argument.

The pattern of 'Socratic dialectic' is familiar from the earlier dialogues. Socrates meets his respondent, who by virtue of his function or of some action in which he is engaged, or of some social, political, or emotional commitment, may be supposed to know the meaning of some abstract term, since he is prepared to translate it into concrete action. Thus Charmides claims to know the true nature of temperance, Euthryphro of piety (since he is prepared to accuse his father of lack of it), Thrasymachus of justice, Lysis of friendship, and so on in the well-known way. After some initial stage-setting the dialogue proper begins. The respondent, called upon to give an account of the principle which justifies his belief and action, usually begins by enumerating examples of justice, piety, friendship, and so on, but Socrates makes plain that what he is after is a *definition* of what each of these examples has in common that enables it to be subsumed under the general term. The respondent then offers a first definition which Socrates examines in quasi-legalistic and even eristic fashion, misunderstanding where misunderstanding is at all possible, and forcing the respondent to refine his original position. Second, third, and subsequent definitions are then offered; all are subjected to criticism employing a variety of devices: 1) the definition is shown to be too broad or too narrow by citing examples which appear to fit, but which the respondent is unwilling to include or exclude; 2) an increasingly precise meaning is given to some of the terms in the definition which have been too loosely used before, so as to restrict ambiguity; 3) analogies and metaphors are employed to discover whether the concept to be defined is 'like' something more familiar among the arts and crafts; 4) spurious as well as genuine etymologies are supplied; 5) logical puzzles (*aporiai*) lead to one impasse after another.[8] Finally, the frustrated respondent leaves on suddenly remembered business, vowing to rid Athens of its Sophists.

Much has been written by way of analysis of the types of argument employed in the aporetic dialogues; here I am not concerned to pursue that analysis in detail, but rather to sketch a broad account of the essentially negative results of this Socratic method, in order the more effectively to contrast it with subsequent developments in Platonic method which complement rather than supersede the method evident in the early dialogues.[9]

The commonest of the objections raised as to the inconclusiveness of this Socratic dialectic is that, while Socrates applies his destructive criticism to the arguments of others, he does not furnish affirmations of his own as to the true nature of the concepts to be defined. Grote's answer to this,[10] intended as an attack, is in fact a defence: Socrates is well aware that any affirmative answers he might give would be equally susceptible to the sorts of criticism he has brought to bear against others. The view, implicit in Grote, that Socrates is engaged in Sophistic eristic, is more likely to be found in antiquity than today, but it is still important to answer the claim that Socrates is more interested in winning the argument and confounding his opponent than he is in establishing the truth of the matter, his frequent assertions to the contrary notwithstanding. The fact is that while Socrates is very devastating in his treatment of cant, pomposity, and pretence where he encounters the redoubled evil of ignorance masquerading as knowledge, he is much tenderer with his respondents where he believes them to be right even for the wrong reasons. He always respects true opinion, if only because he is convinced that real knowledge cannot be taught. Thus he allows Cephalus (*Rep.* I, 331D) to go to his prayers after only the most superficial examination of the proposition that justice is paying what is due to men and gods, and with no suggestion of rebuke or criticism. A different answer to this objection, referring to method alone, rather than to the kind of proposition to be demonstrated, is given by Friedländer,[11] who says, very succinctly: 'Live dialectic, however, does not tolerate any dogmatic thesis'.

A third criticism arises out of a wholly mistaken appraisal of the fallacies and *aporiai* in the arguments. The crudest account of these assumes that Socrates was dishonestly trying to deceive his opponents and, still worse, that Plato tries to pass these off on his readers for sound arguments. Nothing could be further from the truth.[12] There are two elements in any explanation of this point. The first is to be found in Plato's (and almost certainly Socrates') conviction concerning the intransigeance of language, of its incapacity wholly to express universals, of the fatal gap between sign and thing (whether object or idea) signified, such that there is an impossible tension between a nominalist conception of language and a realist conception of universals. The second element grows out of the first: when a respondent says, 'Yes, Socrates', and the reader wants to cry out, 'Absolutely not, Socrates', the reader has risen to the bait. He is in fact invited to join the debate like the third actor in the New Tragedy. However, if he does so, he will discover that although correction of the fallacies may lead him one or several stages further in the argument, it still remains inconclusive.

There are other aspects of the picture of Socrates, not limited to Plato's account, that bear out the contention that the Socratic dialectic is predominantly negative and even sceptical in its conclusions. The most important of them are Socrates' *daimon*, the use of myth, and the historical fate of his position as it was understood by the Sceptics.

Socrates is that rarest of saints and martyrs – he is unwilling to insist, despite his visitations and 'rapts', that his intimacy with the divine has ever afforded him any affirmative sanction for action. The most notable occasions of this are found in the *Apology* at 40, and 41D, and in the *Phaedrus* at 242C; in the first of these Socrates knows by the absence of the sign only that death cannot be evil, though he cannot say what it is; in the second case he is prevented by the sign from leaving until he has purged his 'blasphemy', though he is not told what he should have said. Indeed, it is a cardinal point of Socrates' refusal to escape from prison that private convictions as to the truth and rightness of a course of action that are afforded by intimations of the divine can never be made public justifications of that action. The same paradox that gives Socratic irony its special poignancy also informs the *daimon*: Socratic irony is not of the ordinary variety that simply reverses the meaning of what it says, but in Socrates' case he often concedes to an opponent not the rightness of the opponent's position but the impossibility of demonstrating his own.[13]

Whether the use of myth in the middle dialogues is a Platonic innovation or rests to some extent on some usage of Socrates is not clear;[14] they do not appear at all in the earliest, most Socratic dialogues, and they fade away from the latest dialogues. But the ironical way in which many of the myths are introduced and commented on have a distinctive Socratic ring. We are warned not to take them literally (e.g., *Phaedo* 114D), though Plato makes clear that Socrates takes them seriously. The relation of the myths to Socratic dialectic seems to be a complementary one, rather after the fashion that St Thomas takes faith and reason to be complementary. Certainly, to the extent that Plato resorts to myth, there is at least a partial concession of the inadequacy of dialectic to provide conclusive demonstration of truth. That is a question that will engage us intensely later on.

Socratic dialectic, I have suggested, possesses a negative character of which I take the *daimon* to be a symbol. It may be thought of as laying down some necessary conditions for the use of the abstract terms characteristically brought under its scrutiny, but as despairing of the sufficient conditions. I take the use of myth (including the doctrine of recollection) as an indication of Socrates' awareness of the impossibility of an affirmative demonstration of the truths of which he nonetheless remains convinced. The mark of Socrates lies just in this scepticism. Ample evidence for an interpretation of Socrates in the sceptical sense here suggested is found in the subsequent history of the Academy after Plato's immediate influence had weakened. Aristotle tells us (*Soph. El.* 183b 7) that 'Socrates raised questions, but gave no answers; for he confessed that he did not know.' From Arcesilaus throughout the period of the Middle Academy and in the Cynics and Cyrenaics the appeal was to these aspects of Socrates for support of a sceptical position.

Sextus Empiricus, for example, is at pains to show that Socrates' ethical position was like that of the later Sceptics, and (*Adv. Log.* I, 8) cites Xenophon (*Mem.* i, l, ll ff.) as saying that Socrates 'rejected physics as a subject above our human powers and devoted himself solely to Ethics as the subject which concerns us men.' In the same work (*Adv. Log.* I, 190) Sextus regards the Cyrenaic school as descended directly from Socrates, and elsewhere (*Outl. Pyrrh.* I, 221) denies that Plato's position was likewise derived from Socrates'. Other passages (e.g. *Adv. Log.* I, 264) insist on Socrates' scepticism.[15] I cite these sources rather than the dialogues because while the dialogues can sustain the interpretation that Socrates is merely being ironical about his ignorance, Sextus makes it clear that the appeal of Sceptics to Socrates took his statements about his ignorance as literally supporting their position.[16]

III

I turn now to what, for the purposes of my argument, I am calling Platonic dialectic. Here the attempt is made to supply the sufficient conditions for knowledge. Deductive mathematics is the model, instead of the homely examples and analogies generally associated with Socrates.

Plato's preference for geometry over arithmetic may be seen as an attempt to seek a higher principle capable at once of restoring the 'rationality' of irrational numbers and of furnishing an answer to the Atomists' introduction of line and temporal segments that were not further divisible. I hardly think that anyone identifies the Atomists' atoms with the atoms of modern physics; but it may be useful to recall what their probable function was. The paradoxes of Zeno the Eleatic apparently presuppose that if a line is infinitely divisible then each of the ultimate divisions is zero (instead of converging on zero, as we should say). The sum of an infinite number of such divisions would then evidently itself be zero; and from this the arguments denying change of state or place can be seen to follow. If the result of summing zeros is zero, then there can be no motion from A to B, since B is at zero distance (in space or time) and so precisely corresponds with A.

There is a converse to this proposition that does not appear to have been noticed in antiquity. If one concludes that summing an infinite number of zeros is zero (because any number of zeros is zero), one could as well conclude that summing a small number of infinities is infinity, which would have the effect that everything is in the most extravagant kind of motion through space and time. That would equally apply, on the logic of the zero argument, even if the small number were zero. Both arguments are nonsense if the convention, now adopted as an axiom of arithmetic, that zero is not a number is applied. Thus, a modern solution of the paradoxes is to reject the multiplication of anything by zero or infinity, precisely because it leads to nonsense. But Greek mathematics, though uneasy in the handling of zero and infinity, did not know what to do with them.

Given a logical argument which suggests an outcome incompatible with empirical evidence of change of place or state, the Eleatic rationalists chose one of the alternatives available to them – they preferred to regard the logic as refuting the evidence of sense. But the Atomists chose the other alternative – preferring to save the appearances, they found it necessary to deny the presupposition of infinite divisibility and postulated a smallest division that was 'atomos', not further divisible. What is implied in both positions is the acceptance of the status of zero and infinity as members of the number series, as noted above. Plato was plainly uncomfortable with the consequences of both positions, as his observations concerning the axioms of mathematics show.

The difficulty that the Atomist position entails for Plato, who was also concerned to save the appearances, but in an entirely different metaphysical context, is that an irrational number like $\sqrt{2}$ now became rational, i.e. it must be an integral number of these smallest divisions. But this is incompatible with any geometrical construction available to him (or to us, for that matter). There are many puzzles of this sort, centering about the desire to bring the irrationals within arithmetic.[17] But in the absence of a proof (i.e. a geometrical construction) to solve these puzzles, Plato could not allow empirical measurement to take its place – this would be placing the cart before the horse. Numbers like π and $\sqrt{2}$ are 'irrational' only with reference to arithmetic; but in geometry they are generated in a way that makes them perfectly acceptable, and their appearance is not only evidence against the Atomist position which Plato in any case mistrusted, but also evidence of the 'higher' nature of geometry. This accounts, I think, for the exceptional importance of geometrical examples in Plato,[18] and the use of the geometrico-logical model which distinguishes Platonic from Socratic dialectic. It should, however, be borne in mind throughout the following discussion that Plato's sophistication in the philosophy of mathematics leads him in several places (e.g. *Rep*. VI, 510D, VII, 533/4) to leave room for doubt about the possibility of 1) modelling the rest of knowledge upon mathematics, and 2) demonstrating the *truth* of the first premisses of an axiom system like geometry. In outline the argument is as follows:

If the truth of a set of axiomatic propositions of sufficient generality ('the best of the higher hypotheses' – *Phaedo* 101D) may be presupposed, then any proposition which could be validly deduced from these would be a true theorem, clearly in conformity with empirical fact ('saving the appearances'); but its truth would depend on a valid inference from true premisses, not on empirical verification which is, in the strict sense, always fortuitous.

This has been the dream of rationalists ever since. It is taken quite literally by Descartes, Leibniz, and Spinoza, and finds favour with less respectable mystagogues, cabalists, and those who would demonstrate from the dimensions of the Pyramids that the British are the descendants of the ten Lost Tribes of Israel. Since the post-Kantian upheaval, however, and the rise of fictionalism, conventionalism, reduction chains, and so forth, the claim for the self-evident *truth*[19] of axioms has been abandoned by nearly all except mathematical intuitionists. I say 'nearly all', because one of the most important books on Plato of recent years, J. N. Findlay's *Plato: the Written and the Unwritten Doctrines*,[20] revives and ascribes to Plato a programme of 'mathematicization' entirely at odds with the difficulties that Plato has foreseen and documented.

That programme is sometimes introduced with a degree of caution: 'the passage in question' (Findlay does not say exactly which passage, but the context is the slave boy's 'recollection' of the properties of the square in the *Meno*) 'therefore implies the ontology of the Eide, and perhaps also that of the Objects of Mathematics, and while it does not explicitly endorse the doctrine that *all* Ideal Meanings have a purely mathematical analysis, the examples of definition certainly tend in that direction' (p. 126). He repeats this in almost the same language with reference to the *Phaedo* on p. 130. But the caution disappears in Findlay's treatment of mathematics in the Republic: 'It cannot be doubted that what is here being projected as the program of Dialectic is the complete mapping of all the possible patterns of mathematical being, arithmetical, geometrical, chronometric and dynamic, which for Socrates-Plato are as much normative and axiological as merely ontological – a mapping based, moreover, on principles that are wholly self-justifying, and which leave nothing to mere postulation or unreliable conjecture' (p. 189).

What is so exasperating about this and the many similar statements in Findlay's book is that it is surely true, but not Plato's last word on the subject. Certainly Plato hoped that dialectic would yield a method of attaining truth; equally certainly he took mathematics at least as a metaphor for that method. But he did not, as Findlay does, reify that metaphor. He was surely as aware as Findlay is of the problems of 'mere postulation': 'It is important in this context not to bring in the whole modern machinery of the deductive system which Plato could not have conceived or found interesting' (p. 141). Leaving to one side Plato's interest (I am sure he would have been interested), it seems clear that Plato does foresee the methodological problems of postulation, and sought a way of overcoming the hypothetical status of axioms. But it is astonishing to read in Findlay that Plato did not give us the results of his positive findings concerning Mathematical Objects because that would greatly lengthen the present discussion (*Rep.* VII, 534A and Findlay, p. 188). In anything so central Plato would have given them (perhaps in lieu of the *Parmenides* or any six books of the *Laws*) if he obtained results he believed it prudent to communicate. A famous passage in the Seventh Letter (341BE) suggests both that he did not obtain them and that, even if he did, it would be unwise to present them to the general public. He also warns against writers who, in his opinion, 'have no real acquaintance with the subject' (341C). But Findlay is determined to tell us what Plato would not, and he is invariably half-right. For example he says: 'The postulation of an Eidos is an hypothesis, a postulation of being, and the being it involves is of a kind to involve non-sensuous intuition. Modern philosophers who wish above all things to dispense with non-sensuous intuitions have nothing to put in their place' (p. 156). All these things are true and Plato would agree. But Plato did not want non-sensuous intuitions; where two could be found to agree he would find only a *folie à deux* – what he wanted was proof, and that is not to be had. Findlay, on the other hand, is so terrified that Plato should be mistaken for a logical positivist that he has turned him into a phenomenologist fully equipped with self-serving Eidetic Insights. We had better return to our text and see what Plato actually does say.

Two distinct methods are offered, though both are concerned with classification of concepts in different ways. The method of collection and division (mainly to be found in the *Sophist* and *Statesman*) is primarily concerned with correctness of definition; while the method of hypothesis appears mainly in *Phaedo* (99D–101E) and in the Republic (VII, 531C–539D, with some introductory remarks at VI, 511). Both sets of arguments follow an explicit rejection of empirical methods as furnishing merely probable knowledge; while collection and division are concerned, for example, with sameness and difference to be determined by characteristics 'relevant to a given purpose of definition' (*Rep.* V, 454A), the method of hypothesis expounds the mathematico-deductive method.

IV

Collection and division could as well be called synthesis and analysis; it is the enterprise continued by Aristotle in the *Posterior Analytics*. Division is the attempt to specify those characteristics that correctly define an object or idea, separating these from accidental features, while collection, having correctly identified an object or idea is able to classify it as a member of some class under which it may be subsumed. It may be said of any two objects that there exist between them similarities and differences (cf. *Statesman* 285B), though some of these may be altogether trivial or even misleading. Cabbages and kings may seem utterly unlike, but they are both at least physical objects occupying space and time, having mass, colour, and certain other physical attributes; to a cannibal they are also edible, though this is unlikely to occur to non-cannibals under ordinary circumstances. Two coins, especially if struck from the same die, may be said to be identical, but differences can always be found: the pattern of wear, scratches, or distortions may permit the univocal identification of one coin as different from the other (for example, the particular coin used as a screwdriver to effect a felonious entry) or, more generally, as being a coin rejected by a slot machine as possibly counterfeit, though it might well be accepted by a bank clerk as legal tender. Most trivially, perhaps, it must be allowed that one coin is simply not the other, but is different because it is an other. While some of Plato's examples are every bit as homely as these, and have a like air of seeming triviality, the problem is not trivial and the appearances are deceptive.

The three main examples Plato gives of this method are the definition of women in *Rep.* V, 454 and the 'hunt' for the sophist and statesman in the dialogues so titled. I shall return to the definition of women later on, where I propose to treat it as a sort of anti-myth offered in opposition to the conventional thinking of Plato's day. But for the purposes of the present discussion we must note how the method is applied. Clearly, if we are determined to vindicate current social institutions, we shall stress the differences between men and women and gloss over the similarities; but Plato wants to do the opposite. If one chooses, for example, the role of men and women in procreation, they are utterly different and there is no way within our power (so far) to make them interchangeable. Similarly, one can argue that women are generally shorter and weaker than men, and that these differences are critical; one could also go on with other stereotypes of common thought: women are oriented to home and family, men to work and world. All of these are true in one or another social setting, and some, like the role in procreation, are true regardless of societal forms. There may well be an endless array of facts as well as opinions about the proper definition, but it is important to note that these are not dispositive of the question. We still have to decide which of the facts are material and which superficial in reaching a proper definition. If one decides that certain facts are not dispositive, one has not decided that they are not facts, only that they are not relevant to the purpose of our definition. Plato himself is extremely cautious in advancing the proposition, astonishing to Greek ears, of the essential equality of women despite the manifest differences, but he does so for some very sober and practical reasons. I give these here in summary form, because I shall return to this important issue when dealing with the myths.

The reasons are quite simply that he has noted that genetically it is just as significant who the mother is (not merely who the father is, as was a commonplace of Greek, and later, belief); that women are the equals of men in intelligence and potential for citizenship and that therefore society should not deprive itself of one-half of the available talent; and so on in a sophisticated weighing of the hereditary along with environmental factors. I must contrast this interpretation with Findlay's[21] as illustrating his perilous approach. What he has to say about Plato's insistence on the equality of women is utterly removed from Plato's manifest concern: 'The main point is that it is eidetic insight which alone can decide whether or not there is a genuine difference of Eidos or Phusis – the two are deeply associated in the thought of men and women: procreative, grammatical and conventionally social distinctions do nothing to decide the issue. And logic-chopping or Eristic is precisely the sort of reasoning that confounds genuine distinctions of Eidos or Phusis with conventional, verbal or contingently factual distinctions.' Here myth (the essential inequality of women) and anti-myth (their equality) are contending, and the main point is that it is *not* eidetic insight that can decide. It can, indeed, decide for *me*, but what am I to do with rival lunatics who sheathe themselves in their own impregnable eidetic insights? This removes decision from the realm of rational discourse entirely; whatever the residual problem may be that baffles definitive resolution – and it is of the utmost gravity – it was not Plato's intention to refer it to the very intuitions he most suspected!

The most sustained account and example of the method of division is found in the *Statesman*, where several attempts to define that elusive personage are undertaken, interspersed with some important methodological observations. The *Sophist* is much less important because little or nothing is said about the method as such. Moreover, its three attempts to snare its victim by this method all work backwards, as it were, by examination of the class complements, locating the sophist in the sub-classes to be discarded. We must look for him, we are told, under the rubric of vice not virtue (227D) where he hawks a spurious mode of instruction based on the reduplicated evil of ignorance masked as knowledge. The sophist is a sort of illusionist (235B) who produces fraudulent semblances, not fair likenesses; and (264E) he is both acquisitive and productive of falsity. Finally, he is not a dialectician (253DE) because he does not divide properly.

We shall find much more valuable materials in the *Statesman*: it is a difficult dialogue to follow, even on close reading, because of the surely deliberate dead-ends, comic detours, and other digressions that illustrate the problems involved with this method. We are to dichotomize the class of individuals denoted by some term so as to produce an exhaustive division (261C) between a sub-class and its class complement. This can, of course, be done in a totally random and meaningless way by fragmenting the class along some line of cleavage that does not advance our understanding of the topic. For example, a division between Greeks and barbarians (262E) will not help us to define statecraft because some of the defining characteristics of the statesman are found among barbarians and are lacking among some Greeks. (It is possible to be much more random and arbitrary than this: for example, everything in the universe either is or is not a black cat, and no doubt imagination can suggest circumstances under which it might be useful to assign something to the class of black cats or to its class complement of non-black-cats; but one cannot be certain in advance, or perhaps even later on, which of the unlimited bases on which one might divide will prove useful.) What Plato tells us is that we are to look for 'natural' divisions like the joints into which a sacrificial animal might be carved (287C; cf. *Phaedrus* 265E), so that the section has a specific form (262B); merely semantic contention over the names of things should not confuse us (261E); we should slice down the middle, avoiding odd little bits (262B) – this suggests Plato's quasi-Pythagorean affinity for proceeding by twos that makes such divisions as male and female, odd and even, seem intrinsically more plausible than some others (262E).

My notes on the first ten pages of the dialogue, which it would be utterly boring to reproduce here, show at least twenty such divisions (including most of the misleading ones); fortunately, they are sum-marized at 267AC where the results of this distinctly self-parodistic first effort may be paraphrased as follows: 'Statesmanship is that part of theoretical science concerned with initiating orders given to those beings living on land in herds which are hornless, non-interbreeding (with other species), and two-legged'. For some reason, 'wingless', which kept tame gaggles out of the definition, is omitted here. One is reminded of the plucked chicken that was reported to have been tossed over the garden wall of the Lyceum in order to refute Aristotle's definition of man as a featherless biped. While not totally useless, the definition (back to Plato now) fails because others who also tend such herds – merchants, farmers, and doctors, for example – are not yet excluded. Before proceeding to the second attempt, a myth of the reversal of the motions of the cosmos (to which I shall later return) is interpolated (268D–273E). Its relevance to the hunt for the statesman lies in the moral appended to the myth (273E–274D): since these cataclysms it falls to the universe to govern itself, and to us to find rules for our own guidance. This is a peculiar passage, but it suffices for our immediate purposes to acknowledge that the quest for the definition of the statesman will not be 'natural' in the sense that it will *not* be given in some objective or irrefutable way from outside, but that our own ingenuity will have to supply it; and so the search continues.

Two more attempts at division are made, one of which leads into an analogy with weaving, including a most ingeniously bifurcated analysis of the nature of clothesmaking (279CD); the other introduces the hitherto ignored possibility of multiple division, so that there may be more than two sub-classes (287B–291D). Another valuable meth-odological observation, made almost in passing, offers an answer to the problem of 'relevance' in education: the speakers have no interest in weaving as such in choosing it to illustrate the method (285D). The utility lies in the exercise of one's wits, and in the methods of abstract thought exemplified. But a conclusory definition offered by this method is not reached. Instead the argument is diverted into some important considerations about the nature of analogy, including a discussion of 'examples of examples', for as the Stranger tells us at 277D: 'It is difficult to demonstrate anything of real importance without the use of examples.' Moreover, analogies with the highest things are not available in the visible world, and so these must be demonstrated by reason only (286A).

It is clear that Plato will not give us the desired definition of the statesman by the method of division (or by any other of his dialectic methods) because he says at 284D: ' . . . when one day we come to give a full exposition of true accuracy in dialectic method . . . ' What he in fact offers is an analogy with the art and science of the doctor, such that distinctions among various forms of government (291D), especially as they entail consent of the governed, are on the whole immaterial. What is dispositive is the doctor's (and the statesman's) mastery of an objective body of knowledge which the layman ignores or neglects at his peril (293B) when it is offered in a disinterested way for the patient's benefit.

The Young Socrates (namesake of *the* Socrates, who is mostly a silent listener throughout this dialogue and the *Sophist*) balks at the idea that the best rule would be without laws because authority should vest in the knowledgeable king and not in inflexible laws that cannot meet the varying needs of individuals and changing circumstances. But this, and many other substantive issues of the highest political and ethical interest, owe little or nothing to the method of division. When a definition is presented, at 293D: 'So long as they work on a reasoned scientific principle following essential justice and act to preserve and improve the life of the state so far as may be, we must call them real statesmen . . . ', no further claim is made for the method.

We are not only given a number of analogies, but something of a theory of analogy which, because it is clearly related to collection (i.e. the recognition of similarities that permit the subsumption of particulars under a general principle), likewise forms part of dialectic. As valuable as these methods are, they fail in the promised degree of logical rigour. Analogy compares known features of experience, logical as well as factual, with those newly encountered in quest of an isomorphism between them: these parallelisms are not limited to what we might call first-order similarities (surface resemblances of colour, shape, function), but extend to similarities of higher order (quantifiable relationships, structure), and at sufficiently abstract levels permit the inference that certain properties, mostly of a mathematical kind, found in one system of ordered relationships may also be found in the analogue. Such methods, which of course include metaphors of various kinds, have proven remarkably fruitful in the history of science and, indeed, of abstract thought applied in many other fields as well. But such comparisons are often invidious and may mislead us; not all the properties of one such system are correctly imputable to another, and independent confirmation that those properties in fact exist in the analogue must be sought.

Thus analogy and metaphor (as well as their modern descendants, simulation and modelling) are suggestive and highly valuable as forms of hypothesis, but are not rigorous modes of deductive inference. Plato nowhere argues that they are, but he leaves dangerously open the question how far he thought they might be carried. The most notable weakness lies in the precise role of empirical verification, against which Plato surely had a debilitating *parti pris*. There are indeed very crude sorts which do nothing to advance knowledge: the beginner in algebra, say, who seeks to reassure himself by making an arithmetical substitution at each stage of the algebraic working to confirm that $(x + y)^2$ really is $x^2 + 2xy + y^2$. Or, even cruder, the counter of beans confirming that $7 + 5 = 12$. But even at the most sophisticated level the empirical interpretation of inferences from an abstract and tautologous axiom set must be tested against the physical world; or it must reach, as Plato would have us do, beyond mortal experience for that confirmation.

In fact, common experience is relied upon to a degree much beyond what he is prepared to acknowledge. The dialogues are full of the most homely and everyday examples, drawn from the crafts and the marketplace, and reveal a profound and acute power of observation brought to bear in the most vivid detail on practical concerns. The example from weaving mentioned above would be utterly fatuous if it were not accurate and recognizable by a weaver as such. Nowhere does he explicitly say, and it places the greatest strain on his text to infer, that empirical evidence has at least the function I have ascribed to Socratic dialectic, namely that of disconfirming imprudent and apparently valid inferences from logically antecedent premises that run counter to experience. This is what he in fact does, and it is what I understand by the obscure application of the expression 'saving the appearances' used by his immediate successors in the Academy. But Plato is not, of all people, Karl Popper, and there is no anticipation of any doctrine of disconfirmability to form part of Plato's formal methodology. He is so hostile to the idea that empirical experience could shape the formal structure of our knowledge that he fails to account for the extent and the ways in which he himself relies on it. In the absence of any authority in the text we simply cannot manufacture a sound foundation for the status of such experience in his theory of knowledge. But we may surely infer something from his practice, which is to rely heavily on what the surface of experience can suggest about its depths.

Like analogy and collection, division is also inconclusive, but has its own problems besides. There is an element of question-begging in the requirement (*Rep.* V, 454A) that we must first know the purpose for which we are defining, and for what audience (*Phaedrus* 277C). No rule can be given for the choice among virtually unlimited possible dichotomies; one embarks instead, as Plato does, on a voyage of discovery by trial and error that is not only inconclusive but in fact unconcluded, as we have seen in the *Statesman*, where there is no pretence that the definition finally offered has been reached by this method. Nor should we be surprised at this circularity. The method of collection and division was first defined in the *Phaedrus* at 265D–266A, where it was applied to the several forms of madness; but at 277B Socrates says: 'First you must know the truth about the subject that you speak or write about.' This position is not consistently maintained in the *Statesman* and *Sophist*, where a quest for truth from a condition of ignorance is the aim, but from the *Phaedrus* at least it would seem that we are to argue downward from the highest segment of the Line, not to it from experience. Despite its manifest utility, it is not by this method that we shall establish truth. Perhaps the method of hypothesis will serve us better.

V

In the *Phaedo* Socrates first (99D) sums up the inconclusive results of empirical investigation which blinds the soul to truth just as gazing at the sun (astronomical observation) blinds the eyes. He then moves to the preferred method of hypothesis (100A) where he 'assumes some principle which I judge to be the strongest, and then I approved as true whatever seemed to agree with this . . . and that which disagreed I regarded as untrue.'

What is being pursued here is the idea, familiar enough in the later history of philosophy, but probably novel in Plato's day, that bare observation of facts will not yield explanations of them. Indeed, an 'explanation' for Plato seems to require the subsumption of particulars in a conceptual scheme of great generality and ultimately, of course, of the utmost generality. The *Phaedo* does not go very far in developing this argument which is best worked out in the *Republic*. Here (100B) the theoretical postulates of greatest generality to be assumed are the Forms of 'absolute Beauty and Goodness and Magnitude, and all the rest.' They are invoked in a context (100C) which appears singularly tautologous: 'whatever else is beautiful apart from absolute beauty is beautiful because it partakes of that absolute beauty, and for no other reason.' It is, however, no objection that such propositions should be tautologous because all theorems deduced within a system of axioms, definitions, and rules are, of course, tautologous. This is, no doubt, why Socrates says at 100D that the passage just quoted is 'the safest answer' to give rather than some attempt at locating essential qualities of an object in its fortuitous attributes (100E ff.). So long as the hypothesis is compatible with the observed facts it is adduced to explain one remains safe – it is the hypothesis itself that is subject to attack (101D). In that case it is necessary to show that the hypothesis is a logical consequence of some 'higher' hypothesis, i.e. one of still greater generality; and by a process analogous to the 'ladder of beauty' in the *Symposium* (211C), we hope to rise to a final postulate that is 'befitting' (*hikanos*). We are not told here how this is done – that is attempted in greater detail in the *Republic*. However, an earlier passage in the *Phaedo* (75–9) suggests that the theory of *anamnesis* (reminiscence) is peculiarly suited for this purpose. The problem of a priori knowledge as it appears in the *Phaedo* and *Meno* seems to be raised to solve a curiously pervasive question, by no means confined to Plato's repeated interest in it. How can the mind, if mortal and dependent on the ephemeral data of sense, attain to the knowledge it possesses of, say, geometry? For this is a kind of knowledge wholly different from the probabilistic generalizations of inductive procedures. Since, on the position adopted by Plato, we do possess in mathematics a body of knowledge, none of the propositions of which could possibly be falsified by experience, it cannot be from empirical experience that it is derived; on the contrary, it in fact validates experience! It is impossible to overstate the force of this argument (whatever answers may have been developed later); despite his many objections to rationalist metaphysics, Kant is arguing along substantially the same lines in his discussion of the synthetic a priori.[22] The conclusion of both the *Phaedo* and the *Meno* is that knowledge of this sort must antedate physical existence; and thus in both dialogues it is the basis for a 'proof' of the immortality of the soul: for the soul must be like the eternal qualities of the Forms it perceives and recollects.

The *Republic* supplies us with a much more sophisticated version of the same argument, the precise meaning of which has been the subject of a good deal of scholarly polemic, especially as concerns the role of sense experience. It begins with the image of the Divided Line (VI, 509D), is in essence repeated, after the manner of the weak defence of poetry for the benefit of those who cannot follow the close reasoning of that excessively succinct image, in the allegory of the Cave (VII, 514A), and receives its final expression in the discussion of dialectic at 531C ff. The account of the Line is too familiar to require repetition here, but some points need elaboration. The first of these is the relation of induction, hypothesis, and deduction. For convenience let us number the four segments of the line from the bottom up: 1) *eikasia* (picture thinking); 2) *pistis* (belief); 3) *dianoia* (understanding); and 4) *noesis* (reason or intellection).

In proceeding from the second to the third segment the mind, we are told (510C, 511C), we must employ assumptions, i.e. hypotheses grounded on inductive generalizations, from which we can in turn deduce particular propositions. The illustration Plato uses is geometry (510D) to show in what sense the physical triangle is only an image of the ideal triangle, and he is quite explicit in crediting the geometers with an interest in the triangle present to the mind of which the physical triangle scratched in the sand is the merest image. The properties of that physical triangle are accidental and depend on actual measurement, and so are subject to the errors of sense perception. But if its properties have been deduced from the axioms of geometry (he uses terms interchangeably to denote 'assumptions', 'hypotheses', and 'axioms'), we have a criterion for correcting measurement and sense perception.

The difficulties begin in the transition from the third to the fourth segment of the line, for the validation of the axioms of geometry can occur only within the context of a most general system in which those axioms are no longer primitives but from which they can be deduced. This most general system is, of course, the realm of forms, presided over and illumined by the Good. It would be possible, having attained this level of universality, to deduce the particulars of sense and to confirm *them*, rather than to have this empirical confirmation of the principles,[23] but who could be interested in the Many generated out of the One, if he possessed the One itself?[24]

That the two middle sections of the line are required to be equal, given the proportions stated, is fortuitous, I think, though it had led some commentators into strange speculations as to the meaning possibly intended by so mathematically oriented a thinker. But the most vehement polemics have been devoted to the division of opinion about the extent to which Plato here anticipates modern notions of the logico-deductive method in science and mathematics; and especially about the part played in this by sense perception. Collingwood leads for the idealists, and Findlay for the phenomenologists, and I hope that I can do justice to their reasonable concerns in what follows; the sketchiness of Plato's account, however, leaves more room for ambiguity and dispute than is conducive to any serious reader's comfort.

There are too many references to passing upward and downward among the divisions (510B; twice in 511A; twice in 511B) to be ignored. The temptation, in concluding that 'upward' refers to induction, and 'downward' to deduction, is to read into these passages more of the modern connotations of these terms than Plato is remotely likely to have foreseen. Yet it is impossible to explicate these passages without recourse to some version of these concepts, and one can only hope, in the absence of an unequivocal account of what he meant by Plato himself, that we have not distorted his intentions. On the surface, at least, the dispute centres about whether he has not perhaps overstated the importance of deduction and understated the importance of induction.

Induction, as all would agree, is a mental process rooted in the particulars of sense. At a somewhat primitive level experience is organized by the presence in them of specified properties into classes of objects or events to which a name can be given. That name denotes the class, and may then be applied to objects newly encountered which display the properties specified in the definition. We are still at the level of tables and beds; to the extent that some new object fails to exhibit those properties, we have the choice of denying that it is a member of the class by pointing to the absence of properties included in the definition (or the presence of properties excluded from it); or we may amend the definition so as to include the new object – perhaps being compelled thereby to exclude some object previously thought to be a member of the class, but now seen to have been included in error. This is the sort of enterprise undertaken in the aporetic dialogues, as noted in the discussion of Socratic dialectic above, where successive definitions (of abstract terms, not tables and beds) are offered in a process of refining some intuitively persuasive definition that is soon seen to fail because, among other things, it is too broad or too narrow. The method of division and collection similarly attempts, by a sifting of predicates or properties to specify which of them are essential, which accidental, to correct definition.

The vice of induction is that every definition reached by these methods necessarily remains tentative because it is always subject to correction in light of new experience. It is in fact an hypothesis advanced on the basis of such experience as we have had of some possible class of objects, and so long as we are limited to refining definitions by these methods, there is no way of removing the hypothetical character of any definition currently held because our experience is finite and the future, relatively if not absolutely, is not. But we must not overlook the part played in this inductive process by deduction. Every hypothesis has a prediction built into it: if the hypothesis is true, then we may deduce that every new object to which it correctly applies will display the specified properties. If it does not, we face the choice mentioned above. One can say: 'That is not like any table I ever saw, and therefore it is not a table'; or one can say: 'That is not like any table I ever saw, but I was wrong to suppose the definition based on that earlier experience to be sound.' To the extent that no rigorous rule can be given to determine this choice, above all at this primitive level, induction must appear even more enfeebled, especially if some other method (deduction, say) looks vastly more promising. If, however, it does exhibit the expected properties, we are inclined to subsume the new particular under the hypothetical concept, treating the latter as to that degree confirmed because it correctly predicted the expected properties.

Induction is, of course, not confined to this first level of definition. Tables and chairs may be treated as members of the more inclusive class of, say, furniture or, if that is going too fast, of domestic furniture as opposed to office furniture. (An example of the merely semantic problems about which we are from time to time warned in these discussions not to permit unnecessary confusion, would be to watch out for printer's furniture, which is something altogether different.) Many levels are likely to appear in such systematic classification; perhaps the image of an inverted tree may give some sense of what is intended. The leaves may be thought of as discrete observations unified by the twigs from which they depend; branches of varying thickness unify the twigs, lead into each other, and finally converge on the unitary trunk, which could be thought of as the One, the single principle that lends structure and coherence to the whole. Other images may be more adequate: a 'reticular' network of interrelated concepts joined by lines to indicate a complex and multidimensional set of relationships among them. Whatever the image, we must be on our guard against being seduced by it as a substitute for the reality (or, failing that, as a substitute for a better image).

There is a quantum leap when we shift from the structuring of physical experience in such multilevelled concepts to the analogous structuring of abstract terms: 'But to the highest and most important class of existents there are no corresponding visible resemblances'

(*Statesman* 286A). Nonetheless, it is important to note that the methods of treating the definition of terms is the same in both cases. The early and middle dialogues repeatedly use the analogue of homely objects like tables and beds in seeking a definition of justice, piety, friendship, love, courage, and the like. The first stage is the enumeration of examples of these concepts, much the way we might point to a half-dozen tables to illustrate what we mean by a 'table'. But Socrates expects his respondents to replicate in the case of some abstract term the process that has led to the use of the term 'table' to refer more or less unequivocally to any one of the objects it denotes. In particular he wants them to abandon simple enumeration and move to the higher plane of pattern recognition. What properties do each of the examples exhibit in common that could provide the foundation at least of an hypothetical definition? We have already sufficiently celebrated the negative aspects of Socratic dialectic, and these need no lengthy repetition here.

The special difficulty of definition of abstract terms where no empirical confirmation is possible was surely known to Socrates; it is implied throughout the dialogues. But explicit reference to it, such as the passage from the *Statesman* (286A) cited above, is confined to the mature dialogues, and Plato only vaguely tells us what modification of dialectical method would be appropriate. Findlay, among others, is quite willing to fill the gap with eidetic insight which, as a general indication of method might be a reasonable rendering of the Platonic text, but tells us nothing of the specific content of any particular insight. This may be Husserl's method, but it lacks the rigour and objectivity that Plato insists upon. And so it is that the attempt to define those terms is repeatedly made, some progress and refinement of the definitions certainly emerges, but at the last they fail. The process founders, as it must, because every definition reached by the upward path of induction remains necessarily tentative and subject to further correction dictated by new experience and subtler ingenuity in organizing it.

But the exercise is not worthless. Merely as an exercise it is of great value, sharpening the intellect and accustoming the mind to levels of thought that would never be reached if it were not undertaken. Moreover, the later definitions are superior to the earlier ones, and suggest that other point of departure to which Plato attaches vital importance. It is not difficult to postulate that the series of ever-improving definitions converges on an ideal and incorrigible definition, immune to experience, timeless, and located in a mental/spiritual realm intelligible to mind, not space- and time-bound as are those intermediate definitions based on sense perception in the physical world. He ascribes reality, indeed the only reality, to those ideal definitions – the forms or ideas – with some lesser degree of reality (nowhere clearly expressed under the doctrine of 'participations') for the particulars of sense to the extent that they imperfectly exemplify the ideals they resemble.

The ascription of reality to the Forms is not arbitrary, but springs from Plato's conviction that there exists a branch of our knowledge that comes close to realizing this vision of a foundation for knowledge free of the incurable vice of induction. The upward path of induction is not unlike trying to catch a fluid in an inverted funnel, if I may be permitted this image. Something will be caught, no doubt, but nearly everything is missed; and what is caught is too random a portion to inspire confidence in the method. If the funnel is turned right side up we are certain to do better, even though, as we shall see, not everything can be caught. The downward path of deduction is the funnel set to rights, and the branch of knowledge is geometry. The beauty of geometry does not lie in the fact that its abstract results are confirmed in experience – we can leave that to empiricists, and to the 'narrow' ones at that, as Hempel would say – but it is nonetheless reassuring that we can meet the empiricists on their own ground by pointing to those results. The beauty lies in the fact that upon a minimum of hypothetical presuppositions – and those persuasive in themselves to the point of appearing self-evident – we can prove a vast number of theorems with the utmost rigour. The whole system is internally consistent (as well as corresponding with its empirical interpretation in the world – we do not really need this, but it can do no harm), and if we consider certain theorems as proven, then logically consequent theorems follow with a degree of certainty to which induction can never aspire.

The geometrical proof of the theorem of Pythagoras is a suitable example in this context. The squares on the sides having been constructed, it proceeds by dropping a perpendicular from the apex through the hypotenuse to divide that square into two parts; further lines are drawn from the other corners of the triangle to the opposite squares. The proof relies on a number of theorems previously proven: that equals added to equals are equal; that triangles of equal base and between the same parallels are of equal area, and the like. The theorems previously proven may be traced in an unbroken chain of reasoning through logically antecedent theorems back to the axioms, definitions, and postulates in Book I of Euclid. It may be a common fallacy to suppose that the intermediate theorems have lost the hypothetical character that still invests the axioms. It is not a fallacy committed by Plato, though the meaning of the text is very problematic and the source of much dispute. It is utterly clear to him, though, that deductive inferences cannot be more certain than the postulates from which they are derived. Yet he never abandons mathematics as the best model of knowledge, and so misleads many commentators into the belief that it is his programme to 'mathematicize' philosophy, taking this literally, so that enormous effort is expended in unravelling the Dyad and Ideal Number, as though these were the actual expression of ultimate reality instead of a powerful metaphor pointing toward, but finally inadequate to, the utterance of what at the last must remain ineffable.

If dialectic is to be successful it may indeed begin with assumptions treated 'not as absolute beginnings but literally as hypotheses, underpinnings, footings, and springboards so to speak, to enable it to rise to that which requires no assumption and is the starting point of all . . .' (*Rep.* VI, 511B). If it can do this, then the certainties of deduction lie before by proceeding 'downward to the conclusion, making no use whatever of any object of sense but only of pure ideas moving on through ideas to ideas and ending with ideas' (511BC). The geometers carry out only part of this programme: they 'use their understanding and not their senses' (511D); they correctly treat their drawings and representations of figures as images only, and 'what they really seek is to get sight of those realities which can be seen only by the mind' (510E).

What the geometers fail to do is to validate their axioms, presumably by showing these to be theorems deduced from non-hypothetical premisses. We may gauge the importance of the criticism from the frequency with which it is repeated:

1) '. . . its inability to extricate itself from and rise above its assumptions.' (511A)
2) '. . . dialectic, as something truer and more exact than the object of the so-called arts and sciences whose assumptions are arbitrary starting points.' (511C)
3) '. . . yet because they do not go back to the beginning . . . but start from assumptions . . .' (511D)
4) '. . . it is impossible for them as long as they leave the assumptions which they employ undisturbed and cannot give any account of them.' (533C)

Plato is thus in no doubt that the axioms of geometry are indemonstrable unless they can be derived from the forms in the fourth segment of the Line (511C). As a means of attaining this ultimate knowledge, geometry and the other higher studies are indeed praiseworthy and indispensable (527C), but only as propaedeutic. The task which cannot be executed by geometry must fall to dialectic (533C) by which means alone an 'account of the essence of each thing' (534B) can be given.

From 531C on, Plato becomes increasingly explicit about the benefits of the dialectical progression, and increasingly vague about the manner of attaining those benefits. The mood is conditional and it is evident that these are necessary and not sufficient conditions (531E). We are told (531D) that the whole course of study is wasted unless it 'is carried to the point at which reflection can take a comprehensive view of the mutual relations and affinities which bind all these sciences together.' Glaucon accepts all too readily Socrates' contention that he cannot be sure he possesses the truth himself and that, even if he did, Glaucon, as one not yet trained in dialectic, could not understand it.[25] If successful, however, dialectic would be the only science which dispenses with hypotheses,[26] for its first principles are true. All the same, we search the dialogues in vain for any further realization of this programme, but the rest is silence.

VI

It would be convenient, but improper, to exaggerate the difference between what I have called Socratic and Platonic dialectic in order to claim the discovery of a clear-cut criterion for partial solution of the Socratic problem. But even if it is conceded that no definitive solution is at all likely, some hints are available; and these derive in the first place from studies, like those of Campbell and Lutoslawski,[27] which first date the dialogues on stylistic grounds and on internal historical evidence, and then examine on the basis of a chronology thus established the development of certain key ideas. The general presupposition is that the more distinctively Platonic ideas are to be found at the greatest distance in time from the memory of Socrates. As time wore on, it is assumed, Plato gained confidence in his independent power as a philosopher and so one would expect the later appearance of distinctively Platonic ideas to which nothing in the early dialogues precisely corresponds, or of which those Platonic ideas are a development.

Granting this makes all the more difficult the claim made in this chapter to draw a distinction between the dialectic of master and pupil. For the dialectic here attributed to Plato is not found in dialogues that are unquestionably the latest, but rather in those that are unquestionably from the middle period, where any attempt at a contribution towards solution of the Socratic problem along chronological lines must be seriously compromised by maximum ambiguity in the attribution of these ideas to Plato or to Socrates. The claim, therefore, is only a modest one, and falls under two heads: that Plato, in the middle period, takes a fairly undeveloped idea of Socrates and expands it into a sophisticated anticipation of the hypothetico-deductive method in the philosophy of science; second, that the failure of even this more rigorous system to yield sufficient conditions for certain knowledge led Plato for a time into the employment of myth as a kind of philosophical rhetoric to overcome, in a heuristic way, the shortcomings of dialectic. The myths, and the reasons for their use I mean, of course, to treat in an extended way later. It is to the first of my claims that I wish now to pay closer attention, adding some further considerations on Plato's philosophy of language as a source of the inadequacy of dialectic.

By calling Platonic dialectic an anticipation of the hypothetico-deductive method I do not suggest that the dialogues furnish a completely articulated theory. This would have involved the dissipation of much of the mystery with which Plato is careful to surround the inconclusiveness of his arguments. Something of the same caution is to be found in the discussion of eugenics in the *Republic* (V, 458B), and for the same reasons. From Plato's point of view it is essential somehow to distinguish the extreme rationalism of his own thought, instinct as it is with a firm moral purpose, from the parody of reason coupled with moral irresponsibility that he always sees in eristic and demagogic rhetoric. A frank acknowledgement, along pragmatist lines, say, of the indemonstrability of the truth of his convictions and therefore of their assumption, *faute de mieux*, as fictions or *mythoi*, is more than he is prepared to concede in public. Even the seventh Letter is not explicit in detail, though clearly available in support of this interpretation.[28]

What I am arguing here is that to the extent that the ambiguity of Plato's position leads to the Sceptical *epoché*, it is because of the pervasive (and all but subversive) Socratic element in his thought. The other side has been equally influential – it is the mathematical Plato who, as we are told by Aristotle (in the report of Aristoxenus), startled his hearers with a lecture on the Good couched entirely in mathematical exposition of the One. Any number of commentators have so interpreted the passages from the *Republic* discussed above as referring to an alleged Platonic view that physics is science just to the extent that it is mathematical. They then go on to argue, mainly from the text of the *Timaeus* and the *Laws*, that since Plato appeared to equate mathematics and reality in those later dialogues, he must also have done so in the middle dialogues, including the discussion of the Divided Line. The evidence for this view may be too impressive to discount wholly, especially in light of the activities of Plato's immediate successors in the Academy; but I cannot agree that this interpretation is sound when applied to the *Republic*.

There Plato makes clear that mathematical study as such is so far from being an end in itself that he makes Glaucon say at 531E that hardly any mathematician he has met was a master in dialectic. The argument clearly requires that mathematical study place the would-be dialectician in a position to treat the hypotheses of mathematics as open to question, precisely for the purpose of seeking the still higher hypotheses from which they can be deduced. The end of the programme would be the One – that single, most general principle, from which everything in the cosmos could be derived. That this has been the dream of all rationalist metaphysicians has already been mentioned; it appears again in the nineteenth century religion of scientism which also assumes the ultimate unity of the cosmos as expressible in a single system. Such a hope founders for those who entertain it for a variety of reasons. Plato tells us his reason in the *Timaeus* (28C): 'But the father and maker of all this universe is past finding out, and even if we found him, to tell of him to all men would be impossible.'

There are problems of logic and there are problems of communication. The logical difficulties can be expressed more formally by saying that so long as an axiom in system S_1 can be deduced only within a system S_2 which itself includes axioms not deducible within S_2, our reasoning, if it is not to be circular (i.e. making S_1 and S_2 reciprocally validate one another), must be linear and point to an infinite regress back to the original One – but to know that would entail knowledge of a system logically prior to the One, or identity with the One, which is absurd, at least as concerns human reason. The second half of the remark cited from the *Timaeus* reflects the varying understanding of different men such that even if the first demand were satisfied by someone, and some men could be found to understand it, some other men would not understand it. To the limitations of human understanding the intransigeance of language must be added, since language simply derives from and cannot transcend finite experience.

It may well be, despite his awareness of these surely insuperable difficulties, that toward the end of his life Plato omitted mention of the conditional nature of mathematics, preferring to treat it as symbolic of a profounder truth, mysterious and incommunicable, except to the initiate, if only to justify the asperities of the *Laws*. Certainly he changed his mind for the worse on a number of issues, for example on the question of the value of written language.[29] The tone of the eschatological myths, to take another example, changes very sharply in the *Laws*. They always, on their appearance in the middle dialogues,[30] possess moral overtones in an epistemological and metaphysical setting; but in the *Laws* they furnish background for a savage appraisal of human nature in its more depraved aspects. Among several references to their use in support of morality in the 'second-best' State,[31] there is one, at IX 881B, that tells us that the punishment in this life of those who are not deterred by stories of divine judgment must be as severe as what has been threatened in the afterlife.

Perhaps the differences in the dialectic that have been noted are only one aspect of the many that make up the Socratic problem. What Socrates shows by his negative dialectic is that there are no publicly verifiable truths, but that by self-examination a man might hope to improve, if not perfect, himself. He is reconciled to the necessary imperfection of human existence, and seems on occasion to find it no less comic than tragic. But Plato embarked on an ambitious programme of establishing knowledge by a method of hypotheses that was finally to dispense with its own hypothetical character. His failure is his secret and the only content of the 'esoteric' doctrine that he will never reveal. It leads to the bitterness and violence of the *Laws*. The dialectic is one of the clues we have in understanding two men close in doctrine, but far apart in temperament.

I have made a number of observations in passing about the problem of communication and the intransigence of language. These rest on a large number of scattered remarks found in the dialogues, where I am convinced some sort of theory about the nature of language lies buried. Only part of such a theory is concerned with the problems of being understood by someone who lacks the capacity or training to follow the argument – that part will clearly be related to the 'weak' defence of poetry. The other is much more fundamental and reaches to the question whether the truths Plato seeks are articulable at all with the requisite degree of rigour; if these are expressible only by means of myth, with its appeal to intuition, insight, and emotion, we encounter equally vivid suggestions of the 'strong' defence.

The *Cratylus* offers the most sustained discussion of the related questions of names, etymology, letters, and syllables, and the origins of language. We must look elsewhere for discussion of the relative merits of speech and writing. Here, as in many of the other dialogues, we must face the critical problem of the adequacy of language to its task. The point of departure is the epistemological status of names, especially of proper names. Cratylus is himself a proponent of the view that such names are natural and not conventional (383A), while his friend Hermogenes has been arguing that they are arbitrary sounds invented and adopted by men to denote persons and things. Socrates is to mediate. At first glance we might expect him to support Cratylus because of his characteristic objection to arbitrary, man-made, relativistic doctrines – and surely anything 'conventional' must excite his objections in favour of the 'natural' in the *nomos-physis* dispute in this area, as it already has when raised in the fields of ethics and epistemology. But that is not how he approaches these questions in an inquiry still fresh in its originality. Occasionally the reader is likely to bemoan the recurrent flogging of a dead horse, above all in the etymologies, where a few examples quite adequately illustrate the point, and a couple of hundred are hardly needed.

Socrates' problem emerges clearly enough in the early pages. Things are not relative to each perceiving individual, but have their 'own proper and permanent essence' (386D); if Protagoras were right, then no man could be wiser or better than another (386AC), for each would be the sole and privileged judge of what appeared to him. If this were also true of names, as the conventional argument proposes, would this not constitute acceptance of the Sophist's views? The 'natural' foundation of language must be scrutinized very closely if only to resolve this dilemma. We are not free, he says, to call a horse a 'man' (385A), and there seems to be a natural mode of speech that correctly assigns the proper names of things (387D), much the way an artisan uses the proper tools for his work (387E–388E). It is the legislator whose task it is to find the correct name (389DE), but he is best guided by the dialectician (390C) who knows how to ask and answer questions, for not everyone knows the truth to which the name should correspond (391D).

Some names seem more natural than others. Hector and Astyanax are appropriate for kings and their sons because they contain roots meaning 'ruler' or 'king' (393A); so long as the underlying meaning is the same it does not matter if different syllables are used (389E, 393D), for an instrument may function just as well if made of metal or some other material. But the son of a king who does not inherit a regal nature is not properly called by a name denoting 'king'. Many more examples are given of the aptness of the names of gods and natural forces: the relationship of 'hero' to 'Eros' (398D), because the heroes were born of love (usually between a god and a mortal woman), is one of the few that survives translation from the Greek. In the midst of these far-flung etymologies, however, we are given a hint of the rival view to come: we know nothing, Socrates says, of the gods' natures or of the names they give themselves (400D–401A). And, following pages of dubious etymologies tracing the alleged meanings of the names of heavenly bodies to all sorts of real and imagined roots, comes the next problem: it is all very well to break down the meaning of a complex name into the meaning of its constituent parts, but how are we to get at the meanings of the, presumably more fundamental, primary constituents? (422DE).

He first considers onomatopoeia, but soon dismisses this as imitating, not naming, whatever it resembles (423C), and so it is no more useful for our inquiry than the imitations produced by musicians or painters (423D). Thus the units of meaning, as it were, cannot be the mere sounds, but may perhaps be represented by syllables or letters (424BC). He then engages in a valiant and comic effort to ascribe specific meanings to many of the letters of the Greek alphabet; for example, iota and rho are said to be imitative of motion, lambda of smoothness. This is as far as Socrates claims to be able to go in establishing the natural foundations of language and he calls on Cratylus to improve on this account if he wishes (427D). But this astonishing theory is indeed what Cratylus supports; he is satisfied, but Socrates is not, as becomes clear later, at 437AC, where he is able just as well to find words indicating motion without those letters and words indicating rest that include them; and so he is compelled to examine the opposed view.

After trapping Cratylus in some foolish contradictions, Socrates brings him to acknowledge 'that images are very far from having qualities which are the exact counterpart of the realities which they represent' (432D), and that even if names are erroneously applied or misspelled, they are still names (433A). Cratylus further betrays himself into allowing that, first spelling, then sounds, depend on commonly agreed usage or custom, hence they depend on the very conventions he at first denied. But he does not lightly abandon his preconceptions, because he insists that 'he who knows names knows also the things which are expressed by them' (435D). Socrates balks at this, and his own position becomes clearer: knowledge of names does not of itself give knowledge of the things they name. Even if we simply follow the usage of names handed down from antiquity, those early legislators could only have given names in accordance with their own concepts of things (436A). But there may have been some original error, perhaps compounded over time, and this, like a small flaw in a geometrical proof (436D), would invalidate the whole chain of reasoning. 'And this is the reason why every man should expend his chief thought and attention on the consideration of his first principles' (436D).

Cratylus makes a last effort to claim a divine origin for names; to

Socrates' objection that the gods could not be responsible for the inconsistencies noted at 437AC he replies with the circular argument that some of the problematic names are not really names, but he cannot furnish a criterion by which we know the true from the false names (438D). What he does admit is that we must first know the things and only then can we appraise the aptness of the names (438E). With this cardinal concession Socrates is in a position to give us the clearest indication of his own views: names are an image or likeness of the things they stand for, and knowledge of the things cannot be derived from names (439B).[32] The things we must study are the forms, beauty itself, not this or the other instance of beauty, still less its name (439D). At the end he introduces a new thought, even more disconcerting than the idea that things may be known without names (438E), and that is that perhaps they cannot be known at all: 'Nor yet can they be known by anyone, for at the moment that the observer approaches, then they become other and of another nature, so that you cannot get any further in knowing their nature or state, for you cannot know that which has no state' (440A). The dialogue closes on this sobering note, with the added suggestion that language applies to the Heracleitean flux from which true knowledge cannot derive (440C).

From the frequency of the allusions to them in Plato there must have been a considerable debate about linguistic principles: we know something of the interest and professions of Prodicus and Hippias who made this their study. There are numerous references to Prodicus,[33] including one to his fifty-drachmae course, and two dialogues, one probably spurious, are named for Hippias. If we can infer from Plato's discussion that the effort was widespread to found theories of meaning on words, syllables (what we should call phonemes), and even letters, then his originality lies in rebuffing the attempt. It is not worth listing all the references, but the recurrence of the theme is interesting in itself (see, for example, *Philebus* 17B, 18B; *Republic* III, 402B; *Sophist* 253A; *Hippias major* 285D). The doctrine is rebutted, apart from the *Cratylus*, in *Theaetetus* 202D ff., but is used as an image for the analysis of the simple and compound in *Statesman* 278D and *Timaeus* 48B. It is obviously a false start for an alphabetical language like Greek, but might fit Chinese where complex ideograms are made up of simple ones, or German, which permits lengthy compounds whose meaning is pretty much the sum of their parts. Greek has many similar compounds and these may have been the source of this parody of analysis culminating in the identification of the letter as the smallest unit of meaning. Plato's concern, however, goes well beyond the correction of this error – there is much more the matter with language than this. The clue lies in the reference to the Heracleitean flux: language is rooted in sense perception; names are given to empirical concepts and cannot be any surer than those.

Plato is himself not above punning etymologies when he wants to hint at obscure affinities of ideas. The best known is the play on 'manic-mantic' at *Phaedrus* 244C where the relationship of madness and divine visitation is at issue. But their incidence is fairly rare – I know of only two other examples: *Choros-chara* (the chorus and the delight they give) at *Laws* II, 645A; and *nous-nomos* (mind and law) at *Laws* IV, 714A. Unlike the etymologies in the *Cratylus*, where the theory is reduced to absurdity, these examples illustrate what might have been a mythic device, if Plato had been persuaded that language is wholly rational in its origins and development. Had he thought so there is no doubt that he could have found uses in myth, as a literary device suggesting deeper meanings beneath the surface of overt utterance, for the euphonies and assonances of language where the temptation would be strong to employ his skills in support of doctrines that defied direct expression. He certainly had the skill, as we shall see from the brilliant pastiches of Lysias and Aristophanes, to say nothing of the imitation of the Sicilian dialect of Eryximachus or of his other literary *tours de force*. He is a better poet than most poets, a better rhetor than the rhetors, but knows only too well, as we see from the encounter with Gorgias and his friends, how little connection there is between actual knowledge and the lesser but distinct art of persuasion. His example in this was surely Socrates, who would not speak in the artificial language of the courts, still less play on his hearers' emotions at his trial (*Apology* 17C). Plato's approach to these questions is too austere to exploit either his own facility or the meretricious accidents of language. The symbol is subordinate to the thing symbolized.

'Metaphysics is the science that dispenses with symbols', Bergson said, and looked for a mode of expression that was immediate, that is, without the mediation of symbols. Plato wrestles with that same dilemma, but we shall have some difficulty in shaping a systematic account of his approach to the problem. There are many references to language and to the relative merits of speech and writing, but they are scattered, and some of them are at odds with the others. The core of his doctrine on this question is probably that in the *Cratylus*; most of the discrepant remarks, however, come from the *Laws*, and in that second-best republic the primary concern is with the feasible rather than the ideally desirable, and so there are many compromises.

Names have no real existence we are told at *Sophist* 244D; their meaning is given by their definition, which in turn is based on the facts of experience (*Laws* X, 895D). They are class concepts (*Theaetetus* 157B), based on perception and, therefore, cannot give rise to knowledge (158A). Each person has his own notions of something to which he gives a name (e.g. 'sophist' at *Sophist* 218C), but careful definition is needed to clarify what it means, and to find common ground by dialectical analysis. Names ought to have a constant meaning (*Parmenides* 147D) and, indeed, the names of the Forms themselves will display the desired consistency (*Phaedo* 103E) but 'because of the inadequacy of language' (*Letters* VII, 342E) the relationship of names, definitions, physical objects, and Forms (342BC) will not be stable (343A).

This is perhaps too condensed a summary of such references to the status of names as I can find in the dialogues apart from the *Cratylus*, but its import is clear. We have already been told that we cannot know the names that the gods give, hence the true nature of things eludes our language. We can certainly sift such tentative definitions as we are able to formulate for their consistency and truth to experience, and that is a major task of dialectic (*Phaedrus* 276A). Perhaps we shall be rewarded by those epiphanies of which Plato speaks in the Seventh Letter at 344B, but if we should make that flight of the Alone to the Alone for which Plotinus hopes, and so are carried from the third to the fourth division of the Line, we necessarily fall silent, certain only of that incomprehension if we speak that is the fate of the philosopher who returns to the Cave. There is a stunning reversal of our expectations here, not unlike the surprise in Socrates' defence of a conventional view of language in the *Cratylus*: we are offered a thoroughgoing nominalism in which names are not the names of things, but of our progressive definitions of them; the reality which informs the things is beyond the grasp of language. It does not follow from this that language is without value: we have yet to examine the texts bearing on that topic. But its best efforts, like those of dialectic, can bring us only to the brink of the third division. Between that and the fourth lurks an abyss into which Professors Gaiser, Krämer, Pieper, and Findlay have fallen. This is what I meant by the earlier, somewhat cryptic, remark about the extraordinary combination of Plato's nominalism and his realist theory of universals. Later discussion of this problem, especially in medieval philosophy, presuppose that there are two possible theories of the names of universals: they are either real (which is pseudo-, not neo-Platonic) or they are merely the names with which our empirical concepts are labelled. But Plato himself cuts across these categories, and makes partial use of both theories as I have tried to argue and document here.

We are almost done with this scrutiny of the value and shortcomings of dialectic. Language is indispensable despite its defects, but we must still see why writing is bad, though speech is good, and we shall have to explain the discordant texts in the *Laws*.

Articulate speech and names are a byproduct of that spark of the divine reason that was Prometheus' gift (*Protagoras* 322E). Its rational foundations make it coherent if rules of syntactics and semantics are heeded: not any random juxtaposition of nouns and verbs make a meaningful statement (*Sophist* 261E; *Theaetetus* 165E). These statements must further correspond with the facts, including observed facts in the physical world (*Sophist* 263B). It is characteristic of the approach of Plato and Socrates, as we have already noted, to be impatient of hairsplitting distinctions that becloud the underlying meaning: for them it is the spirit not the letter that counts (*Theaetetus* 184C). Language is a system of signs, and signs must point to things; and undue concern with the signs deflects attention from meaning. Plato repeatedly warns against semantic squabbles such as the sophists engaged in: avoid Prodicus' 'endless distinctions' about words, he warns at *Charmides* 163D; call anything by any name, but specify the referent which it names (cf. *Euthydemus* 277E and elsewhere); plain speaking is preferable to sophistic subtleties (*Meno* 75E; *Theaetetus* 168C; *Statesman* 261E). Actual examples are rare: one from the *Laws* XII, 944B is clear enough. In legislating a penalty for 'losing' weapons in battle it would be easy to go astray if a proper distinction were not made between throwing them away out of cowardice, or losing them involuntarily by accident or misfortune. If the word 'losing' is used without specifying the actual legislative intent, then any instance of being without one's weapons would be culpable.

It is no wonder then that Plato avoids a fixed terminology in philosophy,[34] unlike Aristotle (and a host of lesser lights) who supply as narrowly defined a technical vocabulary as they can manage. In Plato's view this puts the cart before the horse; as we sometimes see in commentary on him it is too easy to become lost in philological minutiae. Elsewhere I shall draw attention to the fifteen or so different words Plato indifferently uses for 'myth': they range from the innocent 'fairy-tale' to the egregious 'lie', yet many readers have missed the common thread of 'indemonstrable conviction' that unifies them. The written word is especially susceptible to this distortion, lying on the printed page as fairly engraved as a 5-billion mark note of the Weimar republic. It seems to have a fixed value, but has lost its connection with reality. That notion is presented mythically in the *Phaedrus* (275A) in the legend of Theuth's invention of writing, which Plato says is bad for memory because it serves as a reminder only of the physically seen, not as a memory or recollection (presumably of the forms). Writing is not permanent and reliable as it seems, but can only remind one of what one knows already (275E); like a painting it maintains a majestic silence and cannot answer questions (cf. also *Protagoras* 329A). 'Words cannot speak in their own defense and present the truth adequately' (*Phaedrus* 276C). He tempers this view a little: there is nothing bad in writing as such, only in writing shamefully and badly (258D). Still, the last word is in the Seventh Letter where he explains that when the mind is sufficiently steeped in its inquiry, knowledge, if it should come, will come finally in a flash (344AC), but there is 'no way of putting it [his philosophy] in words like other studies' (341B).

Living speech, on the other hand, is much more acceptable because of the give and take of discussion, the sifting of meanings of which dialectic is the best example, and the opportunity it furnishes of clarifying definitions as one goes along. Mere declamation without questioning does not achieve this; at best it would be preaching to the converted. The lengthy elaboration of this topic is summarized at *Phaedrus* 277BC:

> First, you must know the truth about the subject that you speak or write about; that is to say, you must be able to isolate it in definition, and having so defined it, you must next understand how to divide it into kinds, until you reach the limit of division; secondly, you must have corresponding discernment of the nature of the soul, discover the type of speech appropriate to each nature, and order and arrange your discourse accordingly, addressing a variegated soul in a variegated style that ranges over the whole gamut of tones, and a simple soul in a simple style.

This is why the dialogues are dialogues, and why the myths are accessible at many levels.

What, in light of this, are we to make of the second-best thoughts on the same subject in the *Laws*? 'The text of the law is the touchstone' (XII, 957D). '. . . legal enactments, once put into writing, remain always on record, as though to challenge the questions of all time to come' (X, 890E–891A). The names of dances and metres enacted by tradition are excellent (VII, 816B). A canon of approved poetry is to be written down and learned by heart; only this may be taught, and teachers who disagree with the canon are to be dismissed (VII, 811). We can perhaps discount these aberrations, as some commentators have, as the product of a Plato grown old, cranky, and disenchanted after the practical failure of his education of a philosopher-king in Sicily. That is very likely true, but a little more needs to be said. I referred earlier to the passage in the *Statesman* (293C) where the Eleatic Stranger suggests that in the best polity there would be no laws; the reason for this is that the statesman works on 'a reasoned scientific principle following essential justice' and so can decide such disputes as might arise in a flexible manner, taking the circumstances of each case into account, and not be bound by the letter of a law where this impedes action dictated by its spirit. One can see how this might work in a very primitive society, and how it might be acceptable in an ideal one. But it will not work in the second-best republic described in the *Laws*, where Plato finally, and distressingly, comes to terms with the dreary practicalities of governing *l'homme moyen sensuel* by politicians no better than that. In such a society less harm is done by the imperfections of jurisprudence written a step behind those ingenious enough to slip between the letter and the spirit than is done by untrammeled discretion vested in self-serving mediocrities. Whether Plato has become wiser in those last writings is unsure, but it is certain that he has become sadder; and so have his readers.

Uncertainty has been my theme in this chapter. The elusiveness of the ultimate truth of existence; the difficulty if not the impossibility of articulating it; the implausibility that one will be understood; amounting almost to the tragic assurance that one will be misunderstood; the imperfections of our rational methods and of the language in which we couch them. Pressed too far, these would make a formula for a less than heroic pessimism, or at best for a debilitating romanticism, but these cannot be ascribed to Plato.

His programme requires that we be as rational as we can, use every method that might advance knowledge, and be alert to the way in which language may properly be used, avoiding the whited sepulchre of overfine analysis. These are the necessary conditions for knowledge, and with them reason reaches its limits and falls silent. The unresolvable problems must be addressed in some other way, one appropriate to the discovered limitations of dialectic. Those methods can indeed whittle away at the periphery of error surrounding truth, but cannot specify it. It falls to myth, predicated on methodological uncertainty, and reflecting it in the modesty of its pretensions, to articulate the indemonstrable premisses of his philosophy.

3 How the Myths have Fared

Fashions in Platonic scholarship have changed a good deal over the years, being mostly coloured by the strains of thought uppermost at the time the scholars have written; with whatever care I take to avoid reading back into Plato some of the leading concerns in contemporary philosophy I hardly expect to escape this criticism altogether. But it will be useful to trace at least some of the dominant approaches to the myths, including the rare and elusive hints that Plato himself gives.

There are many who ignore them, and even some who deny their mythical status (e.g. Findlay), despite Plato's own mostly clear demarcation of the 'stories' he proposes to tell from the passages of dialectic that usually lead up to them. In recent years interest has shifted away from the myths to discussions of rhetoric and Plato's philosophy of language, with little direct attention to the myths themselves. Sustained treatment of the myths has been fairly sparse amid the enormous outpourings of commentary on Plato, with no book in English since Stewart's *The Myths of Plato* in 1905.[1] That book, with its tendency to treat Plato as an early neo-Kantian and an even earlier Christian, has been very influential, leaving a clear trace in Josef Pieper's *Ueber die platonischen Mythen* of 1965. These works regard the myths as little short of divinely inspired (literally so in Pieper's case); such claims go far beyond Plato's own much more modest observations about the myths, and in fact do damage to the rigour of his epistemology, which draws the sharpest distinction between what might be asserted and what can be proved.

Perhaps the two most powerful books on Plato of recent years are the first volume of Popper's *The Open Society and Its Enemies* (4th edn. 1962), and J. N. Findlay's *Plato: The Written and Unwritten Doctrines* (1974). While drastically opposed to each other in method and conclusions, they have in common a remarkable indifference to the myths as such: both writers take the myths pretty literally, Popper treating them as abominable lies and Findlay as sublime truths; and both altogether fail to consider the methodological implications of myth in contrast to dialectic. R. B. Levinson offers an almost line-by-line rebuttal of Popper in his *In Defense of Plato* (1953), defending also against Crossman, Fite, and others, but scarcely touches on the myths at all. In a very recent paper (1978) Findlay goes even further, by explicitly speaking of 'the so-called Myths' as 'themselves a myth'; i.e. they 'are not intended to be mythic, but sober accounts of the geography of Being . . .'[2] Both books are too important to be ignored, and I shall presently say why I believe each to rest on a radical misreading of the text.

The most pervasive interpretation amounts to no more than what I call the 'weak' defence of poetry. Bacon[3] attributed to the classical myths a clarification of matters incomprehensible to ordinary people. Vico[4] attacked him for ascribing this wisdom but even he, up to the *Nova Scienza* (1725), accepted myth as the concealed wisdom of the patricians. Similarly it may be argued, as it was most notably (e.g. by Dryden) in the seventeenth and eighteenth centuries, that the ultimate justification of poetry was its accordance with truth. That truth was secured by the rational certainties of science and natural religion, recourse to the supernatural being regarded as a failure of reason. These earlier thinkers are certainly talking about myth, but the distinction escapes them between the unconscious myth of prephilosophical utterances and Plato's deliberate shaping of myth to his own ends. Yet this failing, pardonable where unconscious myth is held to contain intuitive adumbrations of positive knowledge seen later to emerge, is unpardonable where the Platonic myths are under discussion.

Yet it is this that characterizes most of the literature of the last hundred years on the Platonic myths. Even the best book on the subject, Perceval Frutiger's *Les mythes de Platon* (1930), comprehensive as it is in its survey of the literature to that date, and incisive as it is in its criticism, stops short of furnishing a convincing account of the myths in relation to dialectic and consistent with Plato's epistemology. Frutiger's principal contributions lie in the correction of some spurious definitions of myth in the writings of his predecessors, the minutely detailed tracing of Plato's sources, and the establishment of a canon of the mythical passages that displays methodological sensitivity and finesse. He sees the inconsistencies and weaknesses of earlier treatments, and is the first to detect that 'tone of uncertainty' that invests the language introducing and surrounding the myths, but he does not pursue the matter to its conclusion. Still, he finds, as I do, quite unacceptable any failure to distinguish unconscious myth from Plato's inventions; and he is dissatisfied for unexplained reasons with the weak defence. But there are some hints of the strong defence in Frutiger, especially where he insists that Plato is bound to go beyond what is rationally demonstrable in the myths, thus displaying the insufficiency of the weak defence.

Nonetheless it is the weak defence that dominates the literature. This, as I have already indicated, presupposes that certain rationally demonstrable propositions can only be accessible to the common people by appeal to emotion.[5] It may well be possible to furnish rigorous proof, but only an élite equipped with intellect, leisure, and inclination will be able to master this knowledge and perhaps carry it further. Some earlier writers like Stewart, Willi, and Zeller move, without noting the inconsistency, between the view that Plato spoke in the myths of matters beyond his philosophical means,[6] and the view that the philosopher deliberately chose to clothe dialectically demonstrable arguments in artistic raiment. Later writers, however, mostly confine themselves to the latter view only. Edelstein, for example, in his 1949 article;[7] and Pierre-Maxime Schuhl in *La fabulation platonicienne* (1968), the first chapter of which reprints a justly appreciative review of Frutiger, sums this position up for all those commentators: 'The myths express in concrete terms abstract reasoning inaccessible to the vulgar' (p. 21).

Before looking into this commentary, however, I propose to sketch four relationships often held to obtain between philosophy and literature. These, I hope, will supply a framework within which the various treatments of the myths may be more coherently displayed. Not, I hasten to add, that those treatments are incoherent in themselves; many are quite invaluable and I, as do all Plato scholars, owe a considerable debt of gratitude to the work of our predecessors. But collectively the methods and philosophic aims are so diverse that, without some structure pointing to the different ways in which the myths can be addressed, most of our authors might simply appear to be arguing at cross-purposes.

I

I find four characteristic ways in which poetry has been thought to relate to philosophy that cast some light on the variety of approaches apparent in the literature of the Platonic myths. There may be others, but these, I think, illuminate Plato's attitudes towards the poets and also recur with sufficient frequency later in the history of aesthetics to furnish the basis of a broad theory of the relationship between philosophy and literature. If I draw the lines between them too sharply it will be to compensate for the confusion that often arises in the secondary literature when criticisms of poetry proper under one of these rubrics are misapplied under another.

1) Much of Plato's attack is focussed on what I have earlier referred to as 'unconscious' myths. These may appear as spontaneous folk wisdom, religion, or ritual; they are likely to be handed down through the oral tradition by bards and will contain a core of unchanging beliefs that go far to express and transmit the enduring values of a society. They will not be fixed in written form for many generations, perhaps even millennia, and even then may have a fluidity permitting endless variations, often of a dynastic nature. Their purport is to vindicate the superiority of the people whose history they recite, linking their destiny to the gods under whose special care they flourish, tracing the genealogies of eponymous heroes to those gods, and so justifying the legitimacy of present lawgivers held to be descended from those heroes. A sacred aura invests the recitation of these chronicles, setting limits to improvisation and innovation; yet history is indistinguishable from legend, and where there is some departure from the predominant concern with ethics to speak of matters within factual observation, the facts are likely to suffer, so powerful is the spell of 'the songs my mother taught me'. These are the myths proper, as held by all students of myth and primitive religion.

But they are pre-philosophical precisely because they are unconscious, spontaneous, riddled with paradox and contradiction; indeed, they contain all, for good or ill, that Plato attributes to the poets. They cannot survive rational scrutiny save under the charm of powerful emotion and charismatic effect. This first relationship is the foundation of the battle between the poets and the philosophers, ancient even in Plato's time, and there can be no doubt on which side of the battle Plato aligned himself.

2) Myth later succumbs to philosophical positions which assert truths of some kind (metaphysical, political, religious, ideological), and then literature has a quite different justification. St Thomas, in his discussion of the relation between faith and reason,[8] furnishes a model of why it is plausible that truths demonstrable by reason are nonetheless maintained by faith. It is that many people are too busy, lazy, stupid, or preoccupied to engage in the rigorous and time-consuming labour of elaborating for themselves all that reason is capable of demonstrating. Under this head literature is subordinated to philosophy, much the way

that rationalists at least subordinated theology to philosophy. Literature offers truths painfully arrived at by rational means in palatable form. To the conviction of deductive demonstration it adds the dimension of emotional rightness. It 'mitigates and purifies the passions', as Hegel puts it, because to the extent that a poetic utterance contains material of cognitive or moral significance it has been screened by reason to assure that nothing contrary to truth may sway the credulous by emotion alone, or by a combination of emotion and sophistical rationalization.

What I have said so far is applicable to essentially static notions of truth, such as are found in Plato, Spinoza, and the rationalists generally to the extent that they suppose themselves to be elucidating timeless or eternal truths, usually on a mathematical model. The corresponding literature (and art generally) is didactic, symmetrical and harmonious in form, its genres strictly hedged about with rules designed to assure both truth of content and a perfection of form that is taken to be a microcosm of the order of the universe. But the argument is equally applicable to a conception of truth that is not static, that sees truth as emergent, developing through history. Such positions, found for example in Hegel and in his right- and left-wing successors, still subordinate art to the best truth or 'correct' position available at any given historical moment. The available truths are, to be sure, not merely factual but programmatic, for if a man's grasp does not exceed his reach what's the withering away of government for? But it is not merely that the assertion of an ideal is a necessary precondition for its attainment, nor even that, to be realistic, only those ideals securely founded on correct (or objective) analysis and historical consciousness may properly be advanced. There is yet another factor, the emotional, to be accounted for. Those who cannot grasp the correctness of the postulated ideals on rational grounds alone must be fired by a myth, must be given the direction and purpose that never springs from mere factualness fixed in the here and now. Hence, an indiscriminate appeal to emotion will not do; only those emotions coolly calculated to be edifying and inspiring in the right direction are admissible.

Of the current incumbents of this theory the most important are the Marxist theory of socialist realism in the arts, and assorted psycho-analytic and behavioural notions of the effects of comic books, TV, pornography, and advertising on the general public. The Marxist view has the merit of being the most systematically dogmatic, but I must resist the temptation to spell out its implications here. It will be enough to bear in mind the function of the 'positive hero', of an art that embodies 'socialist principles', and the like. I have not strayed as far from Plato as might appear. The standard treatment of the myths and of Plato's attitude toward poetry remains centred on this subordination of poetry to the whole constellation of philosophical-political-religious-ideological truths. Even on this view the poets will have to be let back into the Republic; but under pretty rotten conditions. From Euripides to Solzhenitsyn they will be tolerated as a necessary evil; but books will have to be burned and so will poets when they overestimate the importance of their tinsel baubles. This, it must be clear by now, is the 'weak' defence of poetry.

3) But imagine a third doctrine, also traceable in Plato, that is neither pre-philosophic, nor subordinates poetry to philosophy. Suppose a failure of reason, suppose the subordination of philosophy to poetry, suppose the assumption by poetry of the expressive functions of philosophy. Such a doctrine is certainly available in a great deal of recent philosophy: the antimetaphysical views of positivists, Wittgensteinians, and existentialists share at least the rejection of classical metaphysics as to ultimate truth claims. Not all of them are ready, however, to elevate poetry to the seat of fallen Philosophy. Where they are, though, the claim runs as follows: man rationalizes rather than is rational; his adoption of given worldviews (*Weltanschauungen*), root metaphors, and attitudes is a varying mix of genetic and environmental factors such that some innate psychological disposition to react in a certain way to experience (if such an innate disposition is acknowledged at all) is subsequently coloured by that experience; there is no uniform human nature (or indeed any given human nature at all) such that uniform response to the world might be expected in the first place; that rationalist claims of an objective body of necessary knowledge about the world was weakened by Kant into a universal subjectivity applicable to all rational or at least to all human beings; that this was further weakened by assorted typologies (such as those of Schiller, Dilthey, Nietzsche, Jung, and James) to yield a small finite number of alternative views no one of which could claim truth in the objective sense, though each may possess a limited adequacy both as to facts and logic.

These theses, which have largely determined the modern sensibility, will not be found explicitly in Plato, but enough hints and anticipations of them are in the text to warrant a rather more extravagant interpretation of the myths than is thus far found in the literature. So long as the metaphysical presuppositions commonly attributed to Plato are taken at face value my thesis will not stand, and Plato will be prized or condemned depending on whether or not his surface objectives are agreeable to the reader. But Plato is much too subtle for so flat-footed an approach. I shall argue from the text that the myths embody truths that are not necessary and that Plato knew this. I do not want to pun on the word 'necessary', so I will make clear now that there are two meanings worth discriminating. My strategy is to show that while the truths contained in the myths are not necessary truths, it *is* necessary that such truths be enunciated, and that what is enunciated be asserted to be true. It is this last that constitutes the strong defence of poetry.

It also constitutes an admission of the failure of philosophy, at least as its task was conceived of by Plato. That task, which I have elaborated at length in the section on Platonic dialectic, was not merely to expose error (the main task of Socratic dialectic), but to affirm positive truths. From grasp of a self-evident One all propositions concerning the world of appearance could be derived with deductive certainty. Plato's search for that One failed, as it must, at least in discursive terms. That failure cannot, however, be made public knowledge – it is too destructive at both the levels of individual and societal stability. It falls to *poiesis*, broadly conceived, to furnish the foundation on which the positive programme of science and statecraft can be asserted.

What distinguishes the position I am attributing to Plato here from contemporary metaphysical anarchy is the singularly important role still assigned to rational discourse. I do not for a moment suggest that Plato is stricken by the enervation that overtook neo-Platonists after Plotinus. Poetry is to be defended because of the limitations of human reason, not because of its bankruptcy.

4) It is, however, precisely the bankruptcy of reason that constitutes the fourth relationship betweeen literature and philosophy. I have already documented in Sextus Empiricus and elsewhere those interpretations of the Socratic enterprise that enabled Sceptics and Cynics to claim him as a founder of their schools of thought. They had their own reasons for this, but surely found some warrant in that strain of uncertainty apparent even to the casual reader. If they are so interpreted, which I do not think is permissible, Socrates (and Plato) would be among the earliest representatives of a desperate doctrine of which Schopenhauer is the leading exponent in modern times. This rejects the power of reason as dispositive, even in the sense of negative dialectic. It proclaims the absurdity of the world as a metaphysical precept and the redoubled absurdity of discourse about the world purporting to be rational. It is most improbable, however, that any of the poets or their works criticized by Plato bore the intention or effect of the works of art afflicting the ears and eyes of modern lovers of the arts. All the same, this fourth position exists and has produced such movements as Dada and Surrealism, as well as others so ephemeral as to become dated upon their very mention.

I have sketched four positions:

1) Pre-philosophical: 'Lying is a privilege of poets because they have not yet reached the level on which truth and error are discernible.' (Santayana)

2) Philosophy tells the truth, and poetry tells the same truth, or is bad poetry if it does not.

3) Good poetry can say only those things that philosophy cannot disprove.

4) Philosophy cannot tell truth, so poetry may say anything.

Of these Plato moves uncomfortably between 2) and 3), though he is perfectly comfortable in attacking 1); he almost certainly never encountered 4). A compromise is needed. It lies in the significance that attaches to the role of reason, the claims for which must now be more modest:

a) it is to sift the spontaneous inspirations, enthusiasms, divine visitations, and intuitions that are all equally acceptable to the uncritical mind; only those may be asserted that survive such rational scrutiny;

b) its limitations are such that the employment of reason, while a necessary condition for truth, is no longer a sufficient condition;

c) imagination and insight are sharpened by cultivation of the rational faculties; it is not true, as asserted by the poets, that sensibility and perception are thereby blunted; it is not true, as asserted by the poets, that it is dangerous, even blasphemous, to look closely at the source of inspiration.

What all this points to is a distinction, entirely neglected in the literature, between two kinds of poets – Schiller calls them naive and sentimental. Plato is a sentimental (or self-conscious) poet attacking the naive poets, much the way Schiller attacked Goethe until illumination dawned and he was able to see the validity of other temperaments and other modes of composition. Most of the commentators whose views are worth serious consideration treat Plato as seeking to substitute 2) for 1) among the positions sketched above; 3) is hardly ever reached, but is, I think, critical if his views are to be correctly understood. For, by its subordination of art to philosophy, 2) decays into propaganda and the death of imagination, while 3) restores autonomy to art and freedom to man.

II

According to Stewart the Platonic myths 'are Dreams expressive of Transcendental Feeling, told in such a manner and such a context that the telling of them regulates, for the service of conduct and science, the feeling expressed' (p. 67). This is the general statement for which the greater part of his lengthy introduction prepares the reader, and it is embedded in language of a vaguely Kantian nature. Much of that language is specifically Kantian, as when he undertakes to show that the myths stimulate the 'imaginative deduction of categories of the understanding and moral virtues' (67). But what dates Stewart's book, in both senses of 'dates', is its wholehearted submission to one of the many strains of post-Kantian thought that sought to understand, expand, or, correct the master. Stewart's point of departure is romantic – a term I prefer to use descriptively rather than pejoratively, however mistaken I take it to be as a foundation for the interpretation of Plato.

Any detailed account of Kant's metaphysics and epistemology would be quite out of place here, for the Kantianism that finds its way into Stewart has been refracted through at least two filters that give it a distinctive colouration. The first is to be found in Schopenhauer's version of Kant; the second is dominated by those forms of idealism which stand in opposition to Schopenhauer's 'pessimism', though they have much in common with his profound mistrust of rational processes. A third strain, of native origin, is found in the Cambridge Platonists, whose impact on the English romantics, above all on Wordsworth, is clearly reflected in Stewart's treatment of the myths. Diffused among these three are some forms of Christian idealism, readily engrafted onto Plato for obvious historical reasons, and the reading back into Plato of a kind of pantheistic transcendentalism most closely associated with Emerson, which has its own origins in some of the sources already cited. All these elements find their way into Stewart's discussion and can legitimately claim Plato as an intellectual ancestor, and so we cannot dismiss them – or Stewart – out of hand; however diverse and contradictory the rival interpretations prove to be, they remain testimony at once to the extraordinary complexity of Plato's arguments and to their living influence.

At the heart of Stewart's approach is a dualism running deeper than the dualism commonly attributed to Plato. It is, perhaps, a Christian disaffection with the world of sense, of the body, and of the order of empirical knowledge ascribable to it. To these are preferred an eternal realm of spirit sometimes illuminated by insights that apparently transcend the limits of time and mortality. Taken by itself such a view is close enough to many of the things Plato says that it is pardonable to see in that coincidence a framework for Platonic interpretation. One is misled, however, if important parts of Plato's doctrines, aims, and methods must be slighted in order to maintain the centrality of that dualism. What Stewart and other commentators following the same critical approach neglect is that Plato is as much concerned with *praxis*, with theory of action, as with the contemplation of pure being. It is as though a full account of Christianity could be given solely in terms of the withdrawn life of the monastic without regard to pastoral concerns in the world. It is surely better to face the jangling complexity and inner tensions of an actual system than to strip it down to simplistic elements that harmonize with each other, but in no way correspond to the concrete problems Plato addressed. It is lamentable, then, though scarcely surprising, that of the half-dozen myths with an explicitly political content Stewart chooses to address only one, the myth of the metals, but he remains oblivious to its obviously political import.

Even more damage is done when such an essentially quietistic view of Christianity is attached to the antirationalism of Schopenhauer (indeed, of the whole early romantic movement). The point of departure is the unknowability of the Kantian thing-in-itself with the concomitant exposure of the debility of reason. That problem is insuperable in Schopenhauer, through a special place is reserved for art as a redeeming feature. It is true, as I have shown in chapter 2, that one can document Plato's own views on the limitations of reason, but it distorts his position entirely to assimilate it to the romantic concept of access to ultimate reality by some leap of imagination and intuitive insight that bypasses ordinary experience and logic, or at least renders them irrelevant. For, to Stewart, combining the Christian and the romantic, myth is revelation: 'the narrow, matter-of-fact, workaday experience, which the argumentative conversation puts in evidence, is suddenly flooded, as it were, and transfused by the inrush of a vast experience, as from another world,' and he certifies this vision by citing Exodus iii, 5: 'Put off thy shoes from thy feet, for the place whereon thou standest is holy ground' (p. 25).

He considers Socrates to be a seer who '*prophesies* . . . the fundamental conditions of conduct and knowledge' (25) and sees evidence of a divine visitation in the Socratic daimon (26). It is easy to discern in these and many other available examples, Stewart's profound and sincere religious beliefs, but what I have called the romantic and transcendental posture needs further scrutiny. In its negative aspect, what Mario Praz called 'the Romantic agony', it despairs of the possibility of discursive knowledge; and in its most extreme form despairs of any kind of knowledge at all, falling into a sort of anarchy of the spirit which feels impelled to perceive the world as irrational and absurd. There is no trace of this extreme position in Stewart; rather he postulates, as we would expect from one whose thought is instinct with religious feeling, a reality benignly governed but surpassing our capacity to grasp it by rational means, although it is held to be accessible to us by other means.

In Schopenhauer's version of this argument those other means are through art, and especially through music. If one cuts through the many ambiguities and difficulties of his language he seems to be saying that a kind of salvation is offered us by art. We are held to be free of self-serving motives in art, liberated from what might be useful or advances our ends; and especially we are free of those obscure impulses that spring from Will (the thing-in-itself in disguise) which we can only rationalize as our own aims when they are in fact beyond our volition. Thus art is taken to be a direct representation of the thing-in-itself, alternatively a direct representation of the Platonic Forms, unmediated by conceptual schemes considered to be a veil over reality rather than illuminating it. Hence what I have referred to as a profound mistrust of reason enters, since whatever explanations we devise suffer irremediably from two defects. The first is that there is no necessary connection between explanations couched in terms of causality and the Kantian categories and the underlying reality to which they can never be adequate, and the second is that our whole epistemological enterprise is vitiated by the impenetrable purposes of Nature, or Will.

The Christian version of this argument brings us closer to Stewart. It shares with Schopenhauer and with certain other positions associated with various forms of idealism the conviction of the inadequacy of human reason to the solution of the human quest for knowledge. But it finds in some kind of revelation of divine origin those insights into truth that are denied us by the medium of reason. If, for example, we take so extreme a position as that of Pieper, which I shall examine in greater detail later, we find no less a claim than that Socrates received the myths directly from God. Stewart's position is less extravagant than this, and one might even charge him with the aestheticism so denounced by Kierkegaard. For Stewart's Christianity is not obtrusive, and he links the arguments set out here by making the poets the instruments and amanuenses of God. It is they who set down in darkling utterances such intimations of a divine order and such radiant assurances of divine beneficence as come to them by an inspiration beyond question. No account of these can be given and, like the composer who was asked what his sonata meant and simply turned in answer to play it again. Stewart can only cite, as he does on pp. 47–57, examples of those poems of Wordsworth, Shelley, Whitman, and Dante (among others) which it seems to him embody those truths.[9]

It is not entirely easy to locate Stewart precisely amid this welter of related views. He is singularly free of the polemics that frequently characterize the defenders of these many forms of Kantianism, neo- and post-Kantianism, idealism, and pantheism, and his sympathies with many of them cloud the sharp distinctions they make among themselves and against empiricists. Stewart is mild by comparison, and even straddles the divide between irreconcilable opponents: 'Judged by the standard of positive science', he says, 'the matter of the context supplied from the dreamworld by the mythopoeic fancy is in itself, of course, worthless; but the mind is enlarged by the mere contemplation of it; the habit of looking for a context in which to read the sense-given is acquired, and matter satisfactory to science is easily received when it afterwards presents itself' (28–9). Here Stewart makes the best of both worlds: in the strict sense he acknowledges that the inspirational mode of receiving knowledge is as discursively inexplicable as the knowledge itself but he does not want to preclude the benefits for 'positive science' of a mode of receiving what from a scientific viewpoint can only be a hypothesis, tentatively accepted until experimental methods, if such can be devised, definitively dispose of it one way or the other.

But he properly excludes from matters, on which the methods of positive science can be brought to bear, questions of value which he locates in a realm of feeling, 'Value of Life itself', 'Universal Nature', and of 'the "higher faculties",' set over in opposition to 'scientific understanding' and the 'world of sense' (p. 45); and here our difficulties begin. I do not want to rest my criticism of Stewart's arguments on the muddle of positions on which he variously relies, on their being hopelessly outdated or unfashionable; rather it is the damage done to Plato which guides my path here. Despite many surface echoes of the Platonic dualism to be found in these idealisms, the most fundamental objection must be to the role of reason, which Plato was never willing to abandon. He never relinquished that most Greek of presuppositions that the world is a rational place, that human reason is of a piece with that which governs the world, which is in consequence intelligible in principle. Furthermore, Plato's mistrust is not directed at reason, despite its imperfections and limitations, but rather at inspiration. His is a terrible dilemma: we gain our sense of the most general principles governing the world only by intuition, inspiration, insight, and the like, but while reason can sift these for error, eliminating those inadequate to fact and logic, it remains powerless to confirm their truth. The vice of Stewart's position, and those whose arguments he uses in support of it, is an all too facile acceptance of those inspirations that suit them, something that Plato was not willing to do and which, if we are to credit the Seventh Letter, he had the soundest of reasons for abjuring.

That need not prevent us from examining what Stewart has to say about the myths, though it will warn us against the defects and limitations of his arguments. Some, indeed, are irrelevant and even misleading, and operate against his own methods. For example, he cites a number of myths from various cultures: Zulu (31–2), Maori (34–6), Greek (36–7), and Japanese (37). The Greek one, cited from Grote, is of particular interest: it deals with the practice of assigning the fat and bones of sacrificial animals to the gods; Zeus apparently regretted his choice, but he had been given the option and the bargain was unalterable. What both Grote and Stewart conclude from this is that the legend is engendered by the practice, not the other way about. This argument, apparently directed against Jane Harrison and other scholars of the relation between myth and ritual, is not without interest. But even if Stewart's position is correct it surely overlooks a much more significant point: the simplest and most obvious reason for retaining the edible portions of the animal for ourselves while exculpating our greed (or need) is to make this the god's choice. This is the sort of story that Plato felt the need to clean up because of the residual impropriety of ascribing baser human motives to the god, to say nothing of the suggestion that men had outsmarted him.

It is, however, a much more serious mistake to offer examples of primitive myths – the kind I have categorized as 'prephilosophical' – as though we can expect to find in them characteristics that will aid us in the interpretation of the Platonic myths. Later students of myth, like Robert Graves, are so clear about this distinction that they reject conscious compositions, which would presumably include Plato's, from being regarded as myths at all. But Stewart is unaware of the distinction: to be fair to him it must be added that so long as he is wedded to the inspiration theory it makes little difference whether a poet supposes himself to be the originator of some myth: such a poet would simply be mistaken, like many who believed themselves to be acting of their own volition and in their own interest when they were but instruments of the gods. Still, if we insist that the gods are responsible for everything, we are nonetheless free to speak of remote as well as proximate responsibility, and there is a vast difference between the spontaneous effusions of popular folk-myth and the nice calculations of a self-conscious artist like Plato.[10]

The manifest danger of failing to draw this distinction is fully realized in Stewart's documentation, with his entire approval, of the 'intoxicating Neo-Platonic atmosphere' (434) to be found in the Cambridge Platonists and in the traditions of the Alexandrian decline on which they rely. A whole chapter (423–68) is devoted to the transformations of Platonism intended to show that he was the 'Attic Moses', and that those elements of Pythagoreanism to be found in his work derive from the ancient Jewish Cabbala. There is no point in repeating this material here, since I am convinced that it carries us still further away from the Platonic text, and I have earlier remarked on the pernicious outcome of the Plotinian tradition. Plotinus' biographer, Porphyry, speaks of 'the severely logical substructure of his thought', and, indeed, we may suppose Plotinus to have pursued with the utmost rigour the full range of rational thought to its limits, before encountering the discovery that the attainment of ultimate knowledge was beyond its grasp. Such a discovery should have been sobering, not intoxicating; but as a matter of historical fact, the successors of Plotinus saw no reason to replicate the quest through reason that he had undertaken, because he had de-monstrated its necessary failure. Instead, in their haste for salvation, they passed reason by and fell prey to mystical intuitions and esoteric doctrines, to enthusiasm and ecstasy, and this, alas, is the vocabulary not only of the Cambridge Platonists, but of Stewart himself. Some of it may be true as an account of God's reality, and some mystics may well have attained union with the One, but all this clamour drowns out the silence of Plato.

Which mystics possess the truth? That is as critical a question for Plato as it has since remained. One of the central problems of his epistemology is just this difference between true opinion and knowledge. Let us for the moment ignore those claims to knowledge that fall of their own inadequacy under the combined scrutiny of fact and logic. There remain doctrines that *may* be true, and some of whose truth we remain convinced. But is there any principle more securely founded in Plato's methods than that unless true opinion can give an account of itself, i.e. offer rational proof of its truth, it may not be claimed as knowledge? Is there any more vivid, even tragic, demonstration of this than Socrates' refusal to escape Athenian jurisdiction, so passionately argued in the *Crito*? He *knew* he was innocent, but because that knowledge could not be made public property, indeed had been falsified by such methods as were available then or now to test it, he was not willing to bring those methods into disrepute by substituting his knowledge for that which is publicly verifiable, claiming a privilege then open to every mountebank and fraud.

The charge that Stewart's mode of interpretation is pernicious, not merely wrong in terms of Plato's epistemological methods, would surely startle and distress him and others who follow similar lines. They write in a spirit of the utmost goodwill and sincerity, and can claim in support nothing less than that 'perennial philosophy' of which Leibniz spoke. This points to the remarkable convergence of the noblest beliefs in the most diverse ages and cultures concerning the benevolence and justice of divine governance. Students of myth, of comparative religion, and cultural anthropologists, with or without benefit of Jungian archetypes, see beyond superficial adaptations to climate or region which may vary on that account, and even beyond the analogous development of social institutions to respond to common human problems, a unifying moral perspective that renders the similarities among human beings more important than the differences. The vice does not lie in postulating the existence of such a universal truth, but in permitting some explicit version of it to harden into dogma, in treating myth as demonstrated truth. It is not a vice of which Plato is guilty.

To be entirely fair to Stewart it must be argued on his behalf that he disclaims dogma; though, as we shall see, the several usages of the term leave the argument rather ambiguous at the last. The clue is given in his employment of the Kantian expression 'regulates' in the passage quoted from p. 67 at the beginning of this section. He elaborates his position in a lengthy excursus towards the end of his Introduction. One is dogmatic in the sense that Kant uses the term (against the rationalist meta-physicians) only when principles held to be constitutive of verifiable knowledge in sense experience are misapplied in the realm of morals and religion, where no such verification can take place. In that realm only those principles of pure reason can be brought to bear, and these are held to be merely regulative, not constitutive of moral judgments. Stewart is therefore quite correctly constrained to defend Plato (pp. 97–8) against the charge brought against him by Kant in the *Critique of Pure Reason*, both in the Introduction and in the Transcendental Dialectic, of the dogmatic abuse of reason. Rather, Stewart insists, keeping to the Kantian idiom, Plato is 'critical', not dogmatic in the myths (98). It is unfortunate that on the very next page Stewart quite unnecessarily allows, with reference to the arguments for the immortality of the soul in the *Phaedo* that Plato was after all dogmatic in the Kantian sense.

There is a larger problem here than can be accounted for merely with reference to Stewart's choice of religious and Kantian terminology. If we begin with the Kantian version we find that those Ideas of Reason (the existence of God, immortality of the soul, and freedom of the will) cannot be asserted 'dogmatically' by treating them as though they were verifiable propositions such as can be subsumed under empirical concepts of the understanding within the ambit of the categories. Instead they are presupposed by Kant as the necessary preconditions for the possibility of morality and natural religion. They cannot be asserted to exist as empirical concepts can – that leads to the internal contradictions of the antinomies – but must instead be accepted 'as if' they exist. And here is the difficulty that leads Stewart into the somewhat ambivalent interpretations noted. We shall be tempted either to accept those Ideas of Reason so strongly that the commitment to them becomes dogmatic (in the broader everyday sense rather than Kant's technical meaning) or, if the 'as-if' is dominant, enough doubt surrounds their status to undermine their utility as the mainsprings of action.

This has its counterpart not only in religious, but in secular terms. From a religious viewpoint the commitment to fundamental precepts of faith and morals constitutes dogma (now in the religious sense); it is the basis of Pindar's 'sweet hope which guides the wayward thought of mortal man', to which Stewart repeatedly refers. No rational demonstration can be given for that act of faith which asserts these things to be true, and such acts of faith are found also in the scientific realm: 'To attempt to rationalise here – to give speculative reasons for such a Hope, or against it, would be to forget that it is the foundation of all our special faculties, including the faculty of scientific explanation; and that science can neither explain away, nor corroborate, its own foundation' (98–9). Later on I shall discuss what Popper calls 'faith in reason', which offers confirmation from an unlikely source of the valuable point Stewart is making here.

Nonetheless it must be concluded that Stewart does not resolve the tensions between the religious and the Kantian meanings of dogma; he defends Plato against Kant, as I have noted, but then leaves Plato at the mercy, as it were, of two disparate foci of religious experience: one goes beyond reason to assert truths insusceptible of rational demonstration, the other falls far short of reason in abandoning itself to ecstasy and enthusiasm. Both strains converge in Plotinus and his successors, by all means, but they do not converge in Plato, the austerity of whose thought does not permit so facile an outcome. Much that Stewart has to say elsewhere in his book on the specific myths he does deal with I shall be glad to draw on in the next chapters, and this will in part compensate for the myths he does not address, and for the lack of a theory of myths adequate to the whole sweep of Plato's systematic thought.

There have been many treatments along these lines, for Stewart's influence has been considerable; it is not necessary to review these in detail because they represent rather more unbalanced versions than his, variously located along a continuum of possibilities ranging from mystical intuitionism at one end, and post-Hegelian rationalist idealism at the other. We shall touch on some of them in reviewing Frutiger's survey in the next section; his sober good sense facilitates our path through the enormous volume of secondary Platonic literature to 1930, when he wrote. Despite that volume, there are only two or three principal themes, often repeated. Some discussions, like Karl Reinhardt's obscure and difficult *Die Mythen Platons* (1927), offer insights of note which I shall be glad to acknowledge as we move along, but of recent books since Frutiger I have space for only one that carries the religious interpretation a stage or two further; but, I fear, a stage or two further from Plato.

Joseph Pieper's *Ueber die platonischen Mythen* (1965) is too short a monograph to undertake systematic review of all the myths; even less than in Stewart might the reader gather from Pieper that Plato is a political thinker of some substance, or that there are political myths. The emphasis throughout is on the eschatological myths and their religious import for those problems of the foundation of faith referred to above. Within this narrow compass Pieper has much of value to say. For example, he makes clear that, even when Plato was advancing mythical accounts of cosmogony in the *Phaedo*, he sought to bring the account into line with the most advanced scientific theories of his day, much the way modern Biblical scholars need to reconcile their interpretations with contemporary geology. Thus, while he accepts Apelt's observation that the description of the circulation of waters out of Tartaros constitutes 'an attempt at a hydrographic theory',[11] he rejects Apelt's further comment, 'made in the same breath', that this is 'a pure phantasmagoria' (44). One can only endorse the evenhandedness of his argument (43–4) that the primary concern of these myths is, however, not cosmogony for its own sake, but to secure through myth the collocation of what is believed and what is known.[12]

Despite Pieper's conviction, first put forward by St Augustine, that Plato could not demonstrate those ultimate truths largely embodied in the myths because he lacked Christian faith (69), he asks rhetorically (56) whether anyone who did not already know their source might not pardonably believe that certain passages from the *Phaedo* come in fact from the New Testament. It is this that sets the tone of the essay, and carries Pieper so far as to argue that Plato is not himself the author of the myths; they are of divine inspiration: 'Whoever accepts the core of the great myths recounted by Plato as true can do so only as Socrates did, *ex akoes*, because he has heard the same voice as must have reached Plato's ear' (34–5).[13]

Pieper thus interprets Socrates' hostility to certain old stories (*Phaedrus* 229C; *Euthyphro* 6A) as meaning that they are not myths at all. Yet surely Socrates' objections are to the immorality of some of the tales about the gods; all he claims for his own myths is that his story is the best he can find to tell (*Gorgias* 527AB). Indeed, all the definitions Pieper is willing to consider impose similar limitations. He cites Paul Tillich: 'Myth is divine history. That is *the* definition of the word that cannot be abandoned . . . it is not a literary, but a religious category.'[14] Walter Willi similarly says that 'almost all that is mythical in Plato' is 'somehow otherworldly.'[15] It would be folly to reject this mode of interpretation entirely; Plato is plainly a religious thinker of enormous depth and influence, but there are two kinds of objection to this insistence on the exclusiveness of his religious concerns. One is obvious enough, yet Pieper does no justice to it at all, and that is the presence of purely political myths; generally, in more 'literary' terms, perhaps: Plato's ability to produce myths at will on any subject is entirely neglected. The second objection, to which great weight must be given, is that even when the surface of the text points unequivocally to religious matters, as in the eschatological myths, Plato is as much concerned with epistemological, ethical, and political implications which need to be harmonized in any interpretation along with the religious ones.

In some ways it is an even profounder misjudgment to make Plato a precursor of Christianity than of one kind or other of the successors of Kant. The necessary failure or inadequacy of reason is in a nonpejorative sense an occasion of rejoicing among the faithful. It bespeaks the greatness of God and the finitude of man, and tilts toward faith away from works. Such a mood of Augustinian submissiveness may be rooted with historical correctness in the Alexandrian period, but it is unidiomatic for Plato and the great era of Greek rationalism. That 'failure of nerve' of which Gilbert Murray speaks was not foreseen by Plato, and in him the classical assurance of the fundamental intelligibility of the world remained intact, even though he was himself unable to solve many of the problems he posed.

III

Perceval Frutiger's *Les Mythes de Platon* is a model of scholarship commanding the respect and admiration of every reader. He is methodical and all but exhaustive in his survey of the earlier literature, his judgment is so sure and nuanced, and his feeling for the Platonic text is so sensitive, that an enormous debt of gratitude is owed to him by all students of this topic and, indeed, of the whole range of Platonic problems. It is a debt that nearly every contributor to the literature has been glad to acknowledge, and I join with them, knowing how immeasurably easier my task has been made by his work. Even my disagreements with him are in part made possible by the clarity with which he has analyzed the issues, and if I point to areas omitted from his discussion it is because my attention has been drawn to them by the suggestiveness and imagination displayed in his book.

One of Frutiger's greatest strengths lies in an approach to a definition of myth in Plato that distinguishes it from the spontaneous and unconscious effusions of prephilosophical myths. He does this with a proper regard for Plato's avoidance of a fixed terminology, pointing to the large number of terms more or less synonymous with *muthos* that Plato uses; moreover, he offers a much more convincing indication of the relationship between myth and dialectic than had ever before appeared. Without turning his back on Plato, the tough-minded rationalist, he is fully appreciative of Plato, the poet; and this feeling for the poet is not perceived as a failure of reason, for Frutiger recognizes the didactic aspect of poetry subordinate to philosophy that constitutes the weak defence, but gives hints also of a suprarational aspiration that explores the limits of reason and beyond.

If there are weaknesses in his book, they lie perhaps in a notable reluctance to offer interpretations of the myths, save along the lines found in Stewart; indeed, he acknowledges that he is in agreement with Stewart at least in principle. Thus, he tends to scant the political myths and does not display the continuity and coherence of Plato's thought in the content of the myths by linking them to the content of the epistemological and political arguments. Having with great caution and good sense reached a definition of myth, Frutiger falls to some degree into an error he has correctly diagnosed in several of his predecessors by allowing that definition to be applied too narrowly, so that he is obliged to deny the status of 'myth' to several passages which, or so his argument might lead us to conclude, are in fact mythical. Indeed, having shown that the spirit of Plato's philosophy is a better guide than the mechanical criteria he has disposed of, he occasionally falls prey himself to the letter of his own criteria. This is all the more startling because having set forth his criteria, he concludes (144) that 'myth' and 'dialectic' are relative to each other and, while some 'ideal line' might be drawn between them, such a classification necessarily retains some trace of artificiality.

But this is hardly a matter for polemic: an entirely conclusive resolution of this problem is most unlikely; some scholars tend to adopt so sweeping a definition that virtually the entire corpus is treated as mythical,[16] while an opposite inclination, of which Professor Findlay is the latest representative, denies that there are any myths at all.[17] Between these, as Frutiger says, a line needs to be drawn; if I draw it more widely than he by using my criterion that the myths contain Plato's axioms, I am unwilling to proclaim the correctness of my method at the expense of his.

In the pages that follow I shall summarize Frutiger's assessment of the earlier literature for substantially the same reason that he undertook it: to establish guideposts and warnings to those following this quest. From this we can see how Frutiger reached his own criteria and so decided which passages are mythical. I shall save for the following chapters what he has to say about particular myths, along with other such interpretations. What follows, then, is largely paraphrase of Frutiger; I have not verified everything he says, but where I have, e.g. Willi, Teichmüller, Döring, Zeller, etc., I have always found Frutiger's own paraphrases of the authors he cites accurate and responsible. I will indicate those rare occasions where I am disagreeing with his judgments of these works, or with him, or when I want to supplement his argument.

Frutiger's brief introduction warns against extremes of interpretation, and especially against the common tendency noted as early as Montaigne and more recently by Paul Shorey to shape Plato to some preconceived principle, usually dictated by the tenets of some currently fashionable school of thought, much as we have already noted Kantian and Hegelian biases. He cites F. C. S. Schiller at length on Plato's elusive and subtle character, and on his literary gifts as ironist and parodist. The latter alone renders doubtful stylometric attempts at a chronology from which the logical development of Plato thought[18] is to be deduced. Frutiger rejects such mechanical schemes, and will look instead for criteria sufficiently flexible to accommodate the range of literary devices of which Plato was master.

It is extraordinary, Frutiger continues in the first chapter, that two interrelated questions have hardly been answered. What is a myth for Plato? And which are the myths? The latter question was answered only by Couturat and Willi, who offer an inventory varying in accordance with their answers to the first question. But other scholars, like Hirzel and Deuschle, tend to identify as mythical whatever does not square with their notions of authentic Platonism, and hence contradict not only each other, but themselves, obliged by their methods to determine what is or is not a myth for irrelevant reasons. He dismisses Couturat's criterion on grounds we have already explored in this chapter. The myths are no more than fairy tales or moral fables for children, or they are superstitious beliefs about the gods and the afterlife, or (what Stewart calls Foundation Myths) legends about the origin of cities and prehistoric events. What is lacking in Couturat is the necessary distinction, of which I have given a fuller account in the first section of this chapter, between the first and the second of the relationships between philosophy and literature. Frutiger simply says that 'this preliminary definition implies nothing less than the complete condemnation of Plato's myths' (13). Instead of concluding, as I have suggested, that the many terms Plato uses for 'myth'[19] imply a reluctance to adopt a technical vocabulary, Couturat permits himself to describe as mythical *all* passages in which these words occur! Since those same words often appear in their other meanings and usages, almost everything becomes a myth for Couturat; given his definition of myth, almost nothing is left of conventionally philosophical value. Apart from Plato's avoidance of a technical vocabulary, to which Frutiger refers and which Jowett, among others, also endorses, Frutiger adds that the particular meaning of these terms must be determined by the context, but Couturat believes that he is being 'objective' in rejecting the discretion entailed by deciding whether or not these terms identify the presence of a myth. Willi follows essentially the same method, differing only in applying it still more consistently and devastatingly.[20]

Hirzel and Croiset offer a different, but equally 'objective' criterion. If a passage is written in the form of a dialogue it is dialectic; but if it is in the form of a sustained discourse it is a myth. What reduces this to absurdity is the *Laws* in which the responses to the Athenian Stranger become increasingly monosyllabic where they appear at all. Save for a few passages, identifiable as myth for altogether different reasons, the *Laws* is a somewhat prosaic treatise on statecraft, yet the criterion of Croiset and Hirzel requires it to be a myth throughout. All the same, Frutiger points out, Hirzel includes the second discourse of Socrates in the *Phaedrus* as mythical, but excludes the discourse of Diotima. If all that is intended is a sort of pun on 'dialogue' (dialectic of course is derived from the same root), then all that we are told is that dialogue is dialogue, and discourse is narrative (*muthos*). But Hirzel and Croiset understand these terms to mean what nearly everyone accepts, namely that dialectic aims at definition and rational demonstration, while myth deals with unproven and perhaps unprovable propositions heavily overlain by poetic images and oblique symbolism. The mechanical application of their criterion, however, leads to the absurd results noted.

Apart from these two criteria – the presence in or about a passage of the key words cited above, or the determination whether a passage is dialogue or narrative – no other systematic basis was advanced before Fruitiger's inquiry for deciding what a myth is in Plato. But that there were Platonic myths was of course universally acknowledged, and there was considerable agreement that many specific passages were mythical. Frutiger lists those on which such agreement was reached (29–31) to see if an examination of them might reveal what they have in common and so lead to a better definition. Part of the problem lies in the common definition of myth. Nearly every such definition – and Frutiger quotes nearly a dozen English, French, and German sources – centres on the primitive, unreflecting, infantile, and spontaneous nature of myth, its inarticulacy before the sublime and ineffable, its incapacity 'to rise from the image to the concept', 'thought . . . which can already give an account, but which cannot yet explain', to take one version, from Bréhier, the French historian of philosophy. Some elements of these on the whole acceptable descriptions clearly do not fit so sophisticated a philosopher as Plato, others do so in part, especially where myth searches for explanations of whatever transcends our finite experience. Finally, the presence of fantastic, magical, and anthropomorphic features is common both to the Platonic myths and to their primitive forebears. That Plato himself drew on the accounts of the gods, of natural forces hypostatized, indeed on all the personae of popular myth, leads to the confusion that led so many commentators (and still does!) either to discount the myths as philosophically unworthy, or as evidence of Plato's limited ability as a philosopher, a defect fortunately remedied by the school of thought to which the commentator adheres. What has gone wrong here, if I may refer back to the first section of this chapter, is failure to distinguish between the first and subsequent relationships between philosophy and literature.

Frutiger has no difficulty with the distinction between the first and second of those relationships (though, as we shall see, he fails to see the difference between the second and the third). He firmly resists the suggestion that Plato is a naif: 'Only primitive minds, chained throughout their lives in a symbolic Cave,' he says severely, 'could be the victims of such an illusion' (33). He has, among others, Couturat and Döring in mind.[21] Apart from some ornaments, which add 'charm and plausibility, nothing of importance in them is left to chance' (34). Having laid down, in his attack on the poets, what the defects of popular mythology are, Plato was fully aware of the standards his own poetry must meet, 'and by a clearly conscious choice has struck out whatever ran counter to his philosophical principles' (34).

This sets the stage for Frutiger's own definition. The three essential characteristics of Platonic myth are: 'Symbolism, liberty of exposition, the careful imprecision of thought voluntarily sustained beyond its frank acknowledgment' (36). The last clause is of particular importance: there is always a peculiarly tentative tone surrounding the myths, which deal with topics that 'surpass his competence as a philosopher' (36); they cannot be treated dialectically and so cannot claim to be rigorous demonstrations. All this is unquestionably a vast improvement on what went on before; but I must interpolate the observation that Frutiger here overlooks those myths which duplicate doctrines that can be and are demonstrated dialectically. For example, the method of hypothesis is a valid account of the role of deduction and induction in scientific inference, but it is duplicated mythically in the Divided Line and even more plainly in the Ladder of Beauty (*Symposium* 211C). These duplicates exemplify the weak defence of poetry, to which Frutiger has much to contribute; but here he hints at what I am calling the strong defence which, however, he never clearly articulates.

With this definition in hand, ambiguous though it still is, Frutiger is able to turn in his third and fourth chapters to the determination of which passages are in fact mythical, and which have erroneously been thought to be so. The number of passages is quite large under both categories; for the present I will confine myself to some generalizations on my disagreements with him and some specific examples of what I believe are erroneous classifications on his part. First, he excludes passages – *Phaedo* 72E–77A on reminiscence is the example I have in mind – from his list of acceptable myths because, although mythical in form, it is offered as part of a chain of dialectical reasoning (69–70) to demonstrate the immortality of the soul. Even if it were true, I would argue against Frutiger, that it constituted a proof, and even if it were true that Plato himself thought so, it would still be a myth in the sense of the weak defence. But both assertions are doubtful, and so by Frutiger's own argument it should be included in the myths. Conversely, to take another argument (*Phaedo* 61C–62C against suicide) which Frutiger includes as mythical, it must be noted that this condemnation of suicide is no less rigorous than, say, Kant's argument in the *Metaphysic of Morals*; if there is any uncertainty in Plato's version, it is not found here, but in Socrates' affecting not to know whether death is neutral or good; but he is quite certain that suicide is evil. On Frutiger's argument this passage should not be a myth. I do not want to press the matter unduly because Frutiger has interesting and sound things to say on all these passages; I would only dispute that the tone of uncertainty is not a necessary characteristic of *all* the Platonic myths, and that Frutiger has been misled by the presence of that uncertainty in some of them into what logicians call the fallacy of composition. Thus I would include within the myths the symbolic and freely expounded duplicates of dialectical arguments as well.

There is another methodological problem related to this that Frutiger does not address. As I shall argue later in detail, Plato has several uses for the doctrine of the immortality of the soul: metaphysical, moral, and epistemological. A vast array of arguments is adduced in support, and one of them is the theory of reminiscence, as encountered in the *Phaedo* and *Meno*. Some of the moral arguments work backwards, as it were, from the deterrent effects on present misconduct of posthumous punishment. This interchangeability of the parts of the argument makes it difficult to locate the axioms. Which are the theorems dialectically inferred from them? We could decide that suicide is wicked because it pre-empts a divine decision and, if we postulate the existence of a certain sort of god, the wickedness of suicide would follow as a theorem. Or we might adopt the possession of a priori knowledge as an axiom, and treat the specific content of that knowledge as inferrable from the general idea that we have such knowledge – a proposition, indeed, that has been much debated in the history of philosophy. I do not propose to elaborate these problems now, though we may return to them later. Here the methodological point is that in these areas we might be (and perhaps Plato was) pursuing a false analogy with the linear reasoning of mathematics in which it is relatively easy to say which propositions are primitive. A better model for this kind of problem than mathematics might well be that of a set or cluster of mutually inferrable propositions which stand or fall together, with no one of them more primitive than the rest.[22] Thus the conclusions that the condemnation of suicide is a myth and that the doctrine of reminiscence in the *Phaedo* is not, would rest on an arbitrary determination (one not made by Plato, by the way) that one of the arguments is uncertain merely because it followed from an uncertain premise, though itself rigorously deduced from that premise; or that it is primitive because uncertain in itself. My approach is safer: when in doubt, treat the passage as mythical.

In fact Frutiger's practice is better than his theory. It does not disturb him, first of all, that Plato's various contributions are not myths in the true sense, if that were to limit the use of the term to the spontaneous and primitive; that would, after all, eliminate his myths from consideration altogether. Furthermore, he excludes allegories (e.g. the Cave, discussed on 101–5) on the grounds that they are 'static, like a picture', not animated like a novel. The distinction rests on the perfectly acceptable notion that in an allegory there is a one-to-one correspondence between the elements of the allegory and the ideas for which each such element stands. Thus one can translate, usually in a rather flat-footed way, from the allegory to its transparent meaning. In contrast to this, the myths that give rise to all the excitement are subtle and complex, and do not so easily yield up the multiplicity of their meanings; like all great works of art they are inexhaustible in their suggestiveness, while the allegories are dull only by comparison. Nonetheless he acknowledges that the two genres are closely related, and in fact discusses their content with great insight.

I must record one further, and more important, disagreement. Frutiger says (40, n. 7) that 'the existence of the intelligible world had always been a self-evident truth for him, a sort of axiom'. He continues this thought later (71–2) to exclude the doctrine of reminiscence from the myths precisely because in the *Phaedo* it is advanced as 'a self-evident principle'. Since this is just as precisely why I include it among the myths, the disagreement cannot be glossed over, admirable as Frutiger's book is. He takes his claim a step further: 'For Plato, the theory of Ideas had the status of an axiom, that is, of a first truth which it is impossible to deny, because it is the indispensable condition of all logical thought and of all science – something comparable to the status for us of the principles of identity and contradiction' (72). The danger in this is twofold: first, the doctrines of reminiscence and Ideas are not on a par with the principles of identity and contradiction – much more falls if the latter are denied; and second, even if Plato thought so (*Phaedo* 92E is cited in support, but speaks to sincerity of belief, not to its logical status), it does not follow from this that they are being advanced with dogmatic certainty. That men must and in fact do believe given propositions strongly enough to act on them, and indeed to die for them, is witness to heuristics of the noblest elevation, not to dogmatics. The whole theory of hypothesis is antidogmatic.

Frutiger continues in the following chapters to establish which passages are truly mythical in accordance with his criteria and, in a lengthy and skilful polemic, those which have been thought in error to be so. I shall pursue these points as they arise later; here I have mostly confined myself to indicating where he has gone astray. It is worthy of special note, however, that he does not regard the eschatology as mythical in itself, but treats the theory of the parts of the soul and the cosmogony as myths; where the eschatology has ethical and epistemological implications, these are taken to be deductions from 'self-evident propositions' and so are dialectical. In the second part of his book he dismisses many of the theories already dealt with above or yet to be addressed: that the myths conceal Plato's scepticism or heterodoxy, that they are confined to religion and the afterlife, that they are pedagogical or moralistic. He is indefatigable in tracing the sources of the myths in the literature prior to Plato, and finally speaks with great eloquence of Plato's skill as a poet. Frutiger's is a wonderful book, for the breadth of its scholarship and for the acuteness of its criticism, clearing the ground of a clutter of partial, misleading, and outright nonsensical interpretations. But at the last, it must be confessed, it falls just short of yielding the insights into Plato it so tantalizingly promises.

IV

Karl Popper calls his autobiography, excerpted from the Schilpp volumes, *Unended Quest*, no doubt because it would be too dogmatic to call it Unending Quest, a possible title for Plato's autobiography. In it he mentions (§ 33) that his wife pointed out that *The Open Society and Its Enemies* (OS) did not represent his central philosophical interests. But there is a link between them that perhaps she overlooked. His leading concerns have been in mathematical logic and the philosophy of science; corrections to current beliefs concerning induction, verifiability and falsifiability, and to the so-called picture theory of language; attacks on subjectivism in mathematics and physics; and important contributions on thus far unresolved problems of entropy and the Second Law of Thermodynamics, indeterminism, and axiomatics; on the broader scene he has tirelessly corrected the excesses of some fashionable currents: the Vienna Circle, analytical philosophy, Wittgenstein; and in many ways has restored to respectability some of the classical inquiries into metaphysics and politics. What unites these central concerns with *The Open Society* is a philosophical motive that underlies them all: a passionate rejection of dogmatism in all its forms, a conviction of the open-endedness and corrigibility of all (or most) currently maintained theories. He attacks Plato because he takes him to be a dogmatist, and especially because he holds him accountable for the roots of totalitarian politics. I am convinced that the case against Plato is much overstated, sometimes grotesquely so, and needs correction in turn.

Popper is not alone in that attack, though his book is so far superior to the others that should be mentioned, that it is on *OS* that I must concentrate attention. Perhaps the best known is R. H. S. Crossman's *Plato Today* (1937); Crossman's background in classics before he stumbled into politics gave him a thorough grounding in the texts, but he is betrayed in this book into a by now dated topicalism. He makes Plato out to be the grandfather of totalitarianism (fatherhood is generally reserved for Rousseau), but cannot quite decide whether Nazism, Fascism, or Communism is the most cherished offspring. Since of these only communism has any intellectual pretensions whatever, and the premise of Crossman's argument misconceives Plato's objectives beyond correction, the book is now of interest only because, after a steady diet of religious mysticism it is refreshing to be reminded that Plato was a political thinker of the first rank. A curiosity, arbitrarily picked out of the many available – the secondary literature on Plato is overwhelming – is Warner Fite's *The Platonic Legend* (New York, 1934). Professor Fite, no doubt despairing of the chastity of the gilded youth of Princeton in the days of F. Scott Fitzgerald, but determined at least to keep them out of irregular courses, presents the entire Platonic oeuvre as an apologia for homosexuality. There is some evidence, of course; about as much evidence against as for this thesis. Since Plato is about 99.44 per cent pure, that is the part I mean to address. None of these authors has a theory of the myths, or pays very much attention to them; Popper occasionally refers to them, observes that they are propaganda of a sort he disapproves, but infers nothing from a distinction between myth and dialectic, wholly failing to see that Plato's preoccupation with method is not far removed from his own. For Popper the myths are lies merely, noble at best, but expressly designed to gull the critical faculties and to conceal the weaknesses where argument has failed. This is close enough to home to be a possible interpretation, and it fits a few of the stories very well indeed. But it can be maintained only by ignoring certain key passages, notably those in which Plato refers to his reasons for employing myth, to the lesser claim these necessarily have on a reader's credence, and to the nature of hypothesis as it bears on the relation between myth and dialectic.

Popper's principal charge against Plato is that he is an 'historicist'. This refers to certain philosophies of history purporting to detect a pattern in history such that events unfold in accordance with a law as immutable as any encountered in the natural sciences. It is perfectly clear that if there is such a law, it is beyond human power to change the outcome of the events it governs, and we would then be bound to acquiesce in the inevitability of that outcome. The worms may sometimes turn: in 1884 the legislature of the State of Indiana passed a bill establishing the ratio of the diameter of a circle to its circumference as just three, instead of the highly inconvenient surd 3.14159 etc. Unfortunately someone induced the governor to veto the bill, so it never became law and in Indiana as elsewhere we continue to suffer the surdity. Historicism will be fatalistic at some level, though not necessarily quietistic. Hegel's doctrine, to which the second volume of Popper's study is devoted, provokes, as Plato's does not, the criticisms brought to bear. History does indeed unfold in time, revealing the emergence of Spirit or Idea by a dialectical rule, the evidence for which Hegel finds in every manifestation of mind. His is a theory of action: we are not called upon to await some inevitable outcome, but to contribute to its advancement, of which we are active agents. How Popper criticizes the views of Hegel is hardly our concern here, fascinating and mostly accurate though it is. There is nothing in Plato, however, that permits assimilation of his doctrines to any version of historicism.

Two ancient theories certainly known to Plato are cited by Popper. One is the straight-line decline of which Hesiod speaks – it offers a vision of unrelieved postlapsarian dreariness. A Golden Age is postulated in remote antiquity, but since that time things have gone badly and will get worse. The other theory is cyclical, the particular one that Plato refers to being the Great Year of 36 000 years (cf. *Timaeus* 39C, and the myth of the age of Cronos at *Statesman* 269C ff.). What exactly these stories mean in Plato is much disputed; I will deal with this myth in the next chapter. But before rushing to the defence of Plato I must first defend Popper. There are, after all, philosophies of history that deserve all the hostility that Popper mistakenly directs at Plato.

Hesiod's is not the only straight-line theory, nor is it a particularly popular one, except perhaps for ancient colonels muttering about the country going to the dogs. People are more likely to propose a straightline ascent from the primitive to the complex – the idea of progress is one such. Sometimes they are a little more sophisticated, like Condorcet's version of a jagged line headed mostly upward, but with a few backward steps, a case of *reculer pour mieux sauter*, as it were, which permits a general optimism without having to fly in the face of the fact that everything is not well all the time. In the *City of God* St Augustine combines both theories, with the earthly city in decline while the Heavenly City is in the ascendant. Cyclical theories fall between the two for cheerfulness because some of the time at any rate the cycle is in the ascendant phase – negentropy, you might say – and hope springs anew.

This manic-depressive aspect is, however, more easily associated with sine-curve theories, of which the one promoted by Toynbee is most familiar in modern times: each civilization has its rise and fall, and this has been repeated throughout whatever history Toynbee has chosen to include in his Study. This is a doctrine usually associated with Alphonse Karr's celebrated remark 'plus ça change, plus c'est la même chose.' A rare combination of cycle and sine-curve is found in Polybius who for quite ingenious reasons sees a rise-and-fall cycle from a state of nature to monarchy, from its corrupt form, tyranny to aristocracy, and then from obligarchy to democracy, which decays into mob rule, and it then all starts again. All these doctrines are as debilitating as Popper says they are, but what has all this to do with Plato?

It is central to Popper's thesis, if he is to maintain Plato's guilt as an 'historicist', that Plato advanced 'a law of historical development' whereby 'all social change is corruption or decay or degeneration' (OS I, 19). Resistance to change is certainly one of the debilitating effects of any philosophy of history that makes change the consequence, not of human initiative which is likely to be fatuous where it is not impertinent, but of processes beyond human control or influence. (Popper altogether ignores the standard conservative argument, best stated by Burke, that resists change for the empirical reasons that most cures are worse than the disease; also the Aristotelian argument against rapid change because it destabilizes society.) But the flat statement that Plato is opposed to all social change is astonishing in view of the indisputable fact that Plato is a reformer, proposing to change practically everything in sight: religion, politics, ethics, poetry, and so on. That is, he is determined to *improve* the existing state of affairs which everybody (including Popper) would agree, Plato found to be corrupt, decayed, or degenerate. Why does Popper quote *Laws* VII, 797D: 'Change is always, we shall find, highly perilous,' but ignore the immediately following words: 'except when it is change from what is bad'?[23]

It is surely false that Plato propounded such a doctrine as Popper asserts against him, because if he were opposed to change, the changes he himself proposes would be bad, and he would know they were bad merely because they were changes. There would no no need of the careful sifting of proposed changes so much in evidence in the dialogues. Clearly some changes are more desirable than others, and those Plato wanted are clearly intended to be among them. The basis of the distinction between whatever social forces bringing about change lead to desirable as opposed to undesirable changes is firmly grounded in Plato's metaphysics. If change comes about mindlessly, in response to selfish or class interests, or out of misjudgment or ignorance, then, as Plato himself has argued, degeneration is inevitable. Nothing historicist about this; what Plato wants, Popper wants: change induced on rational principles, such changes to reduce the degree of corruption. Indeed, when Popper does Plato justice, it is hard to see how his attack can be reconciled with what he concedes: 'Plato believed that the law of historical destiny, the law of decay, can be broken by the moral will of man, supported by the power of human reason' (OS I, 20). He notes that this is not reconcilable with a law of destiny and works out the problem by postulating the solution back to front, as I shall show. Plato's argument is familiar: there is a perfect form of the State, as of everything else, in heaven; earthly states are imperfect copies and, like everything else earthly, pass into and out of being, thus in them change is an evil principle. A state that was perfect would not change, because any change must be for the worse. We leave to one side for the moment, though it must be dealt with later, whether such a state is attainable on earth. Hence change, as a characteristic of imperfection, is inherently vicious.

But, it will be equally clear, changes in the direction of perfecting society, are not evil; indeed, whatever advances toward perfection is inherently good. Popper would acknowledge all this, as his text shows; but he is so bent on pursuit of his *parti pris* that he works backwards from the undesirability of change in the already perfect to the undesirability of change as a fundamental feature of Plato's thought altogether. How else is one to understand what Popper means by the 'arrested state' (OS I, 21)? There is no harm in attributing this to the Golden Age, because this is (or was, or will be) perfect. The tense is unimportant: for Hesiod it 'was'; for St Augustine and other *Perfektionsmänner* it 'will be'; for cyclists all tenses will do, depending where in the cycle you are.

If you challenge, as I do, that Plato has an historical theory at all, most of Popper's attack is beside the point. At this stage in the argument it suffices to say that Plato is not inferring anything from history beyond anecdotal exemplars, and even then with notable reservations. The issue here is logical, tautological if you like. If and only if something is perfect, then change is undesirable. Popper's error is not confined to shifting ground in ascribing to Plato views held by the irreconcilable Heraclitus and Parmenides, but extends to assuming of Plato that he was opposed to change in principle (which makes no sense) and that Plato was certain about how to achieve the perfect state. Far from this, I shall aim to show, Plato seems ultimately to have been certain of very little, and is in any case not the dogmatist Popper makes him out to be. When Popper turns his argument to what he calls a diametrically opposite approach, that of social engineering, we must once again pay attention. There are two kinds (OS I, ch. 9): 'piecemeal' and 'Utopian', and Plato is guilty of the latter. Popper favours piecemeal social engineering because it demands no all-encompassing metaphysical theory, permits mid-course correction, and is generally modest in its claims. How far Plato falls foul of these desiderata will bear close examination indeed, but there is no necessary connection between Utopian social engineering and historicism. If the latter is opposed to change, and the former is dedicated to too much change, or to the wrong kind of change, how can Plato be guilty of both?

It is surely very odd that Popper carries on as long as he does in connection with *Republic* 380D–381C²⁴ against Plato's views on the unchanging nature of the gods and, more generally, of the forms. The nature of the gods, especially, is twice referred to as 'petrified'. What makes this odd is its inconsistency with Popper's philosophical stance as an objectivist, which quite properly requires him to remain sceptical and fallibilist about our knowledge of some ultimate reality, but which permits no doubt that there is a real underlying order. Thus he is entitled to reproach Plato for any assertions he finds in the dialogues that suggest Plato's dogmatic claims to know that reality, but is not entitled to attack him for insisting that such a reality exists. We can save Popper's position by a further argument, but I doubt that he would be grateful for it: let us agree that there is such a reality as Plato refers to in his terminology of 'gods' and 'forms', but postulate that we not only do not know it, but also do not know whether it is static or changing; then it would be dogmatic to assert, as Plato does, that it is static or 'petrified'. The trouble with this for Popper is that, if taken too seriously, it undermines the objectivity that is as important to him as it is to Plato. For, even if we speculate that the underlying reality does change, we should still want it to change according to a rule; we would then merely shift one step back so that reality + change = reality as we had conceived of it before. If we did not do that then we should have to admit that whatever overtook reality was irrational, and so lapse into the subjectivism and psychologism so offensive to Popper.

In *Logik der Forschung* and even more strongly in later writings, Popper believes that he has vindicated the correspondence theory of truth. Scientific theories develop, he has argued, as a series of approximations corresponding to the truth with increasing degrees of accuracy; he does not want to preclude the possibility that we might attain (perhaps here and there have already attained) a precise one-to-one correspondence, though the probability against this is high. But the correspondence theory would be empty indeed, if there were not something for our theories to correspond to, and it makes little difference whether that something has 'change' (whatever that means in noetic terms) built into it. What Popper should be objecting to is the illegitimate and premature transfer of changelessness from the realm of forms to the characteristics of our knowledge. Of course, he does this too, but the objections should not spring from a conception of reality not very different (terminology to one side) from his own. Even in this latter and more modest perspective Popper has misunderstood Plato's position.

Popper's misconception of Plato's dogmatism is fundamental. It is not totally without warrant, of course, since we can find many passages which at least strongly imply that Plato in fact possesses the absolute knowledge that is the goal of his quest. But the opposite is also true: other passages are an embarrassment to Popper because they imply diffidence, fallibilism, and other characteristics that Popper, if he is to save his thesis, must explain away somehow. He does so by ascribing such views to Socrates. For example (p. 281, n. 50 (6), referring to *Theaetetus* 174E), he cites the 'humanitarian' view that, because every man has countless ancestors, the élitism, etc. otherwise argued is inexplicably softened. The only explanation he can find is that this passage is Socratic and, primarily for that reason, he is prepared to argue that the *Theaetetus* is prior to the *Republic*! It does not occur to him that his thesis may perhaps be overstated, and that Plato's arguments are subtler than his treatment allows.

The passage on defective forms of the state that takes up the whole of Book VIII and the beginning of Book IX in the *Republic* has led to some quite unnecessary confusion. Frutiger is alone in treating it as a myth: although the derivation of each type of state – timocratic, oligarchic, democratic, and tyrannical – is 'manifestly dialectical' (41), 'the manner in which these definitions are linked one to another is mythical, because Plato well knew that reality has never presented, and never could present, an example of the decadence he has depicted' (41). Jowett[25] correctly sees that 'The order of constitutions which is adopted by him represents an order of thought rather than succession of time', but he then confuses the issue by continuing, 'and may be considered as the first attempt to frame a philosophy of history.' There is no necessary inconsistency in Jowett, who nowhere explains what he means by a philosophy of history, but in Popper such a view is clearly defined and made one of the central charges against Plato. The model before Popper is the Hegelian succession in time of family, civil society, and state, or the Marxist succession of feudalism, mercantilism, and capitalism (to cut a long story short). These are necessary developments in which the inner contradictions of each form of government necessarily lead to its successor in time. The two key features of Popper's definition are thus a logical nexus that shows how a successor form of government must arise out of the antecedent conditions, and a temporal sequence, which if it is not to be formal and abstract, must be shown to have arisen in historical time.

Neither of these conditions is satisfied by Plato's account, though some version of them may fit Aristotle (*Politics* III, 15, 1286b 8–20) and surely fits Polybius (VI, 5–9). There is no sign whatever of a temporal sequence, and the logical nexus is no more than a showing how each of the four defective types arises out of aristocracy-monarchy (there is no significant difference between these two versions of the best form of government: cf. *Republic* IV, 445D). Popper elaborates his attack in endless detail, but since it rests on an utterly false premise it is hardly worth seeking to refute him on minor points; the best refutation is the text itself. The whole analysis of the ideal state rests on some broad concepts, well explored in the subsequent history of political science, of division of labour, self-sufficiency, security, and the provision of optimal conditions under which individuals can best flourish. The tripartite nature of the soul and the corresponding class structure represent a harmony for which the claim is made that it best suits human needs attuned to the rationale of the cosmos. Such a polity would necessarily be governed by the best man (monarchy) or men (aristocracy), i.e. those most knowledgeable and best equipped to determine and implement the needs of society in accordance with its best interests. But such an ideal harmony is likely in practice to be fractured by an excess or defect in one of the elements compounding it. An overstressing of honour will lead to militaristic excesses, and distortions due to the institutionalizing of property rights or a mindless egalitarianism will lead to plutocracy or mobrule; the worst is tyranny in which the supposed interests of the tyrant override those of society from any aspect. If Plato says he proposes to examine these types one after the other, the 'after' means little or nothing more than that he cannot talk about them all at once. The most perverted, and the most unstable, tyranny, might appear last in time and be the shortest-lived, but there is no substantial ground for seeing any temporal sequence; still less is there any ground for claiming that there is something in the nature of timocracy, say, that necessarily makes oligarchy, say, spring from it or vice versa. Findlay (43), using his own terminology, but clear enough on this point, says that these perversions of the state are 'as eidetic as anything in Plato.'

In opposing Popper here I am certainly not suggesting that Plato's myth of the state is beyond criticism; it can, for example, be criticized in the terms set forth by Ernest Cassirer in *The Myth of the State*, and no doubt in other ways as well. But it cannot be criticized for failings for which there is no evidence in the text. I should add that there is considerable debate in the literature as to the historical or mythical status of these passages. There ought not to be: at *Republic* IX 592AB Socrates tells us 'You mean the city whose establishment we have described, the city whose home is in the ideal, for I think that it can be found nowhere on earth. . . . perhaps there is a pattern of it laid up in heaven.' There is the barest hint at 499C that perhaps it existed at some 'infinite time past', a hint that has sometimes been taken to allude to Atlantis. The line between the dialectical and the mythical is sufficiently blurred in this account of types of government that I have no serious quarrel with Frutiger, who wants to make it fall on the mythical side, whereas I see it as an abstract exercise, closer to dialectic. But the line between a *Gedankenexperiment* and actual history is entirely clear cut, and there is no warrant for Popper's misreading of the text, especially as he then builds so much of his thesis on it.

There are other, equally serious misreadings, that allow Popper to ascribe views to Plato utterly alien to his convictions. Consider these two versions of *Republic* III, 415DE in a passage just following the myth of the metals:

'After having armed and trained the earthborn, let us now make them advance, under the command of the guardians, till they arrive in the city. Then let them look round to find out the best place for their camp – the spot that is most suitable *for keeping down the inhabitants*, should anyone show unwillingness to obey the law, and for holding back external enemies who may come down like wolves on the fold.' (Popper)

'But let us arm these sons of earth and conduct them under the leadership of their rulers. And when they have arrived they must look out for the fairest site in the city for their encampment, a position from which they could best hold down rebellion against the laws from within and repel aggression from without as of a wolf against the fold.' (Shorey)

The addition of the italicized words above in Popper's version enables him to continue: 'This short but triumphant tale of the subjugation of a sedentary population by a conquering war horde . . .' (OS, I 50). But it strains the Greek to add the words 'for keeping down the inhabitants'. The only ambiguity in the text that might permit the inference of an invasion of an inhabited place, as opposed to the founding of a new settlement, is the clause 'in *the* city'. That language is just vague enough that H. D. F. Lee, for example, translates 'and conduct them to *their* city', from which Popper's inference would be impossible.

Consider a further example, this time from *Republic* IV, 434BC:

'Any meddling or changing over from one class to another is a great crime against the city and may rightly be denounced as the basest wickedness.' (Popper, p. 49, n. 31)

'Inference by the three classes with each other's jobs, and interchange of jobs between them, therefore, does the greatest harm to our state, and we are entirely justified in calling it the worst of evils.' (Lee)

First let us note that the Greek refers to a functional analysis of the tasks assigned to each of the classes, and so Lee translates 'jobs'; Shorey translates 'interference with each other's business', which is fair enough. But Popper is determined to minimize or deny the provision for social mobility that Plato has built into his republic. He translates the identical passage again on p. 106 with more embroidery: 'We have three classes in our city, and I take it that *any such plotting* or changing from one class to another is a great crime, etc.' 'Plotting' surely strains the Greek. Popper is bound to admit that *Republic* III, 415C permits social mobility both up and down, but insists that this is 'rescinded' by 434BC, quoted above, and by *Republic* VIII, 547A (see his note 31 on p. 225).[26] He argues (p. 141) from these passages that Plato intends only that children from the upper classes who do not measure up should be demoted, but that superior children from the lower classes will not be promoted. The reference to 547A is a complete non sequitur; it has nothing to do with the point of 415 beyond the allusion to the Hesiodic myth of the metals. He has completely misconstrued that myth; I do not mean merely that he fails to recognize it as a myth in any of the abuses of the term: he could have treated it as a lie, or a fantasy, or as ironical, or as concealing some mystical truth that he either likes or dislikes. But he misses the point entirely, because the myth, of which I shall give a fuller interpretation in the next chapter, is about nepotism, equality of educational opportunity, and social justice, not about a rigid class structure militating against these things. It is tiresome to continue in this vein, but Popper is determined to attribute to Plato every reprehensible social view that has ever existed. Having equated class with caste, he then equates caste with race (n. 23 on p. 240); that will do, if it is simply a matter of the Latin etymology of 'caste', but Popper means to import connotations of the Indian caste system which have no place in Plato's notions of social justice.

There are other and sounder grounds for criticizing Plato that do not rely on distortions of the text. At *Republic* V, 469B is a celebrated plea that Greeks not enslave fellow Greeks; it has distinct overtones of what we should nowadays call racism. Although he thinks slaves should be treated fairly, or even better than equals (*Laws* VI, 777D), there is no consideration of the question whether slavery is in principle tolerable. Aristotle considered the question and found it an entirely natural institution, not peculiar at all.

Popper's animus against Plato has other grounds than those prominent in his book. Even if we dismiss as merely silly or mistaken the ascription to Plato of 'historicism' as Popper has defined it, or of hostility to change on which Popper is so misguidedly insistent, we are still left with a Plato whose character and cast of thought is irreconcilably antithetical and profoundly antipathetic to Popper's. The commingling of matter with spirit is intrinsically vicious to Plato; it irredeemably condemns to imperfection all such mixtures such as we, the material world we inhabit, and our societies represent. This has all the resonance of Platonism and, taken far enough, of neo-Platonism. Here we sense the resignation of the twice-born, the darkling intuitions of the vanity of all aspiration, the impatient shuffling off mortal coils that are commonly associated with Platonism and, it would seem, excite the wrath of Popper. But how much of this is Plato, and how much Plotinus, Augustine, or the *Spätromantik* that is Popper's real target?

But Plato is too complex and elusive to be captured in these few phrases. There is a tragic vision, but it is lightened and redeemed by a comic sense that expresses itself in the most exquisite irony, parody, and good-humoured banter. Popper's device for handling this, where he notices it, is to give the good bits to Socrates and the bad bits to Plato. Socrates is a democratic martyr so that Plato can be a totalitarian; Socrates can be Sancho Panza, so that Plato can be Don Quixote or, more likely, the Grand Inquisitor in *The Brothers Karamazov*. This simplistic rending apart of Plato's work is as much a disservice to Socrates as it is to Plato. It is Plato's account of Socrates that we all rely on – surely not Xenophon's or Aristophanes' – he could not move us with his account of Socrates' life and death if he were not himself moved, and he could not be moved if he were the kind of philosopher Popper takes him to be. The consequences of his theory for Plato are not passivity, resignation, fatalism, or quietism; rather they are analysis, intense critical scrutiny, meliorism, and social activism.

V

Findlay's book seems almost designed to confirm Popper's worst fears. It purports to supply the unwritten doctrines that Plato would never set down, and is reckless in face of the anathema hurled against such an undertaking by the master himself:

> One statement at any rate I can make in regard to all who have written or who may write with a claim to knowledge of the subjects to which I devote myself — no matter how they pretend to have acquired it, whether from my instruction or from others or by their own discovery. Such writers can in my opinion have no real acquaintance with the subject. (*Seventh Letter*, 341BC) [Plato continues:] Acquaintance with it must come rather after a long period of attendance on instruction in the subject itself and of close companionship, when, suddenly, like a blaze kindled by a leaping spark, it is generated in the soul and at once becomes self-sustaining. (341CD)

Plato: The Written and Unwritten Doctrines is J. N. Findlay's blaze kindled on post-Husserlian phenomenology, a book undoubtedly steeped in a life-time of devotion to Plato's work, but astonishingly narrow given the breadth of Findlay's scholarship. It is an exercise in metaphysics, to the virtual exclusion of epistemology (save as 'eidetic insight' is assumed to supplement the limitations of dialectic), of ethics (save as the Good is represented by the One), and of politics (save for some rather conservative remarks in passing). Every page is scattered with Capitalized Words which suffer from the same implication as afflicts translations of Hegel: that the connotations of a large vocabulary are invested with a wider and deeper range of significance than the uncapitalized word can support. Not that Findlay has failed to supply the express content of those deeper meanings: he has, in many pages of intricate prose couched in a style as far removed from the lucidity and suggestiveness of Plato as it is possible to conceive. Only in Karl Reinhardt's *Platons Mythen* have I encountered language as dense as Findlay's, as clogged in the vain effort to articulate the inarticulable.

Findlay cites the passage from *Letter VII*, 341BC quoted above, omitting the second sentence (299), and insists that Plato 'does not hold philosophical insight to be ineffable and private . . . he is merely uttering the common sense of all who attempt to rise above common diction' (301).

The plan of the book is straightforward, its bulk devoted to systematic review of all the dialogues (except the *Menexenus*, often taken to be apocryphal), divided into the early Socratic, the 'Ideological' (the middle dialogues through the *Republic*, held to expound the doctrine of ideas principally in relation to the problem of individuals, their 'instantiations'), the 'Stoicheiological' (middle and late dialogues dealing with the 'Principles' or 'Elements' of the higher dialectic), and Plato's philosophy of the 'concrete' (which includes the *Critias*, *Laws*, and *Epinomis*; and, unexpectedly, the *Timaeus*). Apart from some introductory material and a most interesting appraisal of Platonism and its influence, the heart of the book is Chapter II: 'General Sketch of the Eidetic Theory and of its Arithmetized Version'. There is an appendix concerning the unwritten doctrines (chiefly passages from Aristotle) and another to correct Professor Cherniss' misinterpretation of Aristotle on this question.

It would carry me too far afield in a monograph on the myths to follow Findlay through the range of Platonic problems that seem to him the most important. Indeed, the points of contact between the centre of this study and of his book would seem almost to make them mutually exclusive. I believe that the unwritten doctrines remained unwritten for the best of reasons, namely that they were indemonstrable rather than inarticulable, and Plato was not willing to set forth beliefs, however ardently he may have been committed to them, that could not be deduced by a fully dialectical method of which he despaired at the last. Thus I am more in sympathy with Professor von Fritz[27] who said of the earlier attempts by Gaiser and Krämer[28] along lines similar to Findlay's that he challenged the usefulness of attributing a secret doctrine to Plato: he no doubt had one, but speculations about it are of little epistemological value. On the other side, we have had to wait a little for Findlay's explanation for the complete absence of a theory of the myths, and of other than passing reference to them in his book. In a recent paper[29] Findlay tells us that 'the myths of Plato are themselves a myth', and adds in the summary of this paper in the *Philosopher's Index* that the myths are 'sober accounts of the geography of Being'. This little echo of the language of Ryle in *The Concept of Mind* is a reminder that Findlay is impenitent about his belief that analytical philosophers, empiricists, positivists, and adherents of other contemporary schools of thought with which he is at odds, have their own unavowed presuppositions and remain unconscious of the biases that shape (or distort) arguments for which they are prepared to claim the utmost objectivity. Unlike them, he is prepared to proclaim dogma as dogma. Since his dogma is not mine, I must catch him where I can, which is in those passages in which he says incautious things on method and on the content of the myths. His book is as important as it is exasperating, because it expands the horizons of Platonic scholarship by some not altogether welcome dimensions, but it cannot be ignored.

For Findlay the Eide (Ideas) are central to Plato's thought (47); they are organized in a rational hierarchy which is known by eidetic insight, if it is to be known at all. Findlay insists throughout on the many ways in which the Eide *cannot* be known; despite being willing, unlike proponents of a more disembodied Platonism, to acknowledge the interest in the empirical world that Plato always had, Findlay reveals a sustained animus against empirical observation that does not always square with that interest: 'Plato is not, however, so wholly disdainful of the world of empirical fact as some have supposed: the *Timaeus* bears ample witness to his interest in it' (194). Yet Findlay is more contemptuous of the role of sense experience in, for example, triggering the recollection of the Forms than Plato is. 'Eidetic insight' is a special kind of intuition (cf. 156, to which I shall return), without which real knowledge is impossible. That is surely true, but the state in which Plato has left his written doctrines gives ample evidence of his reluctance to speculate about that elusive reality much beyond what is empirically verifiable. Findlay shows no such reluctance.

Plato's caution is well founded and documentable, as I have shown in chapter 2. The trouble with intuitions is that they are private and unacceptable unless they are subjected to the scrutiny and discipline of public discourse and its methods: ostensive definition (pointing to objects of common experience in the world) and logical exploration (testing the consistency of a proposition both internally and in relation to other propositions). That will reveal the hollow claims of false intuitions, though it will not demonstrate the truth of those that survive. About those, which include all that Plato surely believed, he remained convinced that no proof could be forthcoming, and chose either to remain silent, or to embody those convictions in myth. Findlay's method is rash in the extreme – he certainly acknowledges the inadequacies of dialectic, but insists on supplying as apodictic truth what Plato would only advance as a probability. Unless there is some way of distinguishing true intuitions from false – and Findlay gives no indication of such a way – then he has opened the door that Plato so carefully closed to every charlatan and intellectual adventurer. Findlay's is a counsel of despair: 'Modern philosophers who wish above all to dispense with non-sensuous intuitions have nothing to put in their place' (156). That sounds true, but does not tell the whole story: what many of those philosophers, since Hempel's demolition of 'the narrow thesis of empiricism', have been content to do is to find room for 'theoretical constructs', and other such heuristic devices adopted for the express purpose of advancing highly abstract theories which generate empirical results of immense utility. Imaginary numbers, such as i (the square root of minus 1), will do as an example: nothing in reality corresponds to it, yet its introduction into certain calculations permits the solution of otherwise insoluble problems. Without offering any account or serious critique of the role of art, Findlay suggests (206) that Plato would have to expel himself from the Republic, but I am afraid it is Findlay who would have to be expelled for much more serious violations of Plato's constraints on intuition by ascribing the ontological status of actual knowledge to intuitions that at best have the status of true opinion. For I am certainly willing to allow – it is little enough to give – that every word that Findlay says about Plato's actual beliefs is true, but it fails the requisite test of being discursively demonstrable.

Sometimes Findlay is aware of the overstatement of his own case. He speaks of a group in the Academy 'with a faith in exact argument which was quite alien to a man of insight like Plato, who could make brilliant use of exact argument when he chose, but who knew that it was never stronger than its premises or its working conceptions.' (213) I have no quarrel with this statement; still less would I dispute the need for insights that surpass and shatter an existing framework of concepts. The quarrel begins about what ontological status they are to be accorded: I would be reluctant to accord them any, even if from them a comprehensive set of theories were deducible which enjoyed apparently satisfactory empirical confirmation; I certainly would accord them none so long as they were no more than hypotheses awaiting confirmation.

Where Findlay goes utterly astray, it seems to me, is just in his treatment of the Platonic enterprise as a 'mathematicization' of reality. We would all agree that Plato had before him the model of mathematics, especially of geometry, as representing the best available mode of structuring knowledge. There are two impediments: a) overcoming the problems of axioms which have to be asserted to be self-evident because they cannot be deduced from higher principles; and b) so structuring other bodies of knowledge as to render them assimilable to mathematics. Findlay devotes himself at great length to showing how Plato undertook b). This is utterly vain unless a solution to a) can be propounded, but his approach to the critical passages in the *Republic* do not even fairly state the problem, let alone solve it. He makes use of 511C to indicate the shortcomings of mathematics (189), but he does not conclude from it that, if the mathematical problem cannot be solved, then *a fortiori*, the ontological problems cannot be solved either. Instead he seems to argue from the weakness of mathematics to the strength of metaphysics: 'It cannot be doubted that what is here being projected as the programme of Dialectic is the complete mapping of all the possible patterns of mathematical being . . . based, moreover, on principles that are wholly self-justifying' (189).

Of course, that is the programme, and equally of course, it remains unrealized and unrealizable! The same sort of argument is repeated in connection with 533C: 'This questioning of mathematical Postulations is called by Socrates-Plato their lifting or destruction (533C): we have to abandon them as fixed starting points and proceed to find a truly unquestionable First Principle from which they all can be derived' (195).

But Findlay wavers between what such a programme would be if realized, and seeing it in fact achieved. What is even odder, is that sometimes he accepts mathematics as a mere synecdoche (some kind of metaphor at any rate) for those higher Principles, but goes on to make mathematics the actual expression of reality itself. 'But the higher Dialectic would be nothing beyond an establishment of the foundations of *all* these mathematical sciences, a derivation of all of them from First Principles, and as such it would effectively comprehend Principia Ethica, and Principia Philosophiae Naturalis as well as Principia Mathematica. Plato, we see, was firmly wedded to what Moore called the Naturalistic Fallacy: to him the good form of anything was also the natural form of that thing, and that natural form depended in the last resort on a vast number of Products, Ratios and other functions of Number' (192). Findlay undoes in his second sentence what he has correctly asserted in the first: why go back to number when he has gone beyond number? He reifies the metaphor. And the 'would' of that first sentence soon loses its subjunctive mood.

The *Stoicheia* (Elements) or *Archai* (Principles) are of higher order than the Eide. This 'chosen band of transcendentals' (210) includes the One (as opposed to the Great and Small); Goodness and Unity (as opposed to Badness and Indefinite Multiplicity); Being and Beauty (and their excluded opposites). These may be predicated of Eide or used to speak about them, and therefore cannot be treated at the same logical level as the Eide themselves. There are many elaborations of the problems of type of which Plato was 'only dimly conscious' but they need not delay us here, not because the problem is uninteresting, but because it carries us still further away from the myths, and because my objections to Findlay's arguments are analogous to those already raised.

It will be abundantly clear by now why Findlay pays no special attention to the myths, either from a methodological viewpoint, or as concerns their content. He is quite willing to refer to them in passing as 'myths', but this is no more than a good-natured acceptance of the convention that calls them so. We had to wait for his 1978 article for confirmation that they are not myths at all, but partial realizations of the Platonic programme to be taken more or less literally, if refracted through an eidetic prism. His method betrays him only on those rare occasions when he actually ventures on interpretation of mythical elements. One such occasion is his reaction to the passage on the equality of women (*Republic* V, 455 ff.), In the text the question is initially posed as a problem: How does the women's nature differ from the man's? Plato addresses it in very concrete terms: if, against convention, it should appear that men and women are equal with respect to matters relevant to statecraft, then we must shape our polity accordingly; genetic arguments about the possibly equal biological contribution of women to offspring must also be taken into account, if true; and so forth. I mean to give a fuller account of this topic, which I treat as an 'anti-myth', in the next chapter. Here I note Plato's open mind, and tentative consideration of all the possible evidence, mostly gathered from animal husbandry, not from eidetic insight, at least not as Findlay envisages it. What does he make of this remarkable passage?

> The main point is that it is eidetic insight which alone can decide whether or not there is a genuine difference of Eidos or Phusis – the two are deeply associated in the thought of men and women: procreative, grammatical and conventionally social distinctions do nothing to decide the issue. And logic-chopping or Eristic is precisely the sort of reasoning that confounds genuine distinctions of Eidos or Phusis with conventional, verbal or contingently factual distinctions. (178)

This is a perilous approach – unPlatonic in the extreme – because such insights are indistinguishable from the condemned intuitions of the poets. If they are distinguishable, it is only to the extent that they are submitted to the rigours of logical and empirical scrutiny. But Findlay does not do justice to the manifest surface of the text, insisting instead on the fallacy of supposing that eidetic insight necessarily leads to truth. Even of those phenomenologists of whom it must be admitted that they look before they leap, who can tell where they will land? Plato might conceivably applaud every thought that Findlay ascribes to him, but a diffidence based on the soundest epistemological grounds compels the Platonic silence that Findlay has so unbecomingly violated. What redeems Plato's approach to these problems is the question mark that hovers like the smile of the Cheshire Cat over the desirability of eugenic breeding, say, as opposed to its feasibility.

These are problems to be addressed and perhaps solved, not resolutions to be imposed. Eugenic breeding is surely desirable, though its political feasibility is, if anything, even further removed from the possibility of realization than Plato himself thought. But Findlay's discussion of these passages totally ignores their import for practical politics (on p. 159 he has made it plain that they are not worth pursuing), but surely there are theorems, lemmas, and corollaries in the Platonic scheme as well as axioms and Principles, and there must be a logic that binds them together, and a world in which they are realized. Findlay is so determined that the core of the Platonic enterprise lies in Numbers and Ratios that he reifies these metaphors and assigns to his own subjective convictions of eidetic insight the ontological status of a Reality fathered on Plato. From the Smile he has inferred the Cat.

As noted, Findlay discounts the political implications of the *Republic* as unimportant compared with Plato's primary concern with meaning and value, arguing that he did not understand politics and had nothing of practical value to say (159). But although he ignores Plato's politics for this most unsatisfactory of reasons, he sometimes betrays his own political interest. The feasibility of implementing his proposals, 'Socrates-Plato affirms, with the sickening experiences of the folly and wickedness of the unguided Athenian democracy to back him' (179) depends on making philosophers kings, etc. This unbalances an argument that Socrates-Plato had carefully balanced in the *Apology*, where the excesses of the Thirty Tyrants (32BC) are cited along with those of the democracy (32CD) as evidence of Socrates' regard for the law rather than for the government. 'The *Republic*', Findlay tells us (209), 'is in many ways a strange book, certainly not a manual of practical politics, yet one understands as one reaches the end of it how Benjamin Jowett and others were able to make it, for a brief period, the keystone of an education which produced the best government for the

greatest number of persons that our confused world has ever witnessed.'
So much for Findlay's disclaimer of interest in politics and, for that
matter, in myths.

On the other side, Findlay is strangely silent when Plato actually uses
numbers to hint at a deeper truth. The proper size for society (excluding
women, children, slaves, and foreigners) is factorial seven (= 5040); as a
practical matter this corresponds with Aristotle's 'about 5000'; and both
correspond with the approximate size of Athens at the time. In Findlay
this becomes 'the Commune's sacredly proportioned numbers' (178),
without specification or further comment. And he passes in silence over
a page of numerological gibberish like *Republic* VIII, 546, which
purports to specify the best time for conception. Such passages are
enough of an embarrassment to me, who prefers to see in Plato rational
man at his best and can only deplore his occasional lapse in permitting
the intrusion of Pythagorean cabalism along with Pythagorean
geometry. They are devastating to Findlay's thesis.

After all this, I have a strange confession. It is that in my heart I have a
considerable regard for what Findlay has done in this book; it is possible
that what Plato had in mind was indeed what Findlay attributes to him.
The whole book is a beautiful myth about Plato, written in a spirit close
to the original. But as little as I trust my mind, my heart I trust not at all.

4 Eschatological and Related Myths

The determination which of the many possible passages in Plato are mythical will depend, as already noted, on which definition of myth is adopted. Those who see no myths at all have the easiest task, whether they are defending Plato, like Findlay, or attacking him, like Popper. They may well be willing to refer to 'myths', but this is simply because a misnomer has so passed into common usage that it would be pedantic to insist on some other term. Where, however, the presence of myths in the Platonic dialogues is freely acknowledged, there is still much confusion in the definitions of myth and therewith in the selection of those passages to be interpreted accordingly. Purely mechanical criteria, like the superficial determination whether the form of a passage is narration or dialogue, or detecting the presence in or about it of some characteristic term meaning 'myth' or a near equivalent, are equally useless, as Frutiger has shown. But his own criteria, while much more intelligent and sensitive to the text, founder in part because he insists on treating certain unquestionably mythical passages as dialectical because they embody 'self-evident propositions'. Yet, leaving their alleged self-evidence to one side, that is precisely why I believe they are mythical, as I have argued in the section on Frutiger in chapter 3.

An absolutely unequivocal definition of myth in Plato is impossible if only because at least two rather disparate purposes are served by their introduction, and so generate two different criteria. Those two are not difficult to specify: the first covers what I have called 'duplicates' of dialectical arguments closely related to the 'weak defence' of poetry because Plato is sometimes disposed to repeat in poetic form arguments that he is entirely able to make (and often has made) in dialectical form. The second is related to the 'strong defence' of poetry because these myths contain propositions that are the axioms of Plato's system, and so far from self-evident are they that they can be advanced only in mythic form so that there should be no misconception that they are dogmatic assertions. Thus, on the basis of these two criteria, I will include as myths

119

many passages that Frutiger excludes as 'erroneously considered to be mythical'.

But now my difficulties begin; there are several of them, and some may prove insoluble, or at least I must confess that I cannot solve them all. Some myths are treated in both ways (e.g. the doctrine of reminiscence in the *Meno* and *Phaedo*, as Frutiger has pointed out), without its being possible to draw a clear line between them, so that dialectic and myth are inextricably intermixed, as are the two kinds of myth. Then there is a puzzle which Zeller and other scholars have resolved by treating certain passages as mythical (the second part of the *Parmenides*, and some of the cosmogony of the *Timaeus* and *Phaedo* are examples) because the solution of the problems they address are 'beyond Plato's philosophical competence'. (They often go on to show that those problems were subsequently solved by Kant or Hegel, for example, but I am not interested in that sort of polemic here.) They do alert the reader to merely speculative passages, often in mythical form, in which Plato expounds some possible doctrines to which, however, he does not commit himself: they are 'stronger' than myths easily subsumed under the weak defence, but are 'weaker' than those that fit the strong defence, because they cannot serve as axioms from which a systematic doctrine can be deduced. A third difficulty is posed by passages like the one at *Republic* VIII, 546, which I described above as 'a page of numerological gibberish'. I may here be falling into the common practice of commentators who always find some plausible ground for dismissing inconvenient passages that cannot be made to fit; I cannot make them fit, but am reluctant to find them 'ironical' or 'apocryphal'; nor am I willing to contrive a chronology that makes them early so that they can be superseded by some later passage.

Nearly everybody agrees that there are eschatological myths, and various attempts have been made to classify the others, usually as 'foundation' or 'Aetiological' myths (Stewart). The latter are called 'genetic' myths by Frutiger, who adds 'allegorical' and 'parascientific' categories. All such classifications are bound to be somewhat arbitrary for the reasons given above, to which one might add that myth is in principle, as it were, unclassifiable. While not all myths are prescientific, least of all Plato's, they are produced in what another philosopher-poet, Schiller, called a 'musical mood', in which the hard edge of rigorously structured thought is softened and the mind hovers over its data making tentative explorations of possible structures other than those that govern existing modes of interpretation. In this creative mode the mind is liberated from the shackles of preconception, and new patterns are gestating. System and rigour will no doubt follow, or they should, but they are alien to the musical mood. The narrower and more clearly defined the categories used to label the myths, the more damage is done to a mode of thought that aims at unifying concepts, seeing vast overarching patterns to heal the fragmentation of the analysis that murders to dissect. Thus, if the myths are to be grouped, the groupings should be as loose as possible, with the understanding that there will be considerable overlapping. I will divide them, more for convenience than on any assumption of some underlying system, into three groups: the eschatological and related myths, the political myths, and what I call the methodological myths. The last may be distinguished from the others by a predominant concern, not with the content of possible knowledge, but with the methods by which we secure it.

There are two departures here from the overwhelming preponderance of commentary on the Platonic myths. The political myths have either been neglected in favour of a predominant concern with eschatology, or they have been taken literally (as by Crossman and Popper, for example); I hope in the next chapter to unravel them in a manner consonant with Plato's political sophistication while respecting their connection with his epistemology and ethics. The distinction I am drawing between those myths that deal substantively with religious, ethical, and political matters, and those concerned with method (e.g. the Line, the Cave, reminiscence, the Ladder of Beauty) has not been noticed in the principal works on the myths. I advance these claims to originality with great diffidence: the sheer volume of Platonic scholarship would make it extraordinary for something wholly new to appear, and if I have failed to acknowledge the appearance of any of the ideas I advance as my own in the work of others, it is because I have not seen that work.

I

The four great eschatological myths[1] involve much beyond their concern for the afterlife, and perhaps act most sweepingly to unify Plato's thought in its course from metaphysics and epistemology to ethics and politics.[2] These myths contain many of the key features of his theory of the soul, and it will be useful to recall the four chief ways in which we must understand the use of this term in Plato's writings. The soul is first a life principle, in the sense of the Latin *anima*, distinguishing whatever is alive from the inanimate. Second, the soul is the principle of mind, by which we are able to think and know. Third, if immortal, it is something to be judged, bearing, as he says it does (*Gorgias* 524E–525A), the marks and scars of its actions while in the body. And finally, it bears a meaning not far from its present-day usage in the Black community, 'soul' referring to those unifying attitudes and beliefs adopted consciously or not by a society.

Each of these meanings is intimately related to Plato's metaphysics, epistemology, ethics, and politics, but he has a tendency to focus on the life of the soul as it sustains his religious concerns. All the same, if one assumes that a religious motive is foremost, the danger exists that Plato will be cherished or denounced for the wrong reasons; and, perhaps worse, that the other reasons that he argues as he does will be obscured altogether by a preoccupation with religion. Scholars of the generation and approach of Jowett and Stewart,[3] for example, correctly see the religious-moral aspect, but in isolation, and are led to make of Plato an early Christian.[4] Others, like Popper, are offended by any claim to authority founded on revelation, and precisely because of an anti-religious orientation reject arguments that can be defended on other grounds.[5]

I do not, of course, assert that Plato was not moved by religious concerns. He was a notable reformer in this, as in so many other areas; and his attack on the poets is largely focussed on the account they give of the gods and the afterlife, an account remarkable for its indifference to moral example. But, important as religion is in his works, it must be treated in terms of parity with other considerations, not the least of which is a vindication of knowledge and morality, especially as they bear on social justice. The good, the true, and the beautiful ultimately converge in his thought, becoming inseparable in the One. Whether he is arguing to or from the One will determine whether the religious issue appears uppermost, but since he does both we are surely free to consider his views from either direction.

A less vexed point of departure is the nature of reason and knowledge: even if it emerged that religion can in part be shown to be rational, it does not follow from this that either is subordinate to the other – that is a question we need not reach. We can instead accept Popper's 'faith in reason'[6] as a proposition likely to be assented to by nearly everyone, if only because it nicely obscures whether our religious convictions spring from a rational foundation or vice versa. It is certainly true of Plato that religious beliefs may not run counter to the findings of reason.

Soul as mind, then, is where we begin. The soul knows certain things, as the body does; but each is like the object of its knowledge (cf. the general discussions in *Republic* VII and at *Philebus* 39A ff.). What the body knows, if 'know' is not too strong a word, are the perceptions of sense. They are riddled with error at several levels, the most primitive being optical illusions and other defects of sense (cf. *Theaetetus* 152B, etc.). Beyond these are the problems of inductive knowledge, even when consistent accounts are given of empirical experience by many observers on many occasions – such knowledge is probable only and subject to revision in light of new experience. There is much elegance and artistic verity in Plato's insistence that the ephemeral body can possess only ephemeral knowledge, and that the best that can be said of it is that it is true belief. That elegance is sustained through a lengthy parallel account chiefly in the *Republic* of the kind of knowledge possessed by the soul as mind. In that discussion the nature of knowledge is the unmistakable point of departure.

The claim is for a priori knowledge (conjoined with *anamnesis*, the doctrine of reminiscence), such as is set forth in the *Meno* and the *Phaedo*. The geometrical model is never far in the background of these discussions. If we possess knowledge, as Plato argues, that is irrefutable by experience, then it cannot spring from experience. On the contrary, it is such knowledge that validates and corrects empirical experience. (The converse – that we may not assert apparently rational propositions contradicted by experience – is also dealt with, but we do not need it here.) We seem to possess such knowledge prior to experience, and cannot account for it save by presupposing the existence of the soul prior to birth. In the *Phaedo* this argument is coupled with a cyclical doctrine to propound the further view that 'before birth' is the same as 'after death' and so is adduced to support the immortality of the soul. Our immediate purposes are served if we confine ourselves to the time before birth (which is, for example, as far as the *Meno* goes).

The colourful part of the eschatological myths proposes that in this prenatal state the soul is in the presence of the Forms, perhaps marching in a grand procession through the heavens. We cannot ignore the colour entirely for it serves the purposes of the weak defence of poetry, but it is not needed for review of Plato's metaphysics and epistemology. The philosophical motive for the Forms is our concern, however. They supply a solution to the problem of the status of universals, one indeed that could be maintained independently of their being embedded in the eschatology, and independently also of the other uses Plato has for the eschatology, though I think it does damage to the coherence of his thought to deprive them of this context.

These four myths are shot through with references to the nature of knowledge. The *Phaedrus* is richest in them, with one of the surprisingly small number of explicit definitions of the Forms to be found in the Platonic text: in its sojourn in the other world the soul comes to 'understand the language of forms, passing from a plurality of perceptions to a unity gathered together by reasoning' (249BC). It is the forms that furnish the only true knowledge (247CE) and the ability to recollect at least some of them is a precondition for passage into human form when, in accordance with the doctrine of transmigration of souls, the time comes for the soul to be reincarnated (248C, 249B, E). A somewhat different version of forgetfulness appears in the *Phaedrus* (250A): the soul may have glimpsed the forms only for a moment, or may have forgotten them because of evil deeds in this life. In the *Republic* (621A) the reason is that the newly incarnated soul drinks more or less deeply of Lethe, the river of forgetfulness, depending on the kind of life it has chosen. But it is clear that to the extent we retrieve that memory, we owe the recollection (or reminiscence, remembrance; any of these terms is satisfactory to render *anamnesis* and the other words Plato also uses) to the objects of sense perceived in this life: 'such understanding is a recollection of those things which our souls beheld aforetime as they journeyed with their god, looking down upon the things which now we suppose to be, and gazing up to that which truly is' (249C).

This reminder of the role of empirical experience is often overlooked in more ecstatic accounts of the epistemology; and is certain to be neglected where exaggerated versions of the Platonic dualism lead to a dismissal of this-worldly concerns altogether. It is not entirely without justification. Along with the *Symposium*, the *Phaedrus* is the most 'poetic' (Socrates' own word: 257A). Worldly beauty is a reminder of the true beauty of the forms (249E, 250B, D), and while the exquisite language of these passages may remind us of that 'metaphysics of Beauty' attributed to Plotinus and that this dialogue serves to produce a more acceptable rhetoric than that of the cynical Lysias on love, it may lead us to forget that Plato never loses sight of the need to harmonize his views on morality, final judgement, religion, beauty, and ultimate reality with his epistemology; and the same may be said of the three other eschatological myths.

Two other themes complete that aim: a life devoted to philosophy is the road to salvation because it dwells on the forms and best recalls what was known before incarnation (*Phaedrus* 249A, 256A; *Phaedo* 114C; *Gorgias* 526C). For in an echo of the Allegory of the Cave, we are told in that strange hydrographical cosmogony of the *Phaedo* (109D) that only if we can raise ourselves out of the mists and shoals that gather in the hollow places of the earth shall we see things as they truly are, instead of being like someone who supposes himself to be on the surface, but is under water, the objects of his vision refracted. The truth was and will be seen by the soul – if not irretrievably damaged – in the heavens (*Republic* 615A); and in the Islands of the Blessed the soul is superior in its faculties and can see things as they truly are (*Phaedo* 111BC; *Gorgias* 523A). The harmonizing of epistemology and morality is completed in these myths by the equation of knowledge with goodness (*Phaedo* 114E), a theme pursued elsewhere, of course.

The eschatological myths are not the best place from which to derive an account of the Forms: the best place is probably Book Lambda of Aristotle's *Metaphysics*. But some reference is needed here, because of the affinity of the immortal soul for the immortal Forms. Generalizations derived from experience have the disadvantage already noted: our experience is limited and time-bound, and every such generalization (one might be: 'an encapsulated history of chairs I have known') is subject to correction and improvement in light of fresh experience. Thus any empirical concept based on experience is associated with the limited and time-bound body, at best generating a 'likely story' as Plato characterizes physics in the *Timaeus*. Many philosophers have been content to leave matters in this unsatisfactory state on the grounds that, unsatisfactory or not, it is the best we can attain. But Plato is clearly aiming at something more than this, if only because he believes that we in fact possess something of the sort, as he shows in the *Meno* and *Phaedo*, as well as in the *Phaedrus* passages referred to above.

The geometer's triangle will serve as the model. It is to be distinguished from the sort of triangle scratched out on the ground, or measured with a protractor. Generalizations about triangles so derived are tentative, probabilistic, and so forth. That is to be contrasted with those properties of a triangle deduced from the axioms of geometry. If the axioms are true and the logic of our inferences from the axioms is valid, then the properties so deduced are true of every triangle, past and future, and they are not subject to further correction. There is a further 'if': if we in fact have such a body of knowledge, then it would be the best model for knowledge of any kind. Thus, if it is true, we should be warranted in preferring knowledge of a concept not subject to correction to one that is. Underlying and informing every empirical concept, on this view, is a heavenly concept (form or idea) from which the particulars of sense could be deduced. From an epistemological point of view, therefore, Plato wants the soul to be immortal and to ascribe spiritual and mental properties to it, in contrast with the corporeal and sensuous properties of the body, the soul's properties to be consonant with the eternal incorrigibility of the forms.

This is, however, only the first bird to fall to this stone. The interest Plato has is not limited to rigorous definition of elements of the physical world. It extends, of course, to the moral realm. There are many targets, of which not the least important is an attack on ethical relativism, as it was propounded by the Sophists. The analogue of empirical concepts is found in such precepts as Protagoras' 'Man the measure of all things'. In the realm of moral discourse this means there are no universal prescriptions, but merely such rules of conduct as have sprung up fortuitously in a given culture at a given time. This makes moral rules weaker even than the physical order, because Protagoras would surely agree with Socrates that 'two and two make four here as in Persia.' Plato clearly finds this intolerable: he almost certainly turned to a mathematical model to justify ethics rather than the other way about. So he is compelled to postulate (hypothetically, not dogmatically, no matter what some critics say) Forms of moral ideas also, organized as geometry is to permit deduction from first premisses. Because of their divine origin these are to have the same degree of objectivity and universality as geometry, or, conversely, to the extent that objectivity and universality can be ascribed, one can infer a divine origin.[7]

Greek religion offered a considerable array of notions of the afterlife, variously suited to respond to that fundamental concern that seems to have arisen in virtually every culture. It begins perhaps with the conviction we are all likely to develop of our own uniqueness and irreplaceability, such that we seek assurance of immortality in as many ways as will counterbalance the thought that something as precious as ourselves could wholly pass away. Socrates speaks of some of the ways men seek immortality: it might be through their children,[8] their works, or their public reputation.[9] These are not enough: I leave something behind by all means, but what happens to me? The standard picture of Hades derived from Homer is not very satisfying either: gray shades wandering pointlessly about a dreary landscape. So Achilles would prefer the life of a slave to the colourless eternity he is condemned to.[10] But there are other pictures, finding their way probably from the East into the mystery religions,[11] and it is these that Plato finds apt for his purpose. There is no notion in Homer that Hades is a place of judgement; and so his doctrine fails on both counts, furnishing no prospect either of reward or punishment. The sustained popularity of those versions that promise personal immortality shows how profound the psychological need is that created these myths. It is maintained even in face of the vivid accounts of the damnation more likely to be visited on us than the rewards for our rare virtues. Lucretius turns this argument upside down in the anti-myth of *De Rerum Natura*: if the consolations of religion are our aim, then we should rather seek assurance that, whatever the gods are up to, interfering in human affairs is the last of their concerns. Having set the standards of conduct impossibly high, the proponents of religion then promise us an eternity of misery for our inevitable shortcomings, and proclaim this threat a consolation!

Plato, of course, comes down on the other side. If I draw attention now to those passages in these four myths with an explicitly moral focus, it should not be forgotten that morality is at all times harmonized with epistemology as much as with the explicitly eschatological doctrines, all set against the background of the cosmogonies that are the least assured parts of the myths. It is difficult, and may even be foolish, to separate the issues so cunningly interwoven, and if I do so it is only to draw attention to their presence, often overlooked, for example, by scholars primarily interested in religious questions. At *Phaedo* 108AB we are told that it is attachment to the body that causes suffering, a moral shortcoming isomorphic with the imperfection of the knowledge perceived by the senses. The path to Hades is not straightforward, as Aeschylus said (107E–108A), but has many side turnings and forks, and needs a guide: morality is a rational enterprise, and judgement must be deliberate and not left to hazard: 'the wise and disciplined soul follows its guide' (108A). We are easily deceived, as by all mere seeming, by the appearance of morality – even the judges in the afterworld were so deceived, until they called for those to be judged to appear before them stripped of external pomp that concealed their vices in this life. In a remarkable image, the original Portrait of Dorian Gray, Plato adds in the *Republic* (614D) to the story told in *Gorgias* 523C–525A how the souls now appear naked before the judges, 'full of scars due to perjuries and crime'. The aim of these passages is clear enough, and will become painfully so when we turn later to the *Laws* – it is the reinforcement of morality in this life by the confident assertion that we shall not escape detection and just punishment, however successful we suppose ourselves to be in this life. The vice of ethical relativism, which so exercised Plato, is that it is but a step from arguing that only those actions are crimes that some society more or less arbitrarily declares to be such, to the argument that only those actions are crimes that are detected and punished as such.

From a moral point of view, there is a deeper offence even than that springing from the relativism of ethical principles. It is generated from what has come to be called the problem of evil, and it preoccupies Plato as much as it did the author of the Book of Job. Among the issues debated in the *Republic* is the difference between appearance and reality as it applies to those seeming to be just. Adeimantus and Glaucon attempt to show, albeit halfheartedly, that the appearance of justice is preferable to the reality, giving the best of both worlds. The problem is: since in all our experience it commonly happens that the innocent suffer and the wicked flourish, are we to conclude that there is no divine order to redress the imbalance or, worse, that the divine order is itself indifferent or wicked? The virtuous might indeed conclude with Socrates that virtue is its own reward, and no special assurances or rewards need be held out. But this is cold comfort compared with what is promised the wicked: they are to escape scot-free if only they can die old, fat, and warm in their beds after a lifetime of injuring the innocent. That will not do at all,[12] and so Plato incorporates not only a promise of personal immortality for the individual soul,[13] but the whole panoply of judgement before a tribunal that cannot be gulled, meting out reward and retribution.

It would be quite wrong for anyone who prefers to argue from a naturalistic or pragmatic perspective, as I do, to ascribe the same views to Plato. He surely takes his beliefs about the afterlife seriously. Even in the relative informality of the *Letters* we find allusions to the doctrine advanced with every appearance of conviction. In the *Second Letter*, for example, writing to Dionysius, he says:

> . . . we ought, it appears, to consider as well the time to come, since it is a fact that the most slavish men by a sort of natural law give it no thought, while the best men leave nothing undone to acquire a good reputation with posterity. To me this is a proof that the dead have some perception of events here, for the noblest souls know this truth by intuition, while the vilest souls deny it, but the intuitions of the godlike are more valid than those of other men. (311CD)

He is tireless on this theme, in part perhaps as a sort of memorial to Socrates, the recollection of whose martyrdom is bitter and repeatedly injects a special poignancy into language of incomparable emotional force. So it is not enough that the souls are purged in the interregnum between incarnations: there are those whose offences render them unfit to pass into human form at all (*Phaedrus* 249B) and, drawing on the Pythagorean doctrine of metempsychosis he promises them the miserable existence of some subhuman species bereft of reason. We need not exaggerate, but we should not overlook either, the left-handed comfort this gives to those whose goodness, innocence, or lack of enterprise preserve from the more spectacular vices.

How much of these things Plato himself believed to be literally the case is difficult to determine. The notion of posthumous judgement is clearly of great importance to him, as much for its moral import as for those implications of the immortality of the soul for the validation of his epistemology, and it is the only theme that appears in all four of these myths (*Phaedo* 107D, 113A, D; *Gorgias* 523B; *Phaedrus* 249A; *Republic* X, 614C–616A).[14] Yet, while in the *Gorgias* he will tell his story as 'fact' (523A) of which he is 'convinced' (526D), the *Phaedrus* story is 'poetical' (257A), and he is even more uncertain in the *Phaedo* where he will not insist 'that the facts are exactly' as he describes them, but 'something very like it' is the case (114D). I shall return to these and similar passages in the last chapter in order to assess the justice or otherwise of the charge of dogmatism.

But whether he believes them or not, everybody must agree that, if believed, they act as a powerful deterrent. In his later writings Plato is not above the merely pragmatic benefits that accrue when eschatological doctrines are widely disseminated and believed. Speaking in the *Laws* (XII, 959B) of judgement, he says that the mysteries give 'an account to which the good may look forward without misgiving, but the evil with grievous dismay.' Even more blunt is another passage (XI, 881AB) in which those same accounts 'effect nothing for the deterrence of these criminal souls . . . . Hence we must make the chastisements for such crime here in this present life, if we can, no less stern than those of the life to come.'

The intensely practical aims of Plato's doctrines are displayed in other ways. To the issues concerning deterrence already mentioned, we may add that unjust men are subject to a further year's torture if still unforgiven by those they have wronged (*Phaedo* 114AB) and, if very unjust, will themselves suffer in a future incarnation the fate they inflicted on their victims in this life, or will be irredeemably damned in perpetuity (*Phaedo* 113E, *Gorgias* 525C). But he does not unravel all the implications of this last doctrine: when the apparently just suffer injustice (Socrates assures us in a famous passage that this cannot really happen: *Apology 41D*), we may presume if no nearer crime can be detected that some earlier one is being requited. But the instruments of that divine vengeance, the apparently unjust, may perhaps be exculpated as innocent agents. Leave them to Heaven. Not everything may be so left, though: another remarkable turn of Plato's ingenuity, in the myth of Er, is hardly noted in the literature.

Beginning at *Republic* X, 617D is a passage describing how the souls ready for a new incarnation themselves select their next lives, and so retain responsibility for what they do and for what happens to them. This is far removed from Christian notions of predestination, and it is interesting to compare Plato's treatment of the question with Hugo von Hofmannsthal's in *Das grosse Salzburger Welttheater*. In that play the lives to be endured are imposed on the waiting souls, many of whom object bitterly to the misery they are doomed to enact. But their outcries are overborne by the mystical assurances of the dispensing angel that even lives of wretchedness and crime subserve the impenetrable divine purpose. Other features of the closing passages (*Republic* X, 621AB) link this story to Plato's epistemology. Although the souls know what is to befall them, they drink more or less deeply of the waters of Lethe, and so forget what exactly they have chosen. But the forgetting includes to the same degree what they have seen of the forms, leaving them open to recollect those memories when triggered by the particulars of sense. Plato thus makes elegant use of a punning meaning of the Greek word for truth: *aletheia* = a-letheia: 'unforgetting'.

This insistence, that 'the fault, dear Brutus, lies not in our stars, but in ourselves', may be Plato's reason for saying of Euripides that he was the wisest of the tragedians (*Republic* VIII, 568A).[15] What they share here is a detestation of the disclaimer of the individual's responsibility for his actions implicit in the destiny-spinning of conventional religion and, however sublimely transformed, of the older tragedians. Both Aeschylus and Sophocles are full of gods moving in mysterious ways, and of choruses brooding in helpless acquiescence before an ineluctable destiny. In their plays the Aristotelian catharsis is consummated in ultimate acceptance of divine providence, but a heavy price is exacted for this theodicy. It is the displacement to the gods of the mainsprings of man's actions, so that he is seen to be entoiled in their obscure purposes: their agent or surrogate perhaps, as Oedipus is at Colonus, but not a free agent. Shakespeare has argued on both sides of this terrifying question for, beyond Cassius' words, are those of Hamlet: 'There's a divinity that shapes our ends . . . ' and of the stricken Gloucester: 'As flies to wanton boys . . . ' Euripides permits no catharsis: in his plays the problematics jangle unresolved; hence Aristotle's resistance to him in the *Poetics*, and Aristophanes' outright hostility in *The Frogs*.

That man is free in the required sense is not directly asserted by Plato,[16] but is surely implied in these myths. For all Kant's opposition to rationalist metaphysics he is still impelled to offer his own answer as a necessary presupposition: freedom of the will is one of the ideas of pure reason without which ethics is impossible. But Plato is more modest and advances essentially the same claim in mythical terms. Nor is this casual: the one myth expressly labelled a 'noble lie', the myth of the metals (*Republic* III, 415A), is plainly intended to place the blame for such inequities as are perceived in society, rightly or not, on the gods (for their own unchallengeable reasons) and not on the rulers. One might have difficulty in reconciling the two arguments: holding men accountable for their actions on the one hand, and taxing the gods with the imperfections of society on the other. But that should not distract attention from Plato's shaping of religion to meet his political and ethical goals. For that is what these otherwise disparate examples have in common.

Secular philosophers have very serious difficulty with such an approach. From a certain point of view the retributive uses of eschatology may be considered another example, as in a way to be examined all the myths are, of the 'noble lie'. It is odd to ascribe to Plato a concern for outcomes, instead of for a priori prescriptive principles, yet to take one example, his criticism of the poets largely focusses on the undesirable effects of their works on the naive reader even more than it is concerned with their aesthetic aims. Although as late as the middle dialogues there is little direct reference to the deterrent effect of the final judgement on present conduct,[17] these stories are seen to be beneficial with increasing bluntness as his thought advances. Beyond the question whether Plato believes them or not is the more important question whether they are in fact true; but this we can hardly answer. Yet the posture of agnosticism or outright scepticism adopted by most contemporary philosophers blinds them to the point Plato is after. By embedding the myths in what Frutiger calls 'that tone of uncertainty that is peculiar to the myths',[18] Plato (or, perhaps more properly, Socrates) acknowledges the indemonstrability of beliefs he almost certainly held.

At the very least, even if repelled by doctrines to which they cannot subscribe, readers must be impressed by the ingenuity, to use no more flattering term, with which Plato harmonizes the several uses he has for these stories. They escape the criticisms laid against the other poets by being edifying and promoting morality, by their internal consistency, and by their insusceptibility to charges of irresponsibility and madness. But however ingenious Plato is in finding unifying images to convey his convictions through the epistemological, ethical, and religious spectrum, he has not escaped hostile criticism. From Grote to Popper the attack is launched on his alleged dogmatism and on the mysticism that is supposed to cloud the rational enterprise. Some of this attack may be justified, but not until the myths are better understood.

II

Another group of myths is clearly related to the eschatological myths, dealing with the same topics, without reference, however, to final judgement, but adding to the epistemological and moral significance of the soul's immortality that desire for perfection which chiefly characterizes Plato's notion of love. It has often been argued that the whole Platonic theory of the soul is a myth, and I have no serious quarrel with that conclusion, though the reasoning by which it is sometimes reached seems to me dubious. It is precisely because no clear distinction is drawn between dialogue and narrative forms, between premise and chain of reasoning, between those parts of the argument for which empirical evidence is cited and those parts for which none is or could be found, that the confusions noted arise; and these lead in turn to the extreme positions claiming all or nothing in Plato to be mythical, as they do to those more modest views disposing of one or another passage as mythical or not.

Nobody, so far as I know, treats the swansong of the *Phaedo* (84E–85B) as a myth, though it might be considered a borderline case. It is a beautiful image, somewhat fanciful, that sees the swan as a servant of Apollo singing in welcome anticipation of death, and it is not too far-fetched to associate it with the injunction laid on Socrates to make music, since philosophy, the greatest of the arts, is a preparation for death (*Phaedo* 60E). But not every Platonic trope has the sweep of myth. Another disputed passage has that sweep: the speech of Aristophanes in the *Symposium* (189B–193D). It is certainly a myth, as we shall see, but is it a *Platonic* myth? Almost certainly not, because such metaphysical insight as it has is not reconcilable with Plato's views. (I leave to one side the question of authorship, which I am entirely satisfied rests with Plato; nor am I aware that the sort of dispute rages here as surrounds the speech of Lysias in the *Phaedrus* – 230E ff.) – where so exact is the content and style of Plato's pastiche that editors of Lysias have insisted on including it among his orations!) I include Aristophanes' speech because it is irresistible, and is the perfect foil for Socrates' report of what Diotima told him about love.

On the other hand I exclude the 'proofs' of the immortality of the soul in the *Phaedo* because they are dialectical in form rather than mythical, and because they are like theorems, exploring what may be deduced from the mythical axiom of the soul's immortality. The distinction is essentially that set forth in the introductory pages of this chapter, and an analogy may help to make it clearer. The axioms, postulates, and definitions of Euclid may be thought of as mythical because no proof of them is available; but the theorems, say that of Pythagoras, are dialectical (the added cheer that naive geometricians get from empirical confirmation of a theorem is merely meretricious). Frutiger's mistake is to export the dialectical status of the theorem to the premise, and so he excludes some of these myths; his is the precise converse of the procedure of some other scholars who export the mythical status of the premises to the theorems, and so make, for example, the whole doctrine of the soul mythical. These things said, the passages I propose to deal with in this section are *Timaeus* 69C–72D; *Republic* IV, 434E–441C (this passage needs mention here, but chiefly belongs in chapter 6); *Phaedrus* 243C ff. and *Republic* X, 611B–612A; *Phaedo* 80D–84B; *Symposium* 189B–193D and 201D–212C (the Ladder of Beauty at 211BC overlaps with the myths in chapter 6). So far as possible I will treat them thematically rather than seriatim.

The tripartite nature of the soul is familiar from the account in the *Republic*, where its parts are made to correspond to the three classes of society. The lower two parts are the appetitive and the courageous, and a clear distinction is drawn between these and the rational part which is to govern. Part of the elaborate cosmogony of the *Timaeus* is devoted to the creation of living bodies and in it we find what I think is a unique account in Plato of the soul as *anima*, that is, as life principle, clearly contrasted with the attributes of the higher aspects of soul with which every reader is familiar. The passage (69C–72D) deals with 'that part of soul which desires meat and drinks and the other things of which it has need by reason of the bodily nature' (70D). These assure nourishment, but are set low in the body as far from the rational part as possible, along with the liver and other viscera. A rather extravagant image of the reflections of sight is found in the bitterness of bile and the sweetness of the liver – a sort of allopathic view to maintain the balance between the upper and lower divisions (71CD). The liver itself is the seat of divination (a commonplace of Plato's and later times), which thus belongs to the foolishness of man, not to his wisdom (71E). He remains with this theme rather longer than a purely physiological account would require, presumably to grind an axe, one already encountered in the pun on *manic* and *mantic* at Phaedrus 244C. This becomes the vehicle for grounding his suspicion of inspirations and visions originating in the liver, so that rational interpretation is of greater importance than demented divinations (72AB). This lower part of the soul is contrasted with the middle part, which is the seat of courage and contention, located in the breast nearer the head (70A) to help control the lower part. The lungs are placed near the heart to cool its often overheated passions (70CD). The body needs this different kind of soul (69C) which is mortal, susceptible to pain and pleasure, and to the emotions. The whole account is said to be 'probable' and will become more so on further 'investigation' (72D). The interest this passage has for us lies in its elaboration of the larger myth of tripartite soul and society, filling in some details missing from the *Republic*, and introducing the idea, not found there, that part of the soul is mortal. We might infer that the middle part of the soul is to some degree immortal, since it helps the rational part, much as the Guardians are in alliance with the Philosopher-King to control the appetitive part of soul/society; but Plato nowhere says so.

It is worth noting that *Republic* IV, 434E–441C, which develops the tripartite theory, is in dialectical form and contains some significant methodological observations, and so I propose to deal with it in greater detail among the methodological myths. Here it suffices to say that the whole passage leads to the analogy between the parts of the soul and the parts of the state such that social justice is justice in the individual writ large. A predominance of the spirited element in societies like Thrace and Scythia, for example, is attributable to an excess of that quality in its citizens, whereas Greeks love knowledge, and Phoenicians and Egyptians love money (435E). There is an obvious connection with the doctrine worked out here and the perverted forms of the state in Book VIII, to be discussed in the chapter on the political myths.

The fullest treatment is nonetheless reserved for the soul in its higher manifestations, with relatively little said about the appetitive and spirited parts, and here we turn to those passages describing its nature and attributes as these bear on intellect, morality, and the divine. The soul is a prime mover, hence immortal, for its motion never begins or ends (*Phaedrus* 245CD); the argument is reminiscent of Aristotle's, but without the explicit recourse to an infinite regress as the *reductio ad absurdum*. What it is and what it ought to be is beautifully brought out in the image of the winged charioteer and the two horses, one noble with its vision fixed on the heavens, the other base and always ready to yield to appetite; we are the charioteers striving to keep these conflicting impulses in balance (248B). Some aspects of this image recall the story of the Ring of Gyges (*Republic* II, 359D–360B), for without the external constraints that spring from what others know or may find out about our conduct it is all but impossible for us to check the claims of appetite (*Republic* X, 611C). But if we keep before us that aspiration of the soul to realize its divine heritage, the task will be easier, and we shall not lose our wings. That is the task of philosophy.

Only philosophic natures attain to the divine (*Phaedo* 82C) because they are not attached to money, power, or reputation; philosophy is salvation from desire (a point repeatedly made in the eschatological myths – *Phaedo* 114C, *Gorgias* 526C, *Phaedrus* 249A, 256A), and a release from the deception of the senses (83A). Itself invisible (80D), the soul is devoted to the invisible and intelligible reality (cf. *Phaedrus* 247C), avoiding the extremes of pleasure and pain that rivet the soul to the body (83D), and by following reason it is enabled to exercise self-control, courage, and temperance (83E). By contemplating 'the true and divine and unconjecturable' (84A) it can finally reach a place kindred to its own nature (84B). A more succinct version of essentially the same points is given at *Republic* X, 611B–612C.

Those without philosophy cannot avoid the contamination of the body and do not find the release from folly and uncontrolled desire it brings (*Phaedo* 80E–81A). The complementary versions of the fate that awaits them are found in the hierarchy of incarnations promised: in the *Phaedo* (81C–82B) souls freighted with wickedness lurk as ghosts near the earth from which they cannot rise, and pass into the bodies of animals; the violent become wolves and birds of prey, while those with some sense of the amenities become social insects like ants and bees. *L'homme moyen sensuel* remains a simple citizen. The *Phaedrus* amplifies the spectrum of the prospective incarnations available to those not wholly lost to remembrance of the forms: those recollecting most become seekers after wisdom, followers of the Muses, or lovers; and as we move lower in the scale there comes second, the king who abides by law, third, the statesman or trader, fourth an athlete or physician, fifth the prophet or priest of the Mysteries (compare the denigrating remarks at *Timaeus* 71E on diviners); sixth, the poet or imitative artist, seventh the artisan or farmer, eighth the sophist or demagogue, and last, the tyrant (248DE).

If there is a single theme that characterizes Platonism more than any other it is that disaffection with terrestrial existence for its tragic condemnation to a life for which the nobler hopes of which Plato constantly speaks unfits us. The obverse of that divine discontent is the aspiration of the soul to regain the perfection from which it is for that time cut off. Those who see in Plato one nostalgic for Arcady and attribute to him the conservative or even reactionary longing to recover and restore an idyl long past overlook the quest for Elysium which lies before. Platonic love, of which ordinary usage can say little more than it is an elevated form of friendship into which sex does not enter, is nothing less than the desire for eternal possession of the good (*Symposium* 206A); it should be added that the imagery is rather more sexual than that common usage imagines, especially in Socrates' magnificent second speech in the *Phaedrus* (243C ff.) which leads into the eschatological myth already discussed. The setting in the *Symposium* is a feast to celebrate Agathon's winning the prize for tragedy; each of the participants is to make a speech in praise of love. The six reported speeches are artfully arranged so as to address the grossest forms of sexual love first and then to proceed to the most sublime. Eryximachus, the Sicilian physician, is made to speak in his native accent, and Agathon in the style of Gorgias (198B), further evidence of Plato's literary skill. Two of the speeches are worth including here because of their depth: Aristophanes' story (despite its not being a Platonic myth, though unquestionably of Platonic authorship), because beyond a bawdry worthy of Aristophanes himself, and to which only a prig could object, something of the anguish of Platonic love is intimated. And Socrates' account of what he says Diotima taught him of love conveys this theme in a manner never surpassed.

The chief myth in the *Phaedrus* is the magnificent account of love and the soul at 243C ff.; in structure it is referred to by Socrates as an example of the method of collection and division (cf. *Sophist* 253B). It is also an example of philosophical rhetoric, opposed to the sophistical rhetoric exemplified in Lysias' speech at the beginning of the dialogue. This long and beautiful speech contains so many Platonic doctrines that one commentator (Schleiermacher) at least has tried to treat it, not as a summary of Plato's position on a number of related themes, but as his first work, anticipating their later discussion in the other dialogues.[19] It seems appropriate to list these points briefly here at the outset to show how wide are the ramifications of the issues raised in this myth:

1. The immortality of the soul, a kind of ontological argument, already considered above in relation to the *Phaedo* and *Republic*.
2. Cosmogony: cf. *Republic*, *Timaeus*, *Statesman*.
3. The realm of pure forms: *Phaedo*, *Republic*.
4. The vision of the truth as a precondition of human form; this seems to be unique in this dialogue; discussed above.
5. The theory of recollection: *Meno*, *Phaedo*.

6. The hierarchy of incarnations: *Phaedo*, and the choice offered the souls in *Republic* 617D, discussed above.
7. Eschatology: see section I of this chapter.
8. The image of the soul as charioteer and two horses, compared above with the tripartite division of the soul and of society.
9. The madness of love and its reciprocation: cf. *Symposium*.
10. The best love and the second best.

Except for the argument showing the immortality of the soul at the beginning (245C ff.), the speech is entirely 'one of those chance fancies of the hour' – a myth, and great caution must be exercised in its interpretation. One danger is to attempt to interpret on the level of the imagery alone and to miss the really important meaning which lies beneath the symbolism. In his *Plato*, A. E. Taylor has a very apposite comment on this kind of interpretation: ' . . . it is not really permissible to extract metaphysics from mythical details which are necessitated by simple regard for the coherency of the pictorial representation' (307).

Apart from the large number of Platonic themes represented, the dialogue also contains the most important evidence of Plato's awareness of the function of myth in relation to dialectic and rhetoric that is to be found in his works.

The general context of the myth is the subject matter raised in the speech of Lysias (230E ff.) and Socrates' first speech (237B ff.). Lysias undertook to defend the thesis that a young man should grant his favours to one who does not love him rather than to a lover. As an exercise in rhetoric, this topsy-turvy treatment of 'love' is designed to display the rhetorician's independence of his subject matter, his ability to sway his hearers in any given direction. In his first discourse Socrates claims merely to surpass Lysias as a rhetorician, that is as concerns form, the arrangement of the subject matter without reference to its intrinsic moral worth. But he does this with misgiving, veiling his face for shame at the essential immorality of this treatment; and he provides safeguards in the telling against the same charge of irresponsibility to which Lysias has left himself open. Lysias fails not only from the point of view of the rhetorician, but also because his speech is cynical and depraved, and he makes no attempt to modify its disgraceful propositions by the apologetics which were necessary in the Greek world for such behaviour to be tolerated at all.[20] As Taylor points out: 'The kind of cleverness which sustains such theses by the use of such arguments is a real danger to the community and requires to be countered, as it is by Socrates, with better morality and superior wit' (*Plato*, 302). As Socrates turns to go after his first speech he hears the voice which only prevents him from some act.[21] He cannot leave until he has atoned for his impiety. Eros is the son of Aphrodite and is a god – if love be a divinity it cannot be evil, yet both speeches made it so.

At 243 Socrates begins his second discourse. It was a lie to say that favours should be accorded a non-lover rather than a lover because the one is sane, the other mad. That claim would indeed follow if it were unconditionally true that madness is an evil. But among our greatest goods is a kind of madness which is a divine gift. Socrates distinguishes three forms of madness which have been of inestimable value to men. First prophecy, the gift of Apollo; the value of this is shown by the etymological relationship of *mantikē*, prophecy, and *manikē*, madness, and by the benefits Hellas has obtained through the prophetesses. Second, purgation, the gift of Dionysus; this is the ridding of some ancient blood-guilt upon a house or family: possibly Socrates has the house of Atreus in mind here.[22] Third, poetry, the gift of the Muses; here the benefit is conferred through the true poet, not the poetaster or one whose inspiration is immoral: the poet is moved by a madness which is the source of a truth he cannot explain.[23] At 265A these divine forms of madness, which produce 'a divine release of the soul from the yoke of custom and convention', are distinguished from madness arising out of human affliction.

We have agreed, Socrates continues, that love is a madness, and have found three forms of madness beneficial to men. We shall now show that love also is a beneficial madness, due to the inspiration of Aphrodite, and the greatest gift of the gods. Such a love in its highest form will be philosophical love, such as Diotima speaks of. To place it in its proper perspective we must first find out the truth about the conditions and acts of the soul, both human and divine. The famous passage that follows on the nature of the soul, its immortality and self-motion, has been discussed earlier, as has the image at 246A of the soul as a pair of horses and a charioteer. We are warned that this is only an image because it is only thus that human reason can speak of such matters (cf. *Statesman* 277C); to give a complete account of the soul is only for divine discourse.

Soul is in command of all which is without soul; passing through the totality of the universe it becomes embodied under various guises. When perfect and winged it travels in the heights as an immortal being; but if it becomes imperfect and feeds on ugliness and evil it loses its wings and sinks to earth forming a union with matter. This union is necessarily mortal because the wholly imperfect earthly part must decay. So long, however, as the soul is lifted on its wings into the presence of divine things (the highest Forms of beauty, wisdom, goodness, and justice) it passes in the orderly array of gods and demons through the heavens. No poet has ever sung of this region, but we must dare to do so, Socrates says, and 'It is such as I describe; for I must dare to speak the truth, when truth is my theme' (247C).

This section culminates in a description of ultimate reality, stressing the quintessential rationality that pervades it:

> There abides the very being with which true knowledge is concerned; the colorless, formless, intangible essence, visible only to mind, the pilot of the soul. The divine intelligence, being nurtured upon mind and pure knowledge, . . . rejoices at beholding reality. (247C)

Now we can be shown how the life of the soul before its incarnation bears upon the madness of love. At the sight of earthly beauty one is reminded of the true beauty and the soul takes wings which would fly upward were it not for the body. When moved by love a man is thought mad because he neglects earthly things. Of all the kinds of divine possession this is the highest and only a few souls have so great a recollection of that divine beauty. Those who do, when they see in this world an image of it are amazed and beside themselves. They cannot explain their rapture because they cannot analyze it sufficiently; it is only with difficulty that the higher ideas can be recognized in their earthly images, and then only by the philosopher.

Beauty shone among the other realities, and in this life, too, it shines, palpable to sight, the acutest of the senses (250D, cf. *Republic* 508B). How much more would wisdom and other ideas shine if there were material images of them too! But the man who has become corrupted does not rise from the image to the true beauty, he does not look with veneration but as a beast seeking unnatural pleasure. Beneath the surface, the wanton steed is still bursting with passion and if, under this pressure, the charioteer should cede, his pleasure is only second best because the approval of the whole soul is lacking.

The man, though, who is recently initiated and for whom the object of contemplation is the realities, when he sees in a godlike face or form the expression of divine beauty, he is overcome at first by a shudder of awe, like that he once felt. For him the beautiful is like a god, and were he not afraid of being thought completely mad, he would make sacrifice as to a god. Accompanying the shudder is an unaccustomed warmth which makes the congealed and atrophied wings sprout anew, for once the whole soul was winged. In this condition the soul is shaken and restless, a wave of particles flows from beauty. This men call love, and its reward is great for, after death, even though unwinged, lovers who have resisted carnality are ready to soar and will not sink below. The friendship of a lover, then, brings great and lasting benefits which are not to be compared with the worldly prudence and vulgar caution of the non-lover – these deprive the soul of salvation for the full period of a thousand years.

It should be noted that the conception of love in Lysias' speech was limited to the sexual, or homosexual, level, and to the interest primarily of the active party. In Socrates' first speech there are few hints of the profounder meaning of the second speech; it is in the latter that we find the full blossoming of a concept of love, of philosophical love which is to sexual love as the soul is to the body. Love is thus raised to the utmost level of spirituality where the flesh is not so much despised as irrelevant. It is this irrelevance I would wish to emphasize as far as concerns the object of love here being literally a homosexual one but figuratively and more importantly, the Good. Among those who cannot make this distinction and who, I think, have missed the point, is Warner Fite in *The Platonic Legend,* where he inveighs against the gross immorality which underlies, as he thinks, this view of love. Indeed, the second and fuller reference to the soul considered as two steeds and a charioteer (253C ff.) might, again if taken literally, encourage such a view. But it is not even necessary to be broadminded on the cultural level to see that this sexual imagery constitutes, and only in a limited sense, no more than the outward frame of the myth, and has nothing to do with its inner content. The same kind of people who insist on being literal here shut their eyes to the uxorious appeal of the Song of Solomon and supply page headings like 'Christ the Bride of the Church', etc.

Philosophical love is the basis of the relation between teacher and pupil and is a blessing and a benefit for both – for the mature understanding as for the burgeoning intellect which is able to recognize good and evil but not yet able to give an account of them. It is in this sense that the account of the best love and the second best is to be understood. For that union of souls which is the lovers' highest quest, carnal union is but an inadequate symbol. No wonder that Aristotle said that every animal is sad after intercourse. Throughout our literature the theme is forever recurrent that there is something of regret in physical fulfilment. Our sense of tragedy is affronted by the idea that lovers may have a lasting satisfaction of one another on earth, and our stages are strewn with the bodies of those lovers who could not come to terms with the world, so that the only possible consummation is a spiritual unity in death. Earthly satisfactions, viewed *sub specie aeternitatis*, are necessarily only second best and are inevitably tinged with regret and remorse.

Something of the hopelessness of the lovers' quest is equally apparent in the *Symposium* contribution attributed to Aristophanes (189C–193D). Originally, he is made to tell us, the sexes were three: man, the child of the sun; woman, the child of the earth; and the androgynous combination, the child of the moon. These beings were double, joined together front to front like Münchhausen's hare which, when tired, just flipped over and continued on a second set of legs. So powerful and presumptuous were these creatures that they threatened the peace of the gods, and Zeus ordered that they were to be divided down the middle and adjusted accordingly. If they continued to misbehave, Zeus threatened they would be sliced again, therefore we should not be impious lest we be obliged to hop around on one leg with half a nose! This much is told in Rabelaisian fashion, but the mood changes:

> After the division the two parts of man, each desiring his other half, came together, and throwing their arms about one another, entwined in mutual embraces, longing to grow into one, they were on the point of dying of hunger and self-neglect, because they did not like to do anything apart (191A).

Zeus had pity on them, as well he might, and further arranged the halves that they might have sexual satisfaction of one another. Thus desire is rooted in our original nature, and the longing of love is the impossible desire of lovers to find their other halves and to be reunited again. There is a most eloquent passage at 192C which recalls the lover of beauty in the *Phaedrus* (251A) who is amazed and struck dumb in the presence of beauty. Here too, the lovers, being joined, are amazed and 'cannot explain what they desire of one another.' I will resist the temptation to add to the purple prose inspired by these passages and say only the most arid of souls could remain untouched by this picture of the longing for shared tenderness.

After Agathon has pronounced an elaborate eulogy of love in the flowery style of Gorgias, Socrates declares himself put out of countenance and unable to make another speech half so good.[24] But he recovers sufficiently to extract from Agathon, in a passage of dialectic (199C–201C), the admission that love is not itself beautiful, or great, or good, as he had asserted, but is desirous of all these things, standing in need of them. This sets the tone for Socrates' account of love which then follows, because Diotima forced Socrates to make the same concessions as he has now secured from Agathon.

She told him that love was neither wholly fair and good, nor yet wholly foul and evil. Love is like true opinion, midway between ignorance and knowledge. It is a *daimon* mediating between the mortal and the immortal, the medium by which the divine converses with man:

> For God mingles not with man; but through Love all the intercourse and converse of God with man, whether awake or asleep, is carried on. The wisdom which understands this is spiritual; all other wisdom, such as that of art and handicrafts, is mean and vulgar (203A).

Love is the child of Poros, plenty, and Penia, poverty, conceived at a feast to honour Aphrodite's birthday. On account of this and because love is a lover of the beautiful, he is a follower of Aphrodite. He is as poor as his mother and as scheming as his father; he is both a philosopher and a sophist; mortal or immortal according as his fortunes flourish or decline.

Love is not wise but a lover of wisdom; no god is a seeker after wisdom for he is already wise, and the ignorant do not seek it at all for they feel no need of it. The philosopher is not wise but a seeker after wisdom: he falls, like love, between the two. What does he desire of love? The possession of beauty which, like the possession of the good, leads to happiness. But not all searchers for happiness are lovers: this name is reserved to those only who seek happiness by way of love; and by that he means love of the good:

> You hear people say that lovers are seeking for their other half; but I say that they are seeking neither for the half of themselves, nor for the whole, unless the half or the whole be also a good. And they will cut off their own hands and feet and cast them away, if they are evil; for they love not what is their own, unless perchance there be some one who calls what belongs to him the good, and what belongs to another the evil. For there is nothing which men love but the good (205E–206A).[25]

Socrates and Diotima thus reach the definition of love: it is the desire for the everlasting possession of the good (206B).

One mode of securing this everlasting possession is by sexual generation and the protection of their young by which mortal creatures seek to become immortal. Other ways, to which men devote a passion even greater than that for their families, are the achievement of fame or wealth (208C). And the passion which moves the lover of wisdom is for the immortality of the soul – this underlies the poet's inspiration and is the aim of the legislator who loves temperance and justice (209A).

The concluding section (210A–212A) contains the description of how the lover passes from the various stages of knowledge to the highest stages: the image that Plotinus takes up and develops in his ladder of Beauty.[26] By gradual steps beginning in youth, a man must pass from the contemplation of particulars to the universals or forms in which they share, and from the individual forms to the whole universe of forms crowned by truth and beauty:

> He who from these ascending under the influence of true love begins to perceive their beauty, is not far from the end. And the true order of going . . . to the things of love, is to begin from the beauties of earth and mount upwards for the sake of that other beauty, using these as steps only . . . until he arrives at the notion of absolute beauty, and at last knows what the essence of beauty is. (211C)

A man who has passed through these stages would then no longer be attached to sense, but would behold 'true beauty simple and divine.' The thought which underlies this superlative recital points toward that fulfilment which men, possessors of a reason inadequate to its task, are forever striving to attain. There is that sense of insufficiency, the awareness of a perfection which lies beyond our ability to achieve despite rare glimpses of it, that characterize the saint and mystic and remain wholly inexplicable and incommunicable. There is a kind of heartsickness which accompanies the discovery, a very agony of the spirit which is nonetheless not without a certain serene resignation. Whether Socrates is a saint in that sense is a question best left unanswered but not for nothing did Erasmus say 'O St Socrates, pray for us!'

These three passages, the *Phaedrus* myth and the two from the *Symposium*, can be selected somewhat arbitrarily from the many available as evidence of Plato's indisputable status as a poet. This in no way compromises his status as a philosopher, since the distinction between the two is not that of a technical discipline as opposed to free association. And he is not less a poet because he did not write in metre:

> The distinction between poets and prose-writers is a vulgar error. The distinction between philosophers and poets has been anticipated. Plato was essentially a poet – the truth and splendour of his imagery, and the melody of his language, are the most intense that it is possible to conceive.[27]

Shelley, who, by the way, made a translation of the *Symposium,* is here accepting Plato's invitation to provide a defence of poetry at *Republic* 607C. That invitation is ironic in the extreme, since Plato has provided his own defence of poetry. In the attacks upon the poets they are regarded primarily as imitators, and as incapable of understanding the implications of their own works. What is required for a defence of poetry is that it be shown 'not only that she is pleasant but also useful to States and to human life . . . for if this can be proved we shall surely be the gainers – I mean if there is a use in poetry as well as a delight.' It is to this passage that Shelley refers when he says that 'the poets are the unacknowledged legislators of the world.' For the purposes of the weak defence of poetry art must be didactic; this is its use to state and individual. But beyond that, as these sublime passages make plain, is such expression as we can give to an otherwise ineffable order of being – and there lies the strong defence: we are free to speculate, within disciplined limits, about that ultimate reality, but we may never represent, and Plato never does, that we have articulated that reality as it is.

III

Speculation in Plato is, as we might expect, rifest in the cosmologies. Despite clear evidence that he tempered the transmitted traditions in light of the best scientific evidence available to him, especially mathematical, he came late to physics, probably because of Socrates' distaste for it in favour of ethics and epistemology, to say nothing of more abstract subjects, and equally probably because from a methodological viewpoint physics could never be more than 'a likely story' (*muthos eikos*), and so long as the programme of dialectic remained promising his energies were better directed to its development in the production of positive knowledge. Thus the *Timaeus,* the principal text we must consider, has always posed a problem to its interpreters. Nearly all of them regard it as mythical in its entirety (save for some brief passages), despite the fact that the manner of its telling mostly precludes those comments on its mythical status that are so frequently found in the other myths. It was the only work of Plato known to the Middle Ages until well into the Renaissance, and taken more or less literally has left a heritage to this day as a repository of ancient wisdom and mystical truth. Fortunately much of the damage that approach has done to Plato, the rational philosopher, has been corrected by some important modern studies treating the *Timaeus* as a monument of the history of science, and of ideas generally, but liberating the express information it gives us about ancient notions of astronomy, physics, and biology from the mystical setting. Mysticism has no place in such disciplines, as Plato would himself have agreed. Thus I have no interest here in paraphrasing or interpreting those parts of the Timaeus myth, and they form the greatest part, that are the domain of the historian of science. If they contribute to a study of myth at all, it is as an awful warning not to allow speculation to outrun by too great a distance such facts as will check its course, nor to propose hypotheses of little heuristic value independent of the facts.

We are, however, given some indications of Plato's motive in pursuing these matters. The dialogue begins with a brief recapitulation of parts of the *Republic* (mainly from Books IV and V), and now proposes an elaborate programme, of which only part was completed. Timaeus, who was chiefly an astronomer, is to give an account of the creation of the world and of man, while Critias is to take man from the point where, having been educated as Socrates proposed in the *Republic*, he constituted the citizenry of an ancient Athens 'in fact and not in fiction', able to hold off the powerful warriors of Atlantis until it disappeared beneath the waves. Most of this programme was not completed: the *Timaeus* gives a brief version of the story, and the fragmentary *Critias* is mainly confined to a description of the fabled island. Some scholars think that the unwritten *Hermocrates* may have been superseded by the *Laws*.

These stories are introduced by an account that Solon passed them on to Critias' grandfather (also named Critias), and that he originally heard them from the priests of Egypt. Of special interest for our purposes here is the treatment by the Egyptians of the myth of Phaeton who, unable to control the chariot of his father Helios, burned up the earth and was himself destroyed. This is interpreted by the Egyptians to refer to 'a declination of the bodies moving in the heavens around the earth, and a great conflagration upon the earth which recurs at long intervals' (22E). The Egyptians are represented as proud of their long recorded history, here claimed to be 9000 years, and somewhat patronizing in that, because the Greeks have no written history, they are like children who must always begin all over again. What we are to gather from this, it seems, is not unlike some recent trends in Biblical interpretation: that beneath the surface of legendary chronicles and myths lies a factual history capable of rational and naturalistic interpretation. Strictly speaking that claim is confined to whatever it was that Critias was going to tell, perhaps including the Atlantis myth (which has never ceased to inspire intermittent revivals of belief in its actual existence),[28] but it is not unreasonable, in view of some of Timaeus' remarks, to allow a similar credence to the cosmogony that takes up the largest part of his recital.

That can, of course, be only probable, for we are mortal. Indeed, 'the father and maker of all this universe is past finding out, and even if we found him, to tell of him to all men would be impossible' (28C). Within these limitations, and the limitations of language (29B), we can give an account of creation of the world and of man. It is presented in a distinctly Platonic setting: the Demiurge is supremely rational, and that rationality inheres in the intrinsic intelligibility of the world. He turned disorder into order, though we are not told here, any more than in Genesis, whether he also created the matter of that original chaos. Hebrew, Christian, and Islamic theologies insist that God must have created the matter also, on the principle *ex nihilo nihil fit*, but the Greeks seem to have believed that the disordered matter must have pre-existed.

With himself in mind, the Demiurge created only one cosmos (there are echoes of the Third Man argument at 31A), investing it with soul like a living creature, shaping it into a perfect sphere, and moving it in a perfect circle. It is made of fire and earth, with water and air interpolated in the mean between them. The orbits of the other heavenly bodies are spaced at intervals dictated by powers of two and three, and of the geometrical means between them (35B–36D; 38C). Whatever the Greeks could not reconcile of observed irregularities in the relative motion of the planets was explained away by postulation of a Great Year of 36 000 ordinary years, at the end of which a cycle would be completed. There is much more along these lines, with the origins of mathematics traced to astronomy, but with astronomy much confused in numerology, by which I mean mathematics plus magic. When Kepler found that the planetary orbits were elliptical rather than circular, he abandoned the preconception of the perfection of circularity, and God was discovered to be somewhat more complex than expected. The important thing about these numbers in Plato hardly lies in the pseudoscience of numerological relationships, but that to be intelligible relationships must be lawlike and quantifiable. What cannot so easily be gauged is the extent to which Plato himself, unlike Kepler, was wedded to the specifics of perfect circularity or the properties of the tetractys. I prefer to think that the specific numbers meant little to him, and the quantifiability and lawlikeness meant everything.

When he speaks of the One, for example, I cannot believe that he means the number 'one', but that this is a symbol of unified explanation.

I would go further, and argue that polytheism and religion proceed in tandem with the multiple *ad hoc* explanations of early science; and that polytheism yields to monotheism at the same time and for the same reasons that separate objects and events cease to have separate explanations, but are brought under laws governing classes of objects and events, and under theories of higher order which explain and order those laws. The latter is so close to the stated aims of the higher dialectic that it is no mere prejudice in favour of Plato that persuades me that it is safe to discount the numerology. Jowett and others spare themselves the embarrassment of defending Plato's overlong and excessively detailed account in the *Timaeus* by making him 'playful'; and Findlay embarrasses the respectful reader by seeming to take the metaphor of number literally. Neither of these approaches will do.

In *Plato's Cosmology* (32) Cornford has pointed out that this dialogue is not an allegory in the sense that *Pilgrim's Progress* is. That work can be translated, as it were, into Bunyan's theology by replacing the symbols by the things symbolized. No such one-for-one correspondence exists in the *Timaeus*, or for that matter in any of the important Platonic myths. Thus the *Timaeus* may not be read piecemeal; it is all too easy to lose oneself in the detail that deflects attention from its larger purpose. The whole vast structure of that mythical universe, its harmonies, its numbers, the mathematical relationships with their adherence of magic, its elements in infinite compound, these all must be viewed as an attempt to render a synoptic vision of the unity of all creation.

If we take as a sample of Plato's mathematical reasoning his treatment of triangles and the polyhedra that can be generated out of them, we shall have a suitable illustration of the point I am trying to make. Late in the nineteenth century Poincaré proved why the regular polyhedra are limited to five (in three dimensions; to six in four dimensions). The proof is in terms of the natural limiting condition that not more than five equilateral triangles can be adjacent to each other in different planes. Theaetetus, one of Plato's most brilliant pupils,[29] produced a similar proof, though not so sophisticated and tangled up with the Pythagorean doctrines whose influence is so marked in this dialogue, so that the mysterious relationship of certain numbers to each other was evidence of a divinely rational plan. How the details are incorporated in the vision of that plan is what is so disconcerting, and leads to some internal inconsistencies.

Beginning at 53C Plato offers a kind of atomic theory in which the units are triangles, of which the most beautiful is the $30°-60°-90°$ (half an equilateral) triangle. Out of these, three regular polyhedra can be generated, while the cube is produced by six quadrangular equilaterals, and the dodecahedron has some obscurer and unspecified origin. The elements are held to correspond to these figures (55D): earth (cube); fire (tetrahedron); air (octahedron); water (icosahedron). Of the dodecahedron (which, of course, has pentagonal, not triangular, faces) he says: 'There was yet a fifth combination which God used in the delineation of the universe with figures of animals' (55C), the meaning of which I cannot explain, and even Cornford[30] has not explained it.

This theory has the advantage of supplying different kinds of particles, some of which can combine and be transformed into one another (those based on the half-equilateral triangle); they also come in different sizes. One curiosity is the attempt to reconcile this theory with something rather like the *apeiron* (indefinite stuff) of Anaximander. It is what is called the receptacle of being (52D ff.) that has the property of producing objects of any shape or nature (in accordance with the Forms) without its specifying any shape of its own. These passages are very difficult to understand, and even more difficult to take seriously, except as to their philosophical motive. This seems to be the denial of existence to matter, so that the *apeiron* of Anaximander is not an indefinite substance; rather the receptacle is capable of indefinite transformations; and the triangles and polyhedra it transforms are not atoms of matter to be compounded into things, but mathematical structures to be compounded into the Empedoclean elements similarly deprived of their material character, so that reality subsists in the abstract but intelligible structure. That much is certainly consistent with Plato's epistemology, as is made clear by a short reiteration of his central doctrines at 51D–52C. What is not consistent is the revival of another pre-Socratic belief in rarefaction and condensation (49BC), whereby the four elements are *all* interchangeable, fire being the most rarefied and earth the most condensed. But on the triangular theory earth cannot be transformed into the other elements, being made up of 45° isosceles triangles, while the other three are compounded of half-equilaterals.

At 64A there is an abrupt shift to a detailed account of the body, its organs and senses, and toward the end, of its diseases. I have already dealt with that part of this discussion that treats of soul as life principle, and am reluctant to tax the reader's patience with medical theories long since slain by facts. We are better engaged in examining some of the other cosmological passages which illuminate Plato's metaphysics and his moral insights. He is a great cosmologist and we remain indebted to him for his splendid vision of an intelligible universe; but his physiology is bunk.

But I do not want to fall into the same error I have previously condemned by leaving this beautiful and important dialogue on a note of asperity. The real point is that in it Plato is asserting the place of intelligence and order in the universe, over against the early materialists and the atomists. There is no room for value in a universe mechanically determined; this is the position which Plato is rejecting when he speaks of the world as 'a living organism with soul and reason' (29A). He is interested in the world rather than in the creator when he grounds ethics in intelligence. The little we can say about God belongs to the language of myth and cannot be communicated readily, if at all. The inscrutability of God extends also to his creation and, but for the mythical language used, Plato might be accused of going too far beyond the permissible limits of rational discourse. Where he passes from what might be called matters of faith and morals into the realm of determinable (and subsequently determined) fact, as in the physiology, for example, he incurs the risk, as the Church did in late medieval and Renaissance times, of seeing his valid doctrines discredited along with the invalid ones. Plato saves himself, but in my opinion only just (many other commentators would not agree), by the repeated proviso that what he has to say here is merely probable: all natural philosophy is at best only a likely story because its object is matter, the mere image of the creator's idea.

Apart from the cosmology of the *Phaedo*, which has been dealt with above in the context of the eschatological myth in which it appears, two other passages need to be considered: *Statesman* 268D–274E and *Laws* IV, 713A–714A. They deal with essentially the same topic, connecting a mythical 'reversal' of the motions of the heavens with the political responsibilities of men. Depending on which elements one chooses to emphasize, these myths could be classified as cosmological or as political.[31] The fabric of Plato's thought is too tightly woven to permit portions of it to be dissected out without damage, and he is deliberately unsystematic where system is inappropriate. Thus these passages will do quite well here, at the end of the cosmology and just before the political myths, to which they may furnish something of an introduction.

In the *Statesman,* the Stranger, having amused himself at the expense of the Young Socrates by an intentionally misleading and parodic division, introduces a myth based on the story of the gods' reversing the motion of the heavens so that Atreus may regain his kingdom from his brother Thyestes. The universe is kept in motion by the creator for a certain period of time under his direct governance. But there is an equal period when he 'lets go' and the world, being a living creature (cf.

Timaeus), and having originally received intelligence from its author and creator, turns about and by an inherent necessity revolves in the opposite direction (269C). The logic of that 'necessity' deserves scrutiny; it purports to follow (and after a fashion does) by exclusion of some rival possibilities which reinforce points that Plato has made elsewhere. If the earth moved itself, 'perpetually revolving in one and the same sense', we should have a mechanical world to which God, if he existed, was indifferent (269E). Nor may we say that it is 'God who turns it in its entirety throughout all time in two opposed alternating revolutions' (also 269E), because that would imply both an inconsistency in God, and his responsibility for the ills that befall during the contrary motion; this myth is largely about the problem of evil, as will presently appear. Finally 'we may not say that a pair of divinities make it revolve alternately in these opposed senses because the mind of the one god is contrary to the mind of the other' (270A). It is not an anachronism to call this a rejection of Manicheism, because it was known to Plato, perhaps in some predecessor form, and is repeatedly rejected by him.[32] There is no Form of evil, and God is not its creator; evil is privative, has no existence in its own right, but is measured by the degree to which things fall short of perfection. So, too, are the evils and shortcomings of the world attributable, not to some positive action of God, but to his leaving the world to its own devices for 'the time thereto appointed' (269C).

This reversal of motion brings about the least possible change (presumably because motions relative to each other remain unchanged) and is due to the material element in the universe which mars its perfection. As a result of it, in the age of Cronos, there was a concomitant reversal of the life process as we know it, the old growing young and disappearing. Men sprang fully grown from the earth – the opposite of burial) to 'begin' their lives. The consistency of the story is mentioned with approval at 271B: this is, indeed, one of Plato's criteria in determining the objectionability of the classical myths. Life in those halcyon days was ordered under the direct supervision of demigods who, by their superior nature, were able to prevent any kind of violence or war among the various species of animals. God himself was the shepherd of men (271E) and under his rule there were no laws, governments, possessions or clothes. But there was a drawback which makes it impossible to say that the men of those days were happier than the men of our own (cf., in what follows, the remark of J. S. Mill: 'Better to be Socrates dissatisfied than a fool satisfied'):

Suppose that the nurslings of Cronos, having this boundless leisure
. . . had used all these advantages with a view to philosophy, . . . there
would be no difficulty in deciding that they would be a thousand times
happier than the men of our own day. . . . But until some satisfactory
witness can be found of the love of that age for knowledge and
discussion, we had better let the matter drop, and give the reason why
we have unearthed this tale, and then we shall be able to get on.
(272BD)

Finally the time came when the change was due, and God let the
universe go, retiring to his lookout point. After the initial shock and
catastrophe of the reversed motion, men settled down into the life cycle
we know, masters of themselves and of the beasts, trying to remember,
with ever-decreasing precision, what had been the beneficent rule of the
Father of the world. Forgetfulness and the admixture of matter were
responsible for this fall and corruption, and in time discord grew greater.
Without God, and by virtue of its materiality, the world became so
wicked compared with its former primeval contentment, that God
feared for its utter destruction and took it in hand again. Thus the cycle
was completed.

The myth is introduced to show, as the Stranger points out (275A, B),
how the earlier, playful, definition of the statesman as 'shepherd' applied
to the previous cycle of terrestrial motion, and not to the present one.
Then one could speak of one who has the care of men, for the analogy
with the shepherd who cares for his flock would be exact, but now, when
each man can equally claim, even if it is not so, to know what is best for
individual and state, a new division is required to separate the true
statesman from his rivals.[33] Part of the same story is repeated in the
Laws IV, 713A–714A, which makes the point clearer:

In the primeval world, and a long while before the cities came into
being whose settlements we have described, there is said to have been
in the time of Cronos a blessed rule and life, of which the best-ordered
of existing states is a copy (713B).

This state of affairs was made possible because Cronos, realizing that if
men ruled over men there would be the same chaos as if oxen ruled over
oxen, set demigods to rule over men. He did this for the same reason we
set men over oxen, because a superior order of rulers is required to guide
the destiny of a lower order. Thus, in the ideal statesman we must look

for superiority of judgement and interest. At the same time, a solution to a theological problem is tentatively advanced in these myths. We are spared, in the *Timaeus*, the bland optimism of the 'best of all possible worlds' that so infuriated Voltaire, but we are given reasons why, despite the perfection of God this world necessarily falls short of that perfection. That defect lies in ourselves, not in the divine nature, which is 'ungrudging' (*Timaeus* 29E). With an austerity worthy of Spinoza, and with none of the cringing self-pity of Augustine, Plato summons us to accept responsibility for our own actions, a responsibility unhedged by the expectation of providential intervention. No god out of the machine will appear to unknot our perplexities; the 'distant presence of God' with which Mauriac's severe Catholicism consoled itself is very remote indeed. As we move from theology to politics we must keep these considerations in mind. We shall have little more than the intellectual love of God to sustain us as guarantor of the ultimate justice of the universe. That is, no doubt, the source of that 'great hope' of which Socrates speaks, and of the serenity with which he accepted the death for which his life was a preparation. He lived, as we do, in the penultimate.

This is where Popper goes wrong, for all his respect for Socrates as a 'democratic martyr'. He was a martyr, beyond question, but not to democracy: he was a martyr to fallibilism – of which democracy, as we understand it, is the finest political expression. That fallibilism is Plato's chief inheritance from Socrates, and it pervades his political thought as it does his theology. Here is no tacit acquiescence in the predestined, no subtle apology for the status quo, no resigned acceptance of the inevitability of what must be, but a vigorous deployment of reason, a clear pointer to the direction in which change must occur.

5 Political Myths

To the extent that they have been noticed, the political myths have given Plato a bad name. Part of the reason is the common understanding of 'myth' as something to be exploded, or at least demythologized; it may be innocently false, an old wives' tale that, despite the availability of evidence on which sounder doctrine can be based, continues to be believed, much the way any superstition flourishes on ignorance. More exasperating than that is an attitude of mind that prefers its myths, perhaps because of the comforts of unreason that permit no challenge to what is taken to be well tried and true, even though it may be neither. If one looks for a rationale for the irrational, one discovers that a pervasive anti-intellectualism can be founded, not merely on a misconception, but on explicit rejection of the pretensions as well as the fallibilism of scientific methods. I cannot explore this theme at great length here, because it would carry us too far afield, but some aspects of it are material to Plato's approach, so some comments are to the point.

As to the pretensions: the hard sciences have become partly discredited because too much has been promised. That 'all human problems are in principle soluble by human means', as Mill confidently claimed, now has a hollow ring. The failure is not that of the hard sciences, the advances of which have been staggering over the last few centuries, but of the so-called social sciences which have adopted a parody of scientific method (itself superseded in the hard sciences) in order to address and solve political, economic, and social problems. Had the promises not been so sweeping, the disappointments would not have been so acute; but the more theoretical the social sciences have claimed to be, the greater the failure in practice. Of all the afflictions in this century, none are more vicious than the allegedly 'scientific' theories of race affected by the Nazis, and the social theories of the various stripes of Marxists with their ready sacrifice of present generations (collectivization, the Great Leap Forward, Cambodia) for the sake of highly dubious future benefits.

The fallibilism of science, which is more intrinsic to its methods than the certainties, poses different problems. It entails a willingness to abandon any and all present theories in the light of new evidence. It is conscious that the history of science is a scrap-heap of discarded theories, most of them passionately believed in their day, but that passion now reinforces the uncertainties that surround every present theory. It is also a history, though, of unceasing effort to find better theories to substitute for the old, and of the optimistic expectation that if science is cumulative and progressive ('dwarfs on the shoulders of giants'), we converge on a truth that we shall finally possess. Even if that progress is asymptotic (what J.-P. Sartre called adding 9s to the right of .9999 . . .) and ultimate truth will always be denied, the faith that science is cumulative, with error increasingly left behind, can perhaps be sustained. But that denial places intolerable strains on those who need certainty and, at every intellectual level, we find the rejection of scientific method for this reason. The attempt to leap over or under the limitations of science is apparent as much in those who prefer a lofty intuitionism as in those wedded to an unshakable superstition.

Although Plato addressed all these problems (in terms appropriate to his own time), his discussion of them is not the foundation of the principal charge against him. That charge is that he is willing to invent myths for the good of society,[1] and it has two parts at least. One, of course, is the continuing debate about what the good of society is; the other is stained by the common usage of the term 'myth'. Nobody mistakes Plato's myths for the innocent ignorance of superstition: he is given full credit for his monumental intellect and sophistication, as well as for the rhetorical skills that sway the reader's emotions. What is assumed is that he *knows* that the content of his myths is not true, but cynically persists in promoting them for sinister political ends, or at any rate for political ends with which his critics disagree. The premise is false: there is only one deliberate lie in all this material (one too many, by all means) and that is the rigging of the breeding lotteries (*Republic* V, 460A). For the rest there can be no doubt that he is convinced of the truth of his beliefs; but no less is he convinced of their rational indemonstrability. The strong defence of poetry has its roots in the juxtaposition of these two propositions. To his critics, however, he is damned if he does and damned if he doesn't. Either he is an unbelieving hypocrite, or the road to hell is paved with his good intentions.[2]

The latter observation is the more plausible and deserving of comment. I shall be brief here, but must return to it in the concluding chapter. The vice of sincerely held belief is that it is indistinguishable from dogma, and so closes off paths of further inquiry that should always be held open. Worse, it is an abuse of the credulity of the masses that propositions known to be indemonstrable should be advanced as though they were apodictic truths. These two charges, even more than the unpalatability of any specific political doctrine, are the gravamen of Popper's attack; and I am convinced that Plato is innocent of both. Or, to put it bluntly, if he is guilty, all theorists, including political theorists, are equally guilty.

If I am correct in interpreting 'myth' in Plato in the sense advanced so far, every proposition is either an indemonstrable axiom or deducible from one. On the political plane the fabric of rival social systems is held together by rival myths, i.e. by more or less consciously adopted presuppositions about human nature, values, rights and obligations, and the balance between individual and society, to mention just a few.[3] Some of those presuppositions are discredited, and some of the theorems deduced from them are falsified, by inner contradictions and by the historical catastrophes to which they have led. But among the survivors are seamless arguments in the form of systems internally consistent and so far unexploded, at least in the sense that the political systems predicated on them have proven viable. We may continue to insist on the absolute truth of our favourite system and on the absolute falsity of some other, but the outcome of that insistence is more likely to be the destruction of organized societies altogether and of the high culture which depends on them, than the establishment of a truth of which we can be no more certain than Plato was.

The political myths have mostly been ignored, except for hostility to the idea that our most precious preconceptions are mythical in one or other of the pejorative senses noted above. That is certainly true of Popper and Crossman. Stewart believes only in myths susceptible of translation into the mock King James language into which he renders them, and Findlay does not believe there are any myths. Frutiger is virtually alone in admitting some of them, but is mainly concerned to show why they are myths in accordance with his criteria, rather than showing what they might mean. Some of the political myths, indeed, have no very deep meaning: the two brief *Phaedrus* passages on the origin of writing and the myth of the grasshoppers, for example, are light entertainment; the ring of Gyges poses a test of moral fortitude that few of us could pass, though no Platonic doctrine depends on the story; and I am by no means sure that the Atlantis myth (what we have of it) warrants the attention paid to it. But the others are very important. The accounts of the origins of the state furnish a substantial and influential rival to contract theories; the myth of the metals supplies a device for explaining such inequalities as society seems powerless to correct; the argument for the equality of women is an anti-myth to correct the still prevailing myth of their inferiority, and makes a significant contribution to the nature-nurture controversy; and the decadence of the ideal city, while not a history of anything, is a typology for differential diagnosis of what might ail a polity.

I

The celebrated passage at *Republic* II, 369B–374B is in conversational form, rather than the sustained narrative usually associated with the myths, but it is nonetheless a myth on the criteria I have proposed. It takes its place along with other postulations concerning the origins of society like the various versions of Social Contract theory and the State of Nature. When asked what historical evidence there was for the existence of a state of nature, Hobbes pointed to the dog-eat-dog relationship of sovereign states to one another as an example, while Rousseau pointed to the North American Indian, whose nobility was attested by some early romantic authors who had not seen them either. Locke was rather more cautious, so that he wavers between acknowledgment that his version of contract theory is mere postulation, and the view that it is supported by inference from the development of societies known to him. It is, perhaps, not unreasonable to suggest that what all such theories, including Plato's, have in common is a rationalization to justify how present society should be governed.[4] This is usually accompanied by some generalizations about human nature, as well as even more amorphous notions of the relationship between nature and reason, which may be conceived of as complementary, mutually supportive, or hostile.

For Plato this last question is not directly addressed in the political myths, the answer being found in the discussions of larger metaphysical and epistemological questions. Nor does he rely on historical analysis, real or imagined, for his account of how society began. There are fewer a priori assumptions than are, for example, found in Aristotle who, despite incorporating many of the elements of Plato's version in his own *Politics*, sets the foundation of society on a biological basis, with the family as the irreducible unit.

Plato's is a functional analysis. The real creator of the city, he says, 'will be our needs' (369C). He proceeds at once to the division of labour, for reasons intimately connected with the tripartite structure of the soul and, of course, the three corresponding classes of society. I have earlier referred to the grand analogy here being developed, but it will be useful to recall its aim. The quest for justice in the individual soul will be simplified, we are told at the outset of this myth (368E–369A), if we examine justice in the state, where its nature and problems appear on a larger scale. It is this that links the purely political matters to the larger questions, for not only will justice in the state be a harmony of different and conflicting elements, but it will be both a harmony of the corresponding elements in the individual and a microcosm of the universe.[5] That last consideration is not as explicit in Plato as it became in later political theorists, but it is never far from the surface. It usually seeks to justify the human order, mostly hierarchical (in monarchy and Papacy, for example), as a copy of some heavenly archetype. It is a curiosity of Plato's treatment of political questions that he does not have recourse to this particular metaphor, certainly known to him from Homer, among others, and taken up by later thinkers, beginning with Aristotle. The idea that earthly wars are the counterpart of a heavenly battle between the gods supporting the contending parties below is not only a commonplace of the *Iliad* but also of the early literature of many cultures. We know Plato's reasons for not adopting it: first it implies the possibility of conflict instead of unity among the gods,[6] and second it is unacceptably anthropomorphic by modelling the gods' behaviour on that of men, instead of the other way about.

Nonetheless, the division of labour, as a means of satisfying the physical needs of society with greater efficiency will not of itself produce justice, as presently becomes clear. We shall need a host of trades and crafts so that each person becomes a specialist in whatever his nature equips him to do best, and each will be devoted full-time to his speciality. This will not lead to self-sufficiency, for the society will need to import whatever cannot be produced domestically, and to produce for export to pay for those further needs. In a predominantly agricultural society there will be pressure to expand by annexation of neighbouring land, and this leads to a discussion of the development of a military class. Glaucon is not content with this image of a community based merely on its need of shelter, food, and clothing, and asks: 'If you were founding a city of pigs, Socrates, what other fodder would you provide?' (372D). Appetite feeds on itself, and unless the aims are clarified, we shall not produce a just society, but one based on luxury on the one hand, and on militarism on the other. That clarification follows, of course, in the greater part of the *Republic*. The political myth is, however, confined to the presupposition in this short passage of the division of labour as a basis for organized society. It will be complete only when extended beyond the satisfaction of the needs of the appetitive part of the soul to a balance and harmony of all three parts.

Book III of the *Laws* (676A–702A) pursues the theme of balance in a historical setting, which supposes the ancient myths and legends to have some kind of factual foundation. It proposes to examine the way in which polities developed following the last great deluge. Only mountain dwellers would have survived, and these lived in patriarchal clans under the rigid enforcement of primitive notions of law, sustaining themselves on the meat and milk of their animals. Plato calls this a dynasty (680B), and likens it to Homer's account of the Cyclops (*Odyssey* IX, 112). A second stage is assumed in which larger groups come together on the mountainsides. As an agricultural society succeeds the pastoral, the laws of isolated clans need to be brought into a uniform code throughout the larger community, and so aristocracy (presumably made up of the leaders of each clan) or a monarchy arises (681CD). The third stage leads to the foundation of cities in the valleys, also documented by reference to Homer (though not in this passage to Hesiod, who has similar notions), for under divine inspiration the poets 'often enough hit upon true historical fact' (682A).

That history is of the investment of Troy and the subsequent collapse of the Dorian League. With the establishment of Lacedaemon a larger unit emerges, a nation of unified laws (not unlike those of Crete). Lacedaemon, Argos, and Messene entered into treaties, not just of mutual support, but also to regularize a constitutional monarchy, with the rights of king and subjects clearly set forth (684AB). Of the three only Sparta held to the original constitution, the others falling prey to the effects of legislative innovation and other excesses. These follies sprang from perverted values, setting evil above good, and allowing the pleasures and pains that move the common people to dictate policy against wise counsel (689AB).

Such actual history as we may have here is clearly subordinate to Plato's political purposes in pursuing this recital. Unless a society is so organized as to establish unequivocally who is to govern whom, it will collapse. There are many ways in which that has been defined: parents over children, aristocrats over commoners, the strong over the weak, and so on; or it might be the democratic ballot that is thought to be the most equitable whereby whoever happens to win the most votes rules. But the highest prescription is for the wise to rule over the ignorant: this is 'nature's own ordinance' (690C). Thus two prototypical systems emerge: monarchy and democracy. Both are subject to similar forms of decline: absolute power corrupts absolutely. Under the other monarchies abuse of power began for lack of effective constitutional restraints; while Sparta survived by a mixed system, giving the franchise to men over 28, and adding the ephors. The Persian monarchy worked well so long as a proper balance was struck between the powers of the great king and the liberties of his subjects (694AB). But abuse of those powers after Cyrus led to the disaffection of the common people on whose patriotic fervour the kings must rely (697C).

In Athens there was an opposite cause: 'unqualified and absolute freedom from all authority is a far worse thing than submission to a magistrate' (698B). There is a somewhat Hobbesian flavour about this passage, which suggests that any government, however bad, is better than no government at all – one cannot tell whether this is an argument against democracy or, as it seems, against anarchy. He does not give at this point, as we would expect, historical data about Athens as purportedly factual as those given about the other polities. Instead he chooses an example that must strike the modern reader as very odd and, if anything, reminiscent of de Quincey's dire warning that by subtle degrees murder inevitably leads to sabbath-breaking and minor peccadillos. In a long passage (700A–701B) we are assured that the decline of the Athenian democracy sprang from disregard of the strict rules of musical composition, and the substitution of popular applause for the judgement of experts. It is indeed an example, though a curious one, of that contempt for authority that is the peculiar bane of an unbridled democracy. But there is little to choose between systems, whether democratic or authoritarian, in which the balance between liberty and authority is lost.

And that is the reason 'why we have said what we have' (701D). Without freedom, internal harmony, and wisdom, no society can flourish. The historical examples are cited to identify which kinds of polity have failed or succeeded, and why. They are not used to reveal a pattern of history or a law of historical inevitability. They are not even used as a vehicle of any particular animus against democracy. It seems inconceivable to me how, from the cycle marked by the deluge, Popper can argue (OS I, 210) that the first stage on the mountain-tops represents a Golden Age (everything since being a deterioration), and that the rest is a cycle of necessary stages following a historical law, albeit one that we can influence if we actually know what is coming. Far from that, the history represents Plato's interest in empirical evidence as a limiting condition for speculation about the ideal city that makes up the balance of the *Laws*. In it an Athenian, a Spartan, and a Cretan, each bringing his knowledge and experience of some varied polities to bear, address in highly practical terms what the constitution of a perfect city would be. The emphasis must be on 'practical'. Unlike the ideal city of the *Republic*, of which 'perhaps there is a pattern laid up in heaven' (IX, 592B), the *Laws* are concerned with the 'second-best' city, one capable of actual achievement.

When we turn to the myth of Epimetheus and Prometheus in the *Protagoras* (320C–323A) we may find evidence of an attitude more sympathetic to democracy (ancient, not modern). First, we have to dispose of the problem posed by its being placed in the mouth of the Sophist Protagoras which has led many commentators, including Frutiger, to exclude it from being a Platonic myth. Schleiermacher, Ast, Hermann, and Campbell reject it; Steinhart, Grote and Stewart accept it.[7] Among the objections is that it deals only with the material conditions for survival, without any of the higher more 'Platonic' elements; this despite the fact that *Republic* II, 369C, discussed above, makes those material needs the foundation of human society; and the further and more important fact that the myth plainly goes beyond physical needs to address the share of political wisdom that every man possesses – and must possess to be human at all (323BC). The latter point is so close to the undisputed doctrine of the *Phaedo* and *Phaedrus* that it must be dispositive. Since it contains something of a defence of democracy in that all men share political wisdom, and Plato cannot be shown as supporting such a defence, Popper (OS, I 66) of course attributes it to Protagoras; he can explain why Socrates endorses the story, but not, if Plato was so hostile, why he includes it, and tells it so well to boot.

Epimetheus (Afterthought) persuaded his brother Prometheus (Forethought) to let him carry out the distribution of equipment and capabilities ordered by the gods for the newly created species of mortal creatures. The story is full of ingenious turns: weak creatures need speed, including wings, while strong ones do not; meat-eaters are made less prolific, while the herbivores on whom they prey are more fertile. The whole account is a marvellous anticipation of the argument from design from a religious perspective, and of those aspects of evolutionary theory that deal with the functional and adaptive mechanisms of survival from a scientific viewpoint. But all this is prelude to the appearance of man, evidently a late creation in everybody's Book of Genesis. All the gifts were gone, and when Prometheus came to review his brother's distribution there was man naked, without hide or feathers, speed or strength. So Prometheus stole fire from Hephaestus, a theft for which he paid dearly later, and gave it to man.

He was at first a solitary creature and easy prey to wild beasts, until he gathered in fortified places for mutual protection. But the fire, which it is easy to see was the spark of reason, was not yet sufficient for man. Being divine, that reason gave man an awareness of the gods he worshipped, it gave speech, and the ability to invent houses and clothes and agriculture; everything indeed that a man can do alone. But it did not enable him to live in peace with others of his kind. For that Zeus' intervention was needed, and he sent Hermes to give them respect for others and a sense of justice 'so as to bring order into our cities and create a bond of friendship and union' (322C). Those gifts were not to be distributed to a few individuals, like a talent for medicine or some other expert, but to all (322D). And so it comes about, Protagoras concludes, that all men believe they have something to contribute to political debate.[8]

He is subsequently cross-examined by Socrates, chiefly on the unity of the virtues, but no challenge is offered to the story. One point that cries out for clarification is perhaps wisely left ambiguous. When Zeus says that all are to have a share, he does not say an equal share. That fits Plato's doctrine very well indeed, and we shall be turning to Plato's myth concerning the inequalities among men later in this chapter in considering the myth of the metals. But it does not fit Protagoras' beliefs so well; certainly not on any interpretation like Popper's, which wants to make Protagoras the proponent of an anti-authoritarian egalitarianism. If that is too strong – and it probably is – at least it must be argued that each person has enough of political wisdom to justify his franchise. But if that be allowed, what ought the political consequences to be that some people are wiser than others?

That is a question, central to Plato's political theorizing, that cannot be answered without discomfort. The best answer, beyond question, is found in that handful of western democracies in which the political judgement of the great majority has matured about moderate doctrines, moving within relatively narrow limits between left and right. Changes of regime come about at stated intervals by free elections, which modern sophists in the form of admen and campaign managers seek to sway in the interests of those who have bought their services. Virtually no constraints are placed on what they say, and in the free marketplace of ideas rebuttal follows closely on accusation. Truth, lies, and distortions largely cancel each other out; and the people get the government they deserve. If it disappoints or betrays their expectations they have opportunity to throw the rascals out and elect a fresh batch. The prospect of being turned out of office tempers the extremes of policy that might be adopted even more than those checks and balances built into the separation of executive and legislative powers from each other and from an independent judiciary. An almost institutionalized mistrust of politicians is fed by the regular discovery that they can be bought and sold, often at astonishingly low rates, by self-serving interests little concerned with the public good. The franchise is widened almost indefinitely, and privilege is narrowed. All this works tolerably well in some homogeneous societies, though no society, regardless of its nominal adherence to equality, has found a workable solution of racial, and in some cases, of linguistic and religious differences.

We have no real idea what Plato would have thought of democratic forms utterly unlike those he knew and criticized. That has not, of course, prevented some commentators from equating the primitive political systems he knew with the modern counterparts they loosely approximate. But might Plato not have joined in two cheers for democracy? Might he not have recognized the tyranny of modern totalitarianisms? For every reference to the Nocturnal Council in the *Laws* and *Epinomis*, taken to be the equivalent of the midnight knock by the Gestapo or Soviet notions of psychiatry (*Laws* X, 909A), there are dozens to the need for balance of the *necessarily* conflicting elements in society, including those directed against oligarchies and plutocracies. There is no way of wishing the asperities of these last writings out of existence, and there can be no doubt that Plato changed his mind for the worse at the last. Perhaps his despair at the failure of his experiments in political education in Sicily foreclosed a more temperate judgement.

The grounds for that temperate judgement abound and dominate in his work. It is quite clear that the Philosopher cannot be king, save in an unrealizable ideal society which cannot exist on earth. He would have to be forced to return to the Cave, as we shall see later on. The best treatment of this problem is found in Aristotle's contemplative man in Books VI and X of the *Ethics*. Precisely because his mind dwells on the contemplation of being as such, he is unfitted to rule; he lacks the common touch, and cannot understand the needs and aims of ordinary people. Plato's conclusion is in fact the same. The example of Socrates is one of moral suasion without the exercise of political power, and this is the best that the philosopher can achieve. For the rest, the fallibilism that is the true outcome of Plato's estimate of human knowledge is consonant, of the political systems we know, only with one form or another of democracy. For totalitarianisms rest on the assumption that some one, or some group, knows the truth. That is not an assumption that Plato is willing to make. Even if we allow for the sake of the argument, his and his opponents', that he did make it, the problem remains how to govern in the best interests of those who in principle are incapable of knowing those interests. We compromise uneasily on that question in the name of another myth: *vox populi, vox Dei.* That is no more true than the more aristocratic myths ascribed to Plato. The Epimetheus–Prometheus myth surely makes clear beyond question that the common people share in the political wisdom of which the aristocrats have no monopoly; moreover, even if they did, practical politics do not permit the ruler to function at a level much beyond the aims and vision of the people.

II

The two myths in the *Phaedrus* about the origins of writing and the image of the grasshoppers, and the moral fable of the Ring of Gyges in the *Republic* have nothing in common, not even that they are necessarily myths. I include them because beneath the surface of their imagery lie some insights made more palatable and accessible because of the mode of their telling.

At *Phaedrus* 274C–275B is one of the stories that 'it is easy for you, Socrates, to make up . . . from Egypt or anywhere else you fancy.' Theuth, the inventor of mathematics and astronomy, among other things, also invented writing, which he presented for the approval of the king, Ammon, saying that it would improve their memories and their wisdom. The king replied that it would promote forgetfulness, not memory, but would be a reminder, by means of external signs rather than inner knowledge. It would fill men, then, with the illusion of knowledge.

In general, this little tale fits in with Plato's doubts about language (see the discussion in chapter 2). But it does also have relevance to the immediate setting of the *Phaedrus*, with its preference for the living word or oral discourse, which teaches by the immediate exchange of views, by cross-examination, and increasingly refined definition characteristic of Socratic dialectic. This is contrasted unfavourably at 275D in which the written word appears alive, like a painter's work, but stands lifeless and silent if one seeks to question it. While live dialectic can correct and amplify what one has said, so as to bridge the gap between what one means to say and the inadequacy of language to express that meaning with precision, the written word goes abroad where it is open to misconstrual 'without its parent to come to its help, being unable to defend or help itself' (275E). That same Theuth, we are told at *Philebus* 18BD, also classified sounds into something like phonemes, and so was

led to the alphabet. It illustrates the process of identifying the characteristics of a class, labelling the members with the name of the class.

Socrates remarks on the song of the grasshoppers or cicadas in the
drowsy summer day at *Phaedrus* 230C, and at 259B brings in the little
story that once the grasshoppers were men who became so enamoured of
the Muses when they appeared that they forgot to eat and drink, but sang
all day until they died without noticing it. In honour of them the Muses
gave the grasshoppers the gift of needing no sustenance all their lives,
during which they sing, and report to the Muses which men have
honoured them. So Terpsichore hears about the dancers; and Calliope
and Urania hear of those men 'who live a life of philosophy and so do
honor to the music of those twain whose theme is the heavens and all the
story of gods and men, and whose song is the noblest of them all' (259D).
And so let us not slumber at noon, but sing philosophy.

Almost any comment on this charming image must seem heavy-
handed. It echoes Socrates' music-making which, we are told in the
Phaedo, he was bidden to do by Apollo; he obeyed by pursuing
philosophy, the greatest of the arts (61A). Let us discuss philosophy
instead of sleeping, spiritually or literally.

The ring of Gyges (*Republic* 359D–360B) is a story with a sting. It tells
how Gyges, a Lydian shepherd, found a magic ring which makes him
invisible at will, enabling him to do as he pleases, 'to be like a god among
men' (360C). He uses his power to satisfy his lust, sexual licence being the
most striking symbol of godlike power: witness the accounts of Zeus'
many loves. He slays the king, and possesses his kingdom.

The question posed here and in the discussion following is whether
justice is merely imposed on men, as Thrasymachus had argued, in the
form of the social disapproval and punishment which attend their being
caught. Here the story-telling element has little to do with myth: it is
simply a device for putting an extreme hypothetical case in more
convenient and entertaining form than an abstract presentation would
be. What is striking in his story, as is so often the case in these
illustrations, is the simplicity of the telling, and the broad appeal of
Gyges' being invested with magical powers: the universal charm of the
fairy story. The anecdote in this case is the springboard for a non-
mythical discussion of justice, for the story itself is dismissed by Socrates
(368A) as standing for an answer which Glaucon and Adeimantus
themselves do not believe. The sting lies in the fact that most readers will
be forced to acknowledge the difficulty they would have, if placed in
Gyges' situation, in resisting the temptations to which he succumbed.

III

The myth of the metals (*Republic* III, 414D–415D) is the one myth expressly said to be a noble lie, something the inhabitants of the *polis* are to be persuaded into believing is true for their own good. The image owes something to Hesiod (*Works and Days*, 97ff.), but Plato's purposes are much subtler and further-reaching. The story is simple in the extreme, and falls into two parts. The first is often separately identified as the myth of the earthborn. We must persuade first the rulers, then the soldiers and the rest of the city that although they supposed they had been trained and reared by the laws and institutions of the state, all that was only a dream. What had really happened in that time was that they were gestating in the womb of the earth, along with their weapons and equipment, and were presently given birth by the soil of their native land. They are therefore to consider the earth their mother and all fellow citizens their brothers, and are urged to defend their native land against attack.

This half of the story seems innocent enough, being little more than a device to promote patriotism and the civic bond among citizens.[9] As a lie it seems so implausible, if anyone is actually to believe it, that Glaucon promptly says 'no wonder you were so bashful about coming out with your lie' (414E). That innocence has not prevented some extraordinary observations by the few scholars who have bothered with the myth. Stewart translates its content rather freely, and its style as a sort of Fifth Gospel: 'All the things which they deemed were done unto them and came to pass in their life . . .' His commentary is two paragraphs (422) which pick out as the source and meaning of the myth that in youth we often dream that 'the things here are doubles of things elsewhere' which, although no doubt true, is entirely beside the point. Frutiger does not regard it as a myth, and so mentions it only in passing; Findlay (171) speaks quite usefully about the second half (the metals), but ignores the first half about the earthborn.

It is Popper, never missing an opportunity to vilify Plato even if no opportunity presents itself, who waxes inordinately indignant about this myth, probably because it is announced as a lie. For him all the myths are lies (138 ff.), though the only myths he addresses are a few of the political ones. According to him this myth of the earthborn and the metals is a racial doctrine, a Myth of Blood and Soil (139). The capital letters are meant to intimate a connection between Plato's myth and the Nazis'. 'The motive of Plato's wish that the rulers themselves should believe in the propaganda lie is his hope of increasing its wholesome effect, i.e. of strengthening the rule of the master race, and ultimately, of arresting all political change' (140). I have said enough in chapter 3 about the particular misconception that leads to the clause about arresting change, but the rest of his critique cries out for correction. It is true, of course, that Plato says that the rulers may tell lies for the people's benefit (*Republic* III, 389B), and this is supposed to be one of them, as is clear from the reference in 414B to that earlier passage. How from the first half of the myth paraphrased above can one get a racial doctrine?

It cannot be done, yet Popper does it. There is nothing in Plato's work anywhere that suggests the racial superiority of the citizens of Athens, or of the Republic, or even of Greeks, to other races or groups. There is a plea of *Republic* V, 469BC that Greeks should not enslave Greeks, and a more general pride in being a Greek and not a barbarian that rests on being governed by laws, not by men as in despotic states; and this is a sentiment often repeated in Aeschylus and Euripides, for example. I do not believe that Popper objects to autochthonous feelings, the sense of being rooted in one's country ('This is my own, my native land'), or to a purely defensive policy against attack. He is entitled to object, if he wishes, to that form of patriotism that is the last refuge of a scoundrel ('My country, right or wrong'), or to any doctrine claiming a right to invade and conquer other countries in the name of Manifest Destiny, shouldering the white man's burden, or other expressions of racial or cultural superiority. Now the only place in Plato's works where such a suggestion is made is in the passage where Popper himself strains the meaning to supply words to that effect that are at least ambiguous in the Greek, as I have shown in chapter 3 with reference to *Republic* III, 415DE, which follows directly on this myth. That talks only about maintaining internal order and repelling external aggression, but Popper translates 'for keeping down the inhabitants' so that he can turn colonization of possibly vacant territory into invasion. The second half of the myth may cast some light on how Popper came to his grotesque misunderstanding of this myth.

What the myth of the metals says is: while all citizens are brothers, yet the gods in fashioning them mixed gold into the composition of those to become rulers, silver into the prospective auxiliaries, and iron and brass in the farmers and artisans. Offspring will mostly resemble their fathers, but it may happen that a silver son will be born to a golden father, and vice versa, 'and that the rest would in like manner be born of one another' (415B). The rulers must carefully observe the offspring so that each finds his proper level in society; if sons of iron and brass are born to golden fathers, 'they shall by no means give way to pity . . . but shall assign to each the status due to his nature,' and if artisans and farmers have sons 'with unexpected gold and silver in their composition they shall honor such and bid them go up higher' (415C); all this because of an alleged oracle (another lie!) that the state will be overthrown if ruled by a Guardian of iron or brass. Can we get anyone to believe this tale, Socrates asks. Glaucon says, not at once, but after a generation or two perhaps. Socrates replies 'Even that would have a good effect in making them more inclined to care for the state and one another' (415D).

What Popper has done with this, I think, is to telescope the two halves of the myth and distort their unnatural union by making it seem to argue that Greeks (or Republicans, perhaps, since the inhabitants of Plato's ideal city will not be Democrats) are all made of gold, and barbarians and other foreigners are all of baser metals. The might justify invasion (but only if one shuts one's eyes to what the text actually says). But, of course, you would also have to argue (again shutting your eyes) that golden fathers always had golden sons; otherwise they would have to leave the annexed territory. Also, while we are inventing this text, we must conclude that no golden children are born to the baser peoples; or, if they are, that rulership must pass to them. If it did, as Plato's authentic text requires, there is an end of the so-called racialism that Popper has imported.

He is quite relentless in his use of this passage. He flatly denies, on some very strained reasoning, that any upward mobility is permissible (141).[10] And, casting about the commentators who all seem to have been baffled by this myth, he lights on Adam, who in his note on this passage in his edition of the *Republic* argues that the lie places this matter of religious doctrine on a basis of faith rather than reason. That is a proposition that has meaning, and something like it forms that basis for my own interpretation of the myths. But Popper makes it the springboard for a lengthy excursus (141–4) purporting to show that all Plato's religious beliefs are propaganda lies designed to prop up his racist doctrines; that he had no sincere religious beliefs at all, but mere conventions, the practical utility of religion becoming (n. 15, 273) opium for the people.

The myth has a plain meaning, which should sweep away the hostility, indifference, and misunderstanding that seems to have been its lot. As to the term 'noble lie', most of the agitation has surrounded the precise meaning of *gennaios*, variously translated 'noble' (Stewart, *et al.*), 'lordly' (Popper), 'opportune' (Shorey), 'useful' (Goldschmidt: *mensange utile*), 'convenient' (Cornford), 'spirited' (Richards), and so on. There is not much one can do with *pseudos* and its derivatives, but apart from 'lie' we find 'fiction' (Stewart, Cornford), 'false statement', 'falsehood', and simply 'myth' (Nettleship). *Gennaios* means something like 'well-born', but none of this really matters, not even Popper's 'lordly', with its intended imputation of condescension. The important word is 'lie'; its candour ought to temper criticism, and quite clearly, Plato was not advocating what this word ordinarily means, which is to make a statement knowing it to be false: if he had meant to deceive, he would not have announced his fraud. On the theory of the myths I am offering, 'lie' here means uttering a statement, *not knowing it to be true*, 'knowing' here being used in the characteristically strong Platonic sense of something rigorously demonstrable. It is indeed a fiction or a convention of some kind, but it has nothing whatever to do with lack of sincerity, as I have already argued. On the contrary, it is precisely because Plato does not regard beliefs sincerely held to be true for that reason alone, that he calls the myths 'lies'. The irony of this is over Popper's head. I will heed Plato's warnings against quibbling over the meaning of words, and settle for 'noble lie'.

The myth itself covers a good deal of ground. It is, first, what was said above, a device to promote patriotism and civic unity, 'to care for the state and one another', just as Socrates says (415D). Next, it is an argument against nepotism, which Plato decries elsewhere in the *Republic*. He is fully aware that if class is based on birth damage will be done to society just as if it is based on wealth or any other irrelevant criterion. He provides for controlled breeding among the auxiliaries (459D–460B, to which I will return in the next section) in part to prevent that attachment to their own children that skews the opportunities children have, to the detriment of society. This is one of the reasons for the 'communism' of that class: to assure that selection of the members of each class is based on the merit of the individual alone, and not on the invincible attachment that the ninth transmitter of a foolish face has for the tenth. If anything, Plato is more worried about the damage done by the excessive opportunity of unworthy children of the upper classes, than by the lack of it below, not because he is callous about the poor, but because it is easier in practice to see the actual damage done by the first than merely to speculate about possible Einsteins blushing unseen in the lower classes. Nonetheless, even though he thinks it would be 'unexpected', he does provide for upward mobility in this myth and elsewhere in his writings, and for the universal access to education that this implies.

This preoccupation with inequality is the principal thrust of the myth. It is an entirely practical problem, one that we ourselves are still addressing, and despite the remote times and places that are the best setting for all fairy stories, it is clear that Plato had the concrete events of his own day before him, both in diagnosis and therapy. The problem of inequality may be bluntly, if inelegantly, expressed by the question 'Who gets what?' The inequalities are, of course, not confined to the distribution of material wealth, but extend also to the exercise of authority and to whatever deference to it may be extended. Inequality is not inequity (or unfairness) unless some failure of distributive justice is perceived. The phrase 'from each according to his ability; to each according to his need' plainly provides for inequalities that are not construed as inequities, and can well serve as a point of departure. Formulations of its meaning on the left would aim at something approaching arithmetical equality (no doubt glossing over whatever is not quantifiable) and formulations to the right would seek to justify inequalities, in the form of privilege and prerogative attaching to birth, wealth, social standing, office, and the like.

Every political philosopher has tried to come to terms with this problem. Plato repeatedly stresses at least one good reason for this: where inequality is regarded as inequity, the unfairness rankles and is a prime source of those resentments in society that destroy individual satisfaction and collective stability. This is not the place to repeat in any detail the familiar range of issues in which this question is present in Plato's discussions: the mindlessness of the mob, the avarice of the wealthy, the vice of ignorance joined to power, the damage inflicted on society by its failure to realize the talents of the poor, of women, of the wise. A major portion of the dialogues is devoted to the tireless exploration of ways of resolving the dissatisfactions and injustice springing from these inequities. Let us now suppose, for the sake of the argument, that Plato (or Marx, or anybody) has solved all those inequities: wisdom combined with power bestows authority, opportunity is equalized so that all find their proper level, and the incentives of wealth and power are nicely balanced so as not to distort societal values.

The problem, alas, remains, albeit in a different form. It will have shifted from having objective grounds (removed by the somewhat strained assumptions postulated a moment ago) to having subjective grounds. By definition, those members of a community incapable of exercising the highest authority will be incapable of grasping the reasons for a given course of action. They may well understand in the sense of accepting that those who decided had proper grounds for the decision, even though their reasoning cannot be followed. There is nothing extraordinary in the distinction here drawn: we constantly defer to expert judgement in areas in which we lack expertise. We do not have opinions about brain surgery or transfinite numbers or, Plato would add, about shipbuilding or fluteplaying, unless we know something about those matters. What we can do, short of that knowledge, is to seek another opinion, or assure ourselves that a consensus of expert opinion exists. And then, if we are at all wise, we defer to that judgment.

But many of us are not wise. I do not mean that we are suspicious of claims to expert knowledge, since such suspicion may be well grounded: in *The Doctor's Dilemma* Shaw reminds us that doctors who have brought appendectomy to a high art may be quite unable to diagnose anything but appendicitis; and what is dismal about economics may not be its subject matter so much as its claim to be a science in view of its notorious inability to reach consensus on anything. Nor do I mean that degree of caution vested in the probability we assign to a rational appraisal of facts and goals before thought turns to action. The unwisdom Plato has in mind is incurable. Its symptoms include the irrationalism that systematically mistrusts expertise unless prescription coincides with desire. We blame the bearer for the ill tidings. We dismiss levels of abstract thought beyond our capacity as empty theorizing without application in practice. We have been betrayed by the treachery of the intellectuals, and cannot believe in disinterestedness or altruism at all. 95 per cent of us believe that we are above-average drivers. We have increasingly extravagant notions of the rights due to us, without the historical sense to tell us how novel those claims are. What are we going to do about us?

We are going to have to tell a noble lie. It is that such inequities as we perceive are not attributable to remediable faults of society, but to the mysterious ways of the Gods. The fault, dear Brutus, lies not in ourselves but in our stars. This would be a lie, and a brutal one, if it were designed to conceal self-serving motives. What makes it noble is that it seeks to reconcile us to the shortcomings of existence, not to those of historical accident. This elegant and beautiful myth covers a lot of ground: it is patriotic, directed against nepotism and for social mobility based on merit, and it seeks to console us when we lack grace. Its elegance is independent of the wholly separate question whether one accepts it; I happen to prefer some different myths, especially on the last point, and I wish I had a Plato to tell them for me.

IV

Of the problems of equality that Plato addresses directly, the question of the equality of women has been neglected until the last few years.[11] I have already commented in chapter 3 on Findlay's peculiar treatment of this text: he completely ignores the empirical foundation of Plato's observations based on animal husbandry in order to turn the discussion into an exercise in definition based on eidetic insight. Popper is very interested in the connected issues of eugenic breeding, which he sees as directed to the production of a Master Race (148–53), but has not a word to say about the equality of women.[12] Frutiger and Stewart do not mention the passage (*Republic* V, 451C–457C and related texts in most of Book V), and I am not aware that it has been treated as a myth by anyone. I have earlier referred to it as an anti-myth because it is designed to overthrow a rival myth prevalent in Plato's day, and only a little less so in our own: the inferiority of women. It is one of three 'waves' of paradox treated in Book V that threaten to swamp the development of the argument. Apart from the equality of women, they are the closely connected question of the community of wives and children (anti-nepotism again), and the broad question of the desirability as contrasted with the feasibility of the proposed solutions. This whole section of the Republic has sometimes been thought to be an interpolation breaking the continuity of the argument, but I think that view is mistaken. It all hangs together remarkably well.

The myth to be overthrown is pursued by, of all people, the biologist Aristotle, who remained convinced that women supply the matter (blood, sinew) of the embryo, while the male semen (in part because there is so little of it) supplies the form or essence. Women are thus mere receptacles of the male principle which determines the character of the child. All this forms part of a larger argument showing the natural subordination of women to men, just as barbarians are inferior to Greeks, slaves to masters, and so on. It is astonishing that this canard has died as hard as it has, if indeed it is dead yet. In an age in which the powerful and wealthy had virtually unrestricted access to as many women as they wished (one thinks, say, of the sexual athleticism of Theseus who founded Athens almost single-handed, if we are to credit all his exploits), it seems incredible that the differences among children of the same father but different mothers should never have been attributed to the woman's contribution. Quite often, if the differences were noticed, some other explanation was found.

One delightful example of this is to be seen in Euripides' *Medea* in the baffling scene between Aegeus and Medea in which she obtains a secure haven in Athens following the murder of her children in exchange for unravelling the meaning of an oracular utterance. Aegeus had consulted the oracle because he was not able to produce a male heir, though he had tried very hard with only daughters to show for it. The oracle had said, in one translation, 'Loose not the wineskin's pendant neck', and, not surprisingly, he had no idea what it meant or what he was supposed to do. We are not told what Medea whispered in his ear, but we can guess: the wineskin, usually a goat's bladder, is roughly in the shape of a scrotum and penis. The advice could hardly mean 'don't urinate until you get back to Athens'; it must mean 'don't ejaculate'. Whatever she told him worked a charm, and shortly before his return to Athens the latest Mrs Aegeus (a passing goddess) promptly conceived Theseus.

What the story reveals is another aspect of the putative inferiority of women: sexual overindulgence produces semen of lesser quantity and poorer quality, fit only for the generation of daughters. We know better, of course, in terms of the sex-determining chromosome borne by the father; but some experiments recently reported in the medical press suggest that Medea may have known something we are about to find out. If semen is centrifuged to separate the spermatozoa, those of higher motility are more likely to produce males. Now if it should prove that there is a connection between sexual debility and low motility, Medea may have been right. The myth that it is the woman who determines the sex of offspring is still current, despite the available facts, in many cultures, so that a wife may be divorced if she does not produce a son; quite clearly it is the women who should be divorcing the men or better yet, the rules preferring male succession should be abandoned.

Plato's whole discussion is based on observations drawn from animal husbandry (459). Hunting dogs, horses, and cattle are bred for distinct qualities of speed, skill, milk and meat yield, and in the crossings designed to maximise these qualities the selection of the dam is as important as that of the sire. That is why 'the best men must cohabit with the best women' (459D). To Plato's open mind considerations of heredity may be as significant as those of environment. He is plainly unwilling to deprive society of half its available pool of talent (since women are inferior to men only in matters of relative strength), merely because conventional institutions determining the status of women are in error, and perniciously so. The argument is of a piece with the similar insistence on something close to equal access to the educational system. Plato argues just as firmly against the assumption that the offspring of nobles are necessarily noble, as against the idea that the children of the lower classes are base: the vice of the first assumption leads to the abuses of militarism signalled in Book VIII, but the second deprives society of talents emerging, unexpectedly perhaps, from below.

This upward and downward mobility is crucial to Plato's critique of the defects of present society. There is no inconsistency in the simultaneous use of these arguments from hereditary and environmental influences: he is open to both. What links them is this: while careful selection of the 'best' for purposes of breeding will probably yield better results than random breeding (else animal husbandry – or genetics generally – is nonsense), the proof must still be left to the actual results obtained. There will be no guarantee that the offspring of any particular union will necessarily display the desired characteristics, or even that siblings of the same union will resemble each other closely. (The shortcomings of Pericles' sons were among the commonplaces of Greek literature: cf. *Protagoras* 320AB). Thus, while the probabilities favour the prospect of better offspring of eugenic breeding, and disfavour their emergence from the lower classes, there is nothing certain about these outcomes. The institutions of society must therefore be opened to their optimization; from this the equality of access to education for women (451E) follows.

There is still much to criticize in Plato's approach: he proposes to tilt the balance in favour of eugenics by rigging the lotteries (460A) that determine who breeds with whom. That passage, by the way, contains the one actual piece of deceit in all the myths. Among the devices designed to prevent nepotism is the so-called community of wives and children among the auxiliaries. The children are to be brought up collectively and no one is to know his or her own child. The highly disciplined auxiliaries are to breed once a year, and all the children of a given year are to think of themselves as brothers and sisters. The possibility of inadvertent incest in the further breeding of generations who do not know their genetic antecedents is glossed over by leaving it to the oracle (461E). Infanticide or abortion is to be practised in cases of unauthorized pregnancy (461C). Plato makes no attempt to control breeding among the lowest class, while he will make as much of the odd Alpha who might emerge from the Gammas, Deltas, and Epsilons as education can, he means to leave them alone: they can never be dissuaded from their conviction of the uniqueness of the girl next door as the only possible pebble on the beach.

But the auxiliaries who would, I suppose, be the equivalent of Aldous Huxley's Betas, are under rigorous discipline: they represent true opinion in Plato's hierarchy of knowledge; they know the truth, on the authority of the Rulers' actual knowledge, but unlike the Rulers can give no independent account of it. They will, therefore, accept the rules for breeding; but even they cannot be counted on to breed to order without a further device that they are told about. Lots are to be drawn to determine who breeds with whom. The modern reader should bear in mind that this is not as cold-blooded as it sounds: divination by lots was an established practice in some forms of Greek religion, and it was not taken to be the purely random affair that the drawing of a card under acceptable safeguards would be to us. Chance was a goddess, and the falling out of the lots, while a seemingly arbitrary settling on one of a number of equiprobable possibilities to the modern eye, was in fact a mode of letting the gods decide. That is why, for example, the question of incest referred to above (cf. 461E) could be left to the gods.

But, alas, Plato's orthodoxy here is overridden by the scientific desire to conduct a controlled experiment. Unknown to the auxiliaries, the lots will be rigged, and inferior people will think that the denial of the chance to breed with better ones was the luck of the draw. In fact the Rulers will have decided who is better and will make sure that the best breed only with the best. In view of the use of environmental as well as hereditary factors, it is clear to me at least, that Plato is not convinced in advance who is 'best', still less that such offspring are necessarily best. The whole idea is to test the hypothesis that the breed could be improved by these means.

That will almost certainly fail to redeem it for us, for reasons Plato can hardly be blamed for not anticipating. While we cannot tell how seriously he took his own proposals, we know that they were finally taken seriously only by the Nazis in the notorious experiment to breed a master race by crossing selected members of the SS with the Bund deutscher Mädchen. Such an experiment, however repugnant on moral grounds, might have told us something factually useful one way or the other; in the event, it was bungled and deteriorated into one of the more contemptible forms of brothel-keeping. Too many men as blond as Hitler and as tall and blue-eyed as Goebbels could not keep away from the far from equal partners.[13] Nothing that has happened since in the name of eugenic breeding, or the prevention of dysgenic breeding, offers any encouragement to further experimentation in this area. Some Southern states in the US enforced sterilization in some cases defined by statute in prima facie plausible terms, but in practice the law was applied only to a small number of black women; the whole thing was so shameful that even unabashed racists have dropped the idea, except perhaps on the lunatic fringe. The mismanagement and coercion of Sanjay Gandhi's programme of vasectomy as a birth control device in India (not eugenics, but one of the few examples in a related area) was so crass that it has discredited an important idea, perhaps beyond redemption.

I do not know why Popper holds Plato accountable for the master race doctrine of the Nazis, and for the myths of Blood and Soil. He wanted to breed men and women of high intellect and morality, not thugs; but the point is not worth developing, for Plato would have been as outraged as Popper is. Surely the whole point of the third 'wave' (473C) is the discrepancy between the desirability and the feasibility of many of his proposals. We are late converts to the desirability of treating women as equals, and somewhat patchily are moving toward its practical realization. Eugenics, which is equally desirable, is totally discredited by a *praxis* that has fallen so far short of *lexis* (to use Plato's terms: practice and theory, roughly) that genetic engineering seems more of a threat than a promise of a brave new world. Plato does not expect any of these things to work: the precondition he sets forth in the celebrated passage about philosophers becoming kings (473CD) is one he expects is unattainable in practice, and even if it were, the ruled would have to be philosophers too; then there would be no need of myths, benign or deceptive.

I wish Popper (and Crossman, too), instead of holding Plato responsible for all the abominations of this loathsome century, had held him to a principle enunciated by Kant. In a wonderful essay entitled 'On the Common Saying, "That's all very well in theory, but it won't work in practice",' Kant says that if you have a theory that won't work in practice, you have a bad theory, and should get a better one. If there is anything to be said against Kant's argument, it is that one cannot know in advance what won't work in practice. Plato's notions of the equality of women, an idea that he well knew (452AC) must be regarded as risible, and would not be entertained except as a joke, illustrates this perfectly. It is conceivable that a whole array of problems, say, of medical ethics which now stir the most justifiable alarm – eugenics, euthanasia, surgical intervention in psychopathic disturbances – might after all find workable solutions.

V

The four kinds of perverted forms of the state discussed in the *Republic* (VIII, 545C–IX, 576B) have led to considerable controversy among the commentators. Findlay bases his interpretation (196–200), as one might expect, on the famous mathematical passage at 546, out of which, among other things, the Great Year of 3600 years is generated. By arguing that the several forms of aberrant state are in some coherent way related to the numerology, Findlay plays into Popper's hands, as it were.

In fact, they are derived in a perfectly unmysterious way from the best society as deviations from the balance of classes and interests characterizing an aristocracy of merit. There is no point in repeating here the argument against Popper's view of Plato's alleged 'historicism' set out in chapter 3. In a few words, my rebuttal is that, while there is a logical nexus among the types, there is no necessary temporal sequence.[14] Plato undoubtedly has some actual historical examples in mind: it is quite clear, for example, that Sparta and Crete are timocracies (they are referred to as such in the context of 544C) and this should give pause to those critics who see the political writings as a subterranean defence of Sparta. But those are the only examples explicitly named. What the whole lengthy passage does not permit, whether for good, as Findlay sees it, or for ill, as Popper does, is the derivation of a cyclical history played out in actual time in accordance with an ineluctable formula.

Frutiger offers a much more sober judgement. He concludes (41) that the manner in which the definitions of the four defective forms of the state are connected is mythical precisely because Plato 'well knew that reality had never presented, and never could present an example of decadence such as he depicts for us.' He goes on to say that it is for this reason a philosophy of history; and that is where we get into terminological difficulties, which I have already addressed. Others have also used the term about this typology, but without Popper's insistence (which I believe is perfectly sound) that philosophies of history improvidently demand that history actually unfold in accordance with the pattern specified. That fits Hegel and Toynbee, and others mentioned in the earlier discussion of chapter 3. But it is quite clear that Frutiger and others who see a philosophy of history in Book VIII are using the term in quite another sense, one that I would rather call a 'typology' or a 'schema', if giving it another name will help. It is too 'pure' an analysis, deliberately omitting intermediate and mixed forms such as almost certainly have existed, and still do. Plato's schema purports to be logically exhaustive: 'Can you mention any other type of government', Socrates asks at 544D, 'I mean any other that constitutes a distinct species?' What he is after are the dominant characteristics that define each type, without the incidental and accidental elements that muddle analysis of particular instances.

It is because timocracy is the least bad type that Plato has been supposed to be defending Sparta. What characterizes it (545C ff.) is the exaggerated role played by the spirited element in the soul in disrupting the balance of the ideal society: it is 'contentious and covetous of honor'. An ideal society, if one could be established, would suffer the fate of everything that comes into being: it must decay. This is brought about by begetting out of season (expounded in the mathematical terms I have previously described as gibberish), by neglecting the rationale for important rules, and by failing to test for gold and silver as mandated at 415B. The timocratic society is a parody of the ideal society in which the ruling class is touchy about points of honour, is contemptuous both of intellect and of trades and crafts. Its economy will be run by the latter class, now enslaved (presumably Plato has the Spartan helots in mind), with the land seized by the ruling class. These militarists will 'not admit clever men to office' (547E), preferring simpleminded warriors and hunters preoccupied with war. While at first wealth is little regarded in itself, being held in the public treasury (rather like the 'communism' of Plato's auxiliaries) this collectivism deteriorates so that public thrift is accompanied by private prodigality and secret vices. The pathology increases as a result of the tension between the sobriety of the young officer's father (an aristocrat) and the stimulus to rash points of honour by the more appetitive mother and servants (549B). All the worst aspects of Burke's 'rapacious and licencious soldiery' begin to emerge, as well as the ambiguities of Kipling's

It's Tommy this, an' Tommy that, an' 'Chuck him out, the brute!'
But it's 'Saviour of 'is country' when the guns begin to shoot.

The devotion to wealth displaces honour in the next degradation, oligarchy (550C), which springs out of timocracy. Appetite displaces the spirited element, and poverty, which was not incompatible with honour, is now despised. In this setting the timocratic man, still wedded to honour, becomes poor, but his son sees the value of money. The qualification for office is property instead of knowledge; at 551C Plato returns to one of his favourite examples by asking if one would appoint a pilot because he knew the rocks and shoals or because he was wealthy. It is no longer possible to wage even defensive war for fear that if the poor were armed, they would turn on their rulers instead. Extremes of wealth breed crime among the poor, who have nothing to lose.

The transition from oligarchy to democracy is due to the rapid vicissitudes of fortune of those who become bankrupt because of their improvidence and waste. They are envious of the newly rich who have brought them low, and are 'eager for revolution' (555E). The sons of the wealthy are soft and spoiled, and their effete character is only too evident to the 'lean sinewy pauper' who observes them in the army or in public places. Seduced by ignorance and avid for pleasure the son of the thrifty oligarch (559D) indulges his appetite, angry at his father's reluctant purse. Under a democracy an order based on wealth is overthrown and in its place everybody is to have an equal share. No man being better than another, offices are awarded by lot. There is freedom of speech, for 'has not every man license to do as he likes?' (557B). And since all opinions are of equal validity, there is indifference to truth; disagreements are to be resolved by majority vote; but this may be swayed by demagogues who proclaim their devotion to the people. Those who wish no part in public affairs can withdraw into private lives. Democrats make a fetish of a wholly indiscriminate equality and of a liberty indistinguishable from licence.

And so the foundation is laid for tyranny. Just as lust for wealth undid the oligarchy, so excess of liberty leads to anarchy (562E). As the democracy decays the dominant class is orators, idlers, spendthrifts who seize office in order to mulct the wealthy by taxation, and even despoil the smallholders. They resist this, and a call goes out for a strong man as protector of the people to be 'the leader of faction against the possessors of property' (566A). One appears, to promise the cancellation of debts and the redistribution of lands. The property-owners plot to assassinate him (often he is someone they have exiled, but he is brought back under the democracy). He needs a bodyguard for his protection and to make the city safe for democracy, and he uses this to overthrow his enemies. At this stage he is seemingly a friend to all; the harsh measures are not directed at the people, and he denies that he is a tyrant.

His is government by crisis: he is always scenting enemies and stirring up fear of war, so that a leader is needed. Under this pretext he eliminates those who have detected the danger he poses, but only the brave will speak out and so he disposes of the best in the city and preserves the worst, and of these the most opportunistic flock to him as mercenaries (567E). His rule becomes ever more repressive as he exhausts the diminishing resources, and so he must tax his erstwhile and now impoverished supporters.

There is a recurrent theme that the transitions between the four types are initiated by the sons of the dominant characters representative of each polity to be transformed (cf. 553C, 556B, 559D). The early pages of Book IX examine how the tyrannical man is seduced by the example of his democratic father (572E). It is a theme that Polybius made use of in his cycle of ups and downs in political forms, and no doubt he got it from the *Republic*, though his version of the decline of civic virtue from father to son is much more insistent than anything in Plato, who even allows (at 560A) that there might occur in some individuals at least a reversal of the process, so that a prospective young democrat might turn to oligarchy instead. We shall need to return to that possibility a little later on. Here, however, as we view the development of the tyrannical man (not the tyrant as such; perhaps 'tyrannical temperament' would be clearer), we are asked to note that the extreme indulgence, the conviction that there are no beliefs superior to any others, stimulate excess. Such a man is likened to a drunkard, a madman, an eroto-maniac, who pursues his crazed desires to extremity. Driven by pathological appetite, he resents his father's 'stinginess' which impedes its satisfaction. Having squandered his own wealth, he would lay violent hands on his parents if they deny his demands. It is but a step from this to armed assault and temple-robbing. No early training, no law, can now restrain him – he is the perfect tyrant, a law unto himself. If these characteristics, evil enough in an individual, are present on the larger scale of a polity, the greatest evil befalls. No friend can be true to the tyrant, only flatterers, and only so long as their own interests are served; he is the most miserable of men, and the state he rules for a time is the most wretched of states.

This vivid account is not a history; it is a scenario so broadly sketched that, while Plato no doubt had contemporary examples in mind, we could just as well read into the succession of democracy by tyranny a picture of the supplanting of the Kerensky regime by Lenin and Stalin, or of the Weimar republic by Hitler. With a little shaping of the facts to suit whatever purpose we have in mind, we could make Cromwell, or Napoleon, or a hundred lesser tyrants fit the scenario. It is not so much a history, then, as an analysis of the social forces operating in certain types of polity lacking institutions of sufficient stability to weather crises as they arise, or to assure the functioning of at least minimal notions of equity. One such problem that Plato addresses only obliquely has been solved in the most stable modern societies, and is a source of their stability: it is the mode by which power passes legitimately to a successor government. The only systems known to Plato were primogeniture in the male line, and the election of the Spartan ephors. The first had a sorry history until well into the eighteenth century, with endless wars of succession, the hiding of infant heirs from dynastic assassins, and sons unworthy of their noble fathers. If he preferred Sparta under those circumstances, he was probably right. He could hardly have foreseen the devices by which modern democracies, and there are precious few of them, protect against the abuse of power. Still less would he be enchanted with the imperfect Athenian democracy which put Socrates to death.

Much of the misunderstanding of this book of the *Republic* has generated springs from the engrafting of two myths ill-accommodated to each other. One is the typology itself, and I shall return to it in a moment. The other lies in those traces of Pythagorean number-magic that baffle all readers (an early one who could not make head or tail of 546 was Cicero). These tie the sequence of polities to the Great Year with its suggestion of inevitable decline – hence Popper's agitation at Plato's 'historicism'. But the purpose of the whole account is hardly this. For one thing, a strictly straight-line decline is inconsistent with the suggestion at 560A, mentioned above, that sometimes a young democrat may move up to oligarchy rather than down to tyranny; cold comfort though that may be, it is not the unalleviated Hesiodic misery. The more substantial purposes of the whole account, which make the number-magic irrelevant, are twofold: first, to illustrate the thesis that justice in the state is justice in the individual writ large – hence the argument that the characteristics of the tyrannical man are those of the tyranny, and so of the other individuals and polities described. The second aim is to supply the rebuttal that Thrasymachus did not wait to hear in Book I – against his claim that injustice is better than justice or, more precisely, that justice is what the poweful define it to be, so that the man who can satisfy his every wish, however ignoble, is the happiest of men. Far from this, among all the types of polity, that which corresponds to such a man is the worst.

The other problem causing difficulties lies in the logic of Plato's myth. If it was intended as a philosophy of history, it is singularly unsuccessful. The sequence of polities not only has no foundation in history, since many successions of regimes known to Plato followed other patterns, but it has no clear logical relationship to his other myths. I have tried to show, especially with reference to the eschatological myths (and it is also true of most of the other myths) that in them he did not adopt new and different assumptions merely to justify one aspect of his beliefs in isolation, but sought to harmonize his beliefs in all the major areas of his many interests. The eschatological myths, to limit myself to this one example, aim at religious, epistemological, and moral arguments simultaneously. Some principle of eccnomy, a Platonic Occam's Razor, prevents him from inventing elements of his axiomatics good only for one myth, but inconsistent with the rest. I do not dismiss the importance that mathematics had for Plato, of course, enough has been said already of the centrality in his thought of a structure of knowledge, the very counterpart of cosmological governance, of which axiomatized mathematics is the supreme metaphor. Here it seems obfuscatory and irrelevant.

There is still another sense in which this myth of the several polities is poorly worked out by the standard established everywhere else in his writings. He makes partial use of the tripartite division of the soul, and refers repeatedly to the political evils that spring from the dominance of one of the parts to the detriment of the balance of the whole. What we might have expected, therefore, is a myth treating of the defects of those states in which one of the three parts dominates. The defect would have been attributable to that imbalance alone, and the contrast with aristocracy would have sufficed, without the need to intimate a logical/temporal relationship among them: the logic is too strained and not even consistently applied, and save by accident here and there, no such sequence can be found in history. The image Plato uses is a misleading one, with the faulty states depending from aristocracy and from one another, like links in a chain. If I may be permitted an image of my own, aristocracy could have been likened to a tripod, stable when each of its legs is of the correct length and strength, but unstable if one or other of them (two, perhaps, in the case of oligarchy) is out of proportion.

Some traces of the myth he might have written are evident, if we consider timocracy and oligarchy to be lesser and greater aberrations of the spirited part of the soul, and democracy and tyranny to be counterpart aberrations of the appetitive part. That leaves us without polities based on excess of intellect. I know of none in fact, and of two in fiction: a dreadful novel by Huxley called *Island*, and Hesse's superb *Glasperlenspiel*; perhaps Hamlet might qualify:

> . . . the native hue of resolution
> Is sicklied o'er with the pale cast of thought.

Is it possible that the Platonic invention of a lost island is the missing myth? Since it is incomplete, an unwritten doctrine might be supplied to remedy the defect.

VI

Alas, the Atlantis myth will not do. It promises much more than it delivers, probably because the intolerably long-winded Critias says less of substance in the fifteen or so pages of the fragment named for him than in the two or three pages of the Timaeus that are the only other source of the story. Everyone agrees that the myth is an invention of

Plato's; certainly nothing corresponds to it in the Egyptian mythology and iconography that is alleged to be its source.[15]

Critias claims to possess the notes that Solon took after he had been told of the ancient island kingdom by Egyptian priests. Their account purports to be a history dating back 9000 years to the foundation of Athens under Hephaestus (the arts and crafts) and Athena (wisdom), a history of which the Athenians have no record, the Greeks being children compared with the sophisticated and stable institutions of the Egyptians, which presumably included historical records. They could not have been quite as childlike as *Timaeus* 22B (also cf. 23B) suggests, because the polity of ancient Athens was apparently nothing less than the very perfect form of government described in the *Republic*. Little detail is given beyond the establishment of the class of auxiliaries who held in common the little they needed for sustenance: '. . . in short they followed all the practices we spoke of yesterday when we talked of those feigned guardians' (*Critias* 110D). The reference is to the opening pages of the *Timaeus* which partly recapitulate a recital of the *Republic* the previous day.

Much more has been made of the myth of Atlantis than need concern us here. The elaborate account of the erosion of the soil of that primitive Athens (111–12) has led at least one commentator to claim Plato as one of the earliest geologists. And the fabulous wealth of the sunken island still attracts science fiction writers and treasure hunters; most of the *Critias* is devoted to the geography and architecture of the island. Bacon started, but did not finish, a *New Atlantis* (located in the Pacific, oddly enough); it has a political programme with Utopian aims, which at least brings us back to Plato.

To the extent that we can extricate from the wordy Critias any points of philosophical interest, these are quickly told. It is essentially a story of the political decline of Atlantis through the stages described in Book VIII of the *Republic* just discussed. From their divine origins under Poseidon, the Atlanteans passed through timocracy and oligarchy, though the specific hallmarks of these polities are not clearly set out. Their wealth came in part from an overseas empire (114D), which implies both conquest and trade. It was this, no doubt, that brought them into conflict with Athens, for they had already conquered northern Africa and southern Italy, and now they proposed to subdue Athens (*Timaeus* 25B). But Athens, standing alone, defeated them (25C).

Meanwhile, the gods were disturbed by the moral decline of Atlantis, attributable to the infusions of mortal blood into the original divine stock; by now, perhaps, they had slumped into democracy or even tyranny (though we are not told). Zeus summoned the gods, and began to address them . . . At this point the *Critias* breaks off. From the *Timaeus* (25C) we may infer that it was Zeus' and the other gods' judgement of Atlantis that it be destroyed by earthquakes and inundated. The parallel to the stories of Noah and of Sodom and Gomorrah have often been remarked. The claim that the fate of Atlantis was intended as a warning to Sparta seems implausible, certainly if Plato is held to prize timocracy above democracy. As a warning, moreover, it came too late to deter the defeat of Athens in the Peloponnesian War.

Plato's purpose, of which we gain only a few hints, was probably to produce a didactic tale asserting the actual existence of his ideal society in remote antiquity, and of proclaiming its moral and (for that reason) military ascendancy over the commercial and expansionist Atlanteans. It was a commonplace of ancient literatures to claim some tutelary deity to found and oversee the welfare of the city. Athena was, of course, the eponymous goddess; but the addition of Hephaestus is an ingenious touch. Perhaps Plato wanted to supply a god for his lowest class of artisans and craftsmen; in any case we will have suppressed the story how Hephaestus was crippled by Zeus. If the story is a warning to anyone, it must be to the Athenians themselves, against foreign conquest and trade which undermine self-sufficiency and just balance. Speculations beyond these are hazardous.

6 Methodological Myths

A new distinction now needs to be introduced in order to set off the myths with a specific doctrinal content, discussed in the last two chapters, from myths invented for the purpose of specifying how thought is shaped. The first kind deal, as we have seen, with metaphysical, epistemological, religious, moral, and political questions; sometimes they overlap with or duplicate arguments that Plato has demonstrated dialectically, sometimes they are little more than ingenious moral fables, more or less transparent in their meaning, and occasionally they are fanciful images in which the poet indulges himself without any considerable freight of meaning. In all these cases they tell us what Plato believed about the nature of ultimate reality, the governance of the cosmos, the content of our knowledge, and they tell us also of his religious, moral, and political principles. Those might be called the substantive myths.

The discussion in chapter 2 of the variety of dialectical methods used by Plato was called 'the inconclusiveness of dialectic' because those methods did not yield the demonstrative proof he hoped for in adopting and refining them. The difficulties he encountered cannot be explained solely in terms of the inaccessibility of the objective world to our imperfect senses; that could perhaps be overcome if the higher mental equipment we possess were capable of grasping the world – in some other fashion, no doubt, as idiomatic to the entertainment of abstract knowledge as sense perception is for such grasp of the physical world as we have. That the latter suffers from all the defects that Plato ascribes to it we need not assert (or correct), not because his position is beyond argument – I shall have something to say about this in the final chapter – but because the direction he takes, having established the defectiveness of sense perception to his satisfaction, is to explore the ways in which a more reliable foundation for knowledge can be found. This, of course, is the method, or methods, of dialectic. It fails, as I tried to show in chapter 2, primarily because the primitives of any system cannot be proven within that system, though when postulated as true, many propositions can be deduced from them that are in fact confirmed experientially. Among those propositions are the content of his doctrines mentioned above.

But among them also are a number of topics addressed to the foundations of dialectical method. Here we are concerned with the structure of knowledge, not its content. What assumptions does Plato make concerning that structure? We know how sensitive he was about the foundations of mathematics: he seems to have been alone in his own times in raising the questions he does about the axioms of geometry (cf., especially, *Republic* VI, 511 and VII, 533), though some doubt about the parallel postulate appears in the literature not long after him. Some of the myths are clearly about the structure of knowledge, the most obvious being the doctrine of *anamnesis*. This does not speak to the specific things or ideas recollected, but to the role of recollection *überhaupt*. Similarly, the method of hypothesis is a schema for organizing knowledge in such a way that as much as possible can be deduced, and as little as possible assumed; the version of it that is most obviously in the form of a myth is the ladder of beauty in the *Symposium* (211). The allegory of the Cave is the obviously mythical version of the divided line. But the latter is no less a myth merely because it is written in dialectical form. Like the others mentioned, it embodies some undemonstrated and indemonstrable assumptions about the methods by which we structure our knowledge. A little noticed passage in the *Philebus* (16C–17A) tells us something about the origins of dialectic itself. The whole theory of forms is, like these other examples, a myth; indeed, of all the myths, it is probably the most contested. And, of course, the rival modes of structuring knowledge are rival myths.

I

The theory of forms or ideas is the most familiar aspect of Platonism, known even to those who have perhaps never read any of the dialogues. It is all the more surprising, therefore, to observe that nowhere in those texts is an account given of the forms that is sufficiently complete and detailed to be an authoritative version of Plato's central doctrine. There are, indeed, innumerable references scattered throughout his writings and a few places, notably in the first part of the *Parmenides*, where we encounter something close to a coherent and systematic discussion of the forms. The special interest of the *Parmenides* is that in the opening pages the claims for the theory of forms are not merely asserted or mentioned in passing, as is the case almost everywhere else in the dialogues, but a serious challenge to them is raised to which Socrates' answers are far from satisfactory. This has baffled many commentators – certainly the exercise in dialectic that makes up the greater part of the dialogue is baffling – but I think that we need not be disturbed by the tentative and uncertain way in which Socrates replies to Parmenides' questions about the forms. It is not simply a matter of Parmenides giving as good as he got in response to Socrates' rejection of the Parmenidean One, which denies the possibility of becoming and of change. Rather, it seems to me, Socrates is in genuine doubt whether the puzzles and apparent inconsistencies or incompletenesses of his theory can be resolved. He does not fall back on dogmatic assertion in defence of his theory, but acknowledges his uncertainty (130D).

What we are to understand is that the form of anything (objects, ideas) exists independently and prior to its exemplifications in particulars which derive their reality from the extent to which they participate (or partake = *metechein, metexis*) in it. The forms are distinct from the things participating in them (130B); their existence is thus independent of the world of appearances and is the only true existence. For the most part Socrates is thinking of abstract ideas, like rightness, beauty, goodness, and he expresses puzzlement about forms of man, fire, or water, perhaps because of their complexity. But he has no difficulty about forms of things, even unworthy or trivial ones like mud, hair, or dirt (130D). It is the sense in which particulars partake in the forms that gives the most trouble. He makes a quite unnecessary concession to Parmenides when asked how the form is present in the particulars. At first he says it is like a day that is the same everywhere, though in many places (131B); but he then allows that it is also like a sail that covers many men (131C). In that case part of the sail covers each man, and so (he incautiously agrees) the sail is of many parts, each covering one man. Is the form such that it is fragmented, so that one of its many parts 'covers' each particular?[1] Socrates says yes to this; he should have said no, because Parmenides is then able to argue that a part of largeness is smaller than the whole, and so a large object is no longer large (or, perhaps, as large as it was); similarly, something equal becomes less equal because covered only by part of equality. Had Socrates said no, we may be assured that he would have been trapped some other way by the ingenious Parmenides, just as Socrates had himself trapped many an unwary interlocutor.

The Third Man is the next argument (132): if there is a form of man, say, then there must be some respects in which man resembles that form, and to the extent that man and the form have certain properties in common, those properties constitute another form, a third man. But the third man and the form have certain properties in common, and these constitute a fourth man, and so *ad infinitum*. This argument was revived by Aristotle (*Metaphysics* 990b, 18), and rests on a mistake best explained by Russell's theory of types, which displays the paradoxes that arise when propositions are made about a class of which the proposition is itself a member. But Socrates does not have this answer to hand.

There are more devastating arguments to come. If the forms are indeed independent, and if their relation to the objects of perception is so tenuous, then they are strictly unknowable (133CD). All we know are the objects of perception and the names we give them, but these bear no clearly specifiable relationship beyond a vague likeness to the forms they are said to resemble. They will be known to the gods, but so complete is the dichotomy that Parmenides has drawn from Socrates' concessions, that it now appears that the gods and we inhabit separate worlds, such that not only do we know nothing of the divine world of forms, but the gods know nothing of our world, and would not intervene in its governance (134CE). Parmenides' purpose is not to destroy the theory of forms. If one 'has nothing on which to fix his thought' (135C), then knowledge is impossible and he 'will completely destroy the significance of all discourse.' I can only conclude from this that Plato places in Parmenides' mouth his own conviction that no theory of knowledge can be developed without indemonstrable premises. We must fix our thought on some principle, as a hypothesis, for its heuristic value, analysing its consequences, and so forth. Many objections can no doubt be raised against it, and some may prove fatal, but the fact that it cannot be proved is not such an objection. If it is believed to be fatal, then no theory of knowledge is possible.

What is especially noteworthy from the perspective adopted in this book is that it is precisely in the *Parmenides* that the difficulties and problematics of the theory of forms are broached and left unresolved. The setting of the dialogue is curious, as has often been observed, in that it invents a meeting that could hardly have taken place in actuality between the aged philosopher of Elea and the young Socrates. As young as he is represented to be, Socrates is nonetheless known to the proponent of unchanging being grasped only by the mind, as holding a rival doctrine in which the things of sense in some way embody or exemplify the essences which, to Parmenides, are the only objects of knowledge. And so he challenges the young man's claim that physical objects somehow share or participate in those essences so as to acquire a degree of reality corresponding to the adequacy with which they reflect the essences. As we have seen, the answers Socrates gives in response to Parmenides' searching questions are far from satisfactory.

Yet the *Parmenides* is a late dialogue, written as everyone agrees in Plato's philosophical maturity, and so one might have expected arguments of greater penetration that we in fact find in the first part, arguments that Socrates might have won without damage to the extraordinary deference shown to the venerable Eleatic. There are important grounds for that deference. In the array of philosophical beliefs current in Plato's day that of Parmenides and his school might be thought of as one extreme. It argued for the total unreliability of the senses, as shown, for example, in the paradoxes of Zeno the Eleatic; it denied the reality of change, whether of place (i.e. motion) or of state (coming into or passing out of being): 'Whatever is, is, and what is not, is not.' Not far from that position one might locate the Pythagoreans, who combined religious mysticism with mathematics; the latter, for all it advanced knowledge of geometry and the even more influential notion that our science is most reliable when quantifiable[2] and axiomatically structured, was inseparable from the hermetic mystery religion in which it was embedded, so that mathematics gave insight into reality.

At the other extreme of that array may be found an assortment of materialists, of whom the most important was Democritus, a contemporary of Plato who never refers directly to him, but to whose doctrines, political as well as metaphysical, he was bitterly hostile. It is difficult to say what Democritus' doctrines were because almost nothing that he wrote or said has survived save at second-hand; but they have been taken to be descended in part from certain aspects of earlier philosophies, notably those of the Milesian and nearby schools, which argued that all things are made of matter of some kind. It might be water, or air, or the tiny likenesses (*homoiomeriai*)[3] of things of which a great number make up an object palpable to sense because the eye, for example, is struck by some of the tiny trees, say, emanating from a visible tree so that it can be seen. Or all things might be composed of some substance so indeterminate (the *apeiron*) that it was capable of being changed into any of the specific things encountered in ordinary experience, or they might be compounded of the four elements; or of atoms, as Democritus said, small determinate particles (*atomos*: not further divisible), the basic constituents of matter, of various shapes, sizes, and properties.

What brought about combinations and changes in these substances was the subject of further speculations; I have referred to some of them in chapter 2 and elsewhere , when Plato comments on them. In purely physical terms changes of state, like that of water to steam or ice, were thought of by some of these earlier thinkers as attributable to compression and rarefaction; changes of place as the result of objects originally in motion as striking and caroming off one another like so many billiard balls. But beyond postulations so closely linked to familiar experience lay other and more obscure speculations concerning the cause of change. It might be Love and Strife (Empedocles), or Mind (Anaxagoras), or simply that the whole natural order was necessarily in a state of Flux (Heraclitus);[4] or, without necessity, which implies a logical principle of some kind, change might be the result of Chance. These terms need to be capitalized to indicate that to their ordinary meanings has been added some weightier import, raising them to the status of an explanatory principle of ultimate universality. Alongside all these schools and drawing on their doctrines, we find the sceptics, some of whom as I have noted earlier claimed Socrates as a fellow-spirit in part because of the unsolved problematics of definition and the forms.

Plato's sympathies quite clearly lie closer to the Parmenidean – Pythagorean end of the spectrum, but he differs from it in important ways which owe more of a debt to the materialistic end than is generally acknowledged. The interpretation of his work divides sharply about this question and, as I have several times indicated, I believe that he is disserved by denying or minimizing the role of the physical world in his thought. If he were in fact as hostile to or as contemptuous of the physical world of appearances and of the senses as he is so often taken to be, we could not account for the need of such assumptions as recollection, the obscurely but insistently stated relationship between forms and things, the analogy between the sun and the form of the good, each illuminating its realm, and the isomorphism between the two principal divisions of the line. And in the ceaseless quest for definition we find two outcomes that likewise reflect the relationship between the two realms: the first is the constant need, in what I have called Socratic dialectic, to verify (falsify, in most cases) tentative definitions by reference to examples drawn from common experience; the second, its counterpart, is the acknowledgement that the highest ideas can be shown only by means of examples (*Statesman* 277D).

There is, however, an equally clear sense in which he *is* hostile to the world of matter,[5] and it is this that no doubt leads many commentators to tilt the balance towards a one-sided rationalism, idealism, or mysticism. But they have misconstrued, I think, the nature of that hostility. It springs from the failure of the materialists to postulate a corrective to the shortcomings of their position. Of those defects the first and most obvious is that, while individual objects and events can be observed, unifying patterns that imply coherence and causality are not observable, but must be inferred. Some materialists are prepared, of course, to postulate some principle of order, but then their materialism is no longer consistent; and those not willing to do so are condemned to view each object and event as unique,[6] facing what James called 'the booming, buzzing confusion of sense', and the dilemma that Hume could neither explain away nor act upon. Materialism, at least in its purer forms, cannot consistently import the notion of purpose any more than that of order; on the contrary, chance plays a role in the unfolding of events that undermines the possibility of stable knowledge; moreover, the ideas of harmony, uniformity, simplicity, and rationality are superimpositions on the observable that materialists quite intelligently adopt, but at the price of consistency.[7]

I do not say that these problems have not after a fashion been solved; they have been solved in important ways in this century, at least as concerns mathematics and science – and classical materialism has been significantly modified in the process. Those solutions, which are perfectly intelligible, whether one agrees with them or not, were certainly not available to Plato. When, for example, Anaxagoras postulated the notion of Mind to explain how change comes about, Socrates was very excited, he tells us (*Phaedo* 97C–98E), but was disappointed to discover that Mind was merely an *ad hoc* explanation drawn in at random to help him over some of the difficulties of his argument; but Anaxagoras did not employ it as a coherent and consistently applied principle.

It is when we shift from science to ethics that the problems of materialism appear totally intractable. Certainly that was the case in the versions known to Plato. Materialists committed to observation of what *is* can hardly infer what *ought* to be the case, even if they are able to permit inference of anything from anything. They are likely to be unable to distinguish whether some thing should be done from the fact that it can be done; instead, and this was Plato's experience, they base morality on the observed practices of a society, or on what as matter of fact it proclaims to be its moral principles; and so they might reach what Kant described as anthropology and what we might call ethical relativism, but they could not possibly reach what Plato would call morality. I might, for example, be deterred from doing something that I am physically able to do because I am afraid of being caught and punished, or held in low esteem, or, to be more modern and sophisticated, because I have so internalized certain values that my superego or self-image will not permit the act. But if I can be sure that I will not be caught, my self-image will quickly adapt, and if I can find no other foundation for morality I will behave exactly as Gyges did after a few fairly innocuous experiments with his ring to make sure it was working. The point about relativism (including its modern descendant, emotivism) is not just that it is a rival myth; rather, it is a vicious myth.

However ill these problems may be addressed as they bear on morality, they are quite insoluble in the domains of religion and metaphysics. The materialist simply splutters here; we are so far removed from the observable that nothing meaningful can be said. The agnostic may be willing to suspend judgement, but the dogmatic materialist cannot afford to be so indulgent; hence the hostility to principles which from his point of view are gratuitously assumed, probably for sinister purposes; and hence, too, the antipathy as roundly reciprocated, as I have shown in chapter 1.

Given Plato's undoubted loathing of materialism, the mistake of Findlay, Stewart, and many others, is to disregard what is of value in materialism, and by an exaggerated dichotomy between it and the doctrines of the Eleatics and Pythagoreans, make of Plato an adherent of mysticism, intuition, and the more arcane regions of an idealism so abstract that it can hardly speak of the world we inhabit. For there is a middle ground, and Plato, along with some materialists, may be seen to occupy it, though they are still far apart. What they have in common is a considerable sense of the fallibility of all our explanations, and they recognize that to the extent that empirical confirmation is available it must be sought and brought to bear. Where empirical confirmation is not available or is inapplicable we are free to speculate. The process does not end there, however. For the beliefs adopted, even tentatively, have consequences, and Plato gives evidence of shaping his myths in light of those consequences. There is thus a reciprocal interplay between the loftiest of abstract formulations and their practical outcomes, of which the best examples are to be found in the political myths.

The theory of forms is presented in a number of ways, of which the most concise is the summary of his views that Plato gives at *Timaeus* 51D–52C. Much of the version dealing with problems of definition has already been discussed in chapter 2, so I will be brief here. When Socrates calls on one of his interlocutors for the meaning of some, generally abstract, term like piety or friendship, he is usually given examples of what is meant when the term is applied to some action. He rejects this approach and asks instead for specification of those properties that all examples of the term have in common (cf. *Phaedrus* 249C: 'passing from a plurality of perceptions to a unity gathered by reasoning'), the presence of which permits the application of the term and so defines it. Inferring what the definition is by induction from the examples may be a necessary part of the process, it is clearly not a sufficient one. For induction, the upward path from particulars to the universal, suffers as we have often enough noted from being merely probabilistic (cf. *Timaeus* 28A and *Republic* IX, 585C) and subject to correction in light of new particulars encountered later. If we already knew the definition (or form, idea, essence) we could proceed by the assured downward path of deduction (*Republic* VI, 511B) from the definition to the particulars: such knowledge would be a check-list, as it were, of the defining properties, and our task the presumably much easier one of verifying the presence in an object or event of the requisite properties (cf. *Philebus* 17E).

I have tried to make clear in the last few pages why it is so important to Plato that there be forms of objects and events. He might have been content that, as concerns beds and tables (*Republic* X, 596A), all we have is empirical concepts subject to indefinite future correction. We can live with that – and, on the whole, we do – but much more is at stake. First, of course, if the problem of deductive knowledge is insoluble at the level of objects of sense, then it is all the further removed in the realms of morals, religion, and metaphysics, with the consequences just noted. But, second, we appear to possess a priori knowledge of the desired sort in geometry; our definition of a triangle is not an induction from the limited selection of triangles physically encountered, but is deduced from a system of axioms such that it applies to every triangle, whether encountered or not.

While, therefore, we might regard the question of the form of triangle to be settled, we are bound to add, as Plato does, that the problem has been pushed back to a higher level, so that doubts about whether we really know triangles become doubts about whether we really know the truth of the axioms of geometry. The methods of collection and division carry forward in a more sophisticated way the same problem of definition: if we are examining a class of apparently related matters, but need to divide into subsets so as to refine our understanding of what those matters have in common, 'we must divide where there is a real cleavage between specific forms' (*Statesman* 262D). That language begs the question, in the sense that if we know where the line of cleavage is that sets the boundary between some class in which an individual properly belongs and some other class(es) in which it might incorrectly be included, then we should hardly need a method to establish that line. This is not a fatal objection (or if it is we are all dead); what validates it is that underlying the process is an assumption, not always clearly expressed or clearly avowed, and that is that we are dealing with hypotheses, not apodictic certainties. Sometimes, at least, Plato is very clear on this: 'I am assuming the existence of absolute beauty and goodness . . . and all the rest of them' (*Phaedo* 100B); and again: 'If all these absolute realities . . . really exist' (*Phaedo* 76D). It is permissible to postulate forms of which inductive generalizations are approximations, provided that we do not forget that they are hypothetical, and provided also that no inconsistency is ignored in the propositions deduced from the hypotheses, and that they are not contradicted by empirical fact.

The theory of forms is itself such a hypothesis, one to which Plato is impelled by the unsatisfactoriness of the rival hypotheses of his predecessors and contemporaries. His theory satisfies the conditions set forth above, and it has the advantage over those other theories of being continuous in its epistemological conclusions with its conclusions in those areas in which empirical confirmation is much harder or impossible to bring to bear. The sense in which the application of an ethical rule, say, is falsified by experience is much less rigorous than the falsification of a proposition predicted by a physical law that runs counter to the facts. To argue that the relative vagueness of such rational and experiential methods as we use to test ethical rules makes those methods worthless is to reduce ethics to the level of taste or emotional preference.

That has, of course, been argued at various times, and proponents of that view and its variants will not be short of suitable terms of opprobrium: from those perspectives Plato will be guilty of the Naturalistic Fallacy (assimilating ethical to physical laws), and of using 'flag-waving words' (signalling that he feels strongly about something by asserting that it is true). Those rival myths are as coherent and have no worse problems than Plato's; and as guides to conduct fare no worse than his. By one test no ethical theory has been notably successful: for every practising Platonist, Christian, or Kantian whose life honours those precepts, there are thousands affecting them whose lives range from ethical mediocrity to outright villainy. Those who three times denied Charles Bradlaugh the seat in Parliament to which he was repeatedly re-elected were astonished when he was finally seated in 1886 to discover how moral a man can be who would make no acknowledgement of religion. My point is that, independent of the discrepancy between theory and practice, there may well be several theories that satisfy with rough approximation whatever tests we can devise of their validity, and it is quite unnecessary to prove all the others wrong in order to be assured that one's own theory is true. Yet philosophers have been tireless in the ingenuity and pertinacity displayed in revealing the errors of their opponents; they have not always noticed that even if all other theories are demonstrably false it does not follow from this that their own theory is true. What philosophers have not often paid attention to are the grounds, more likely psychological than philosophical, why they are attracted to some theories and repelled by others.

II

The theory of recollection (or reminiscence = *anamnesis*) is perhaps not a myth in the sense of being a separate axiom or hypothesis of Plato's system. It could simply be treated as a theorem deducible from the theory of forms with which it is obviously linked. It has rarely been treated as a myth, and among the few scholars who accept it as such Frutiger treats its appearance in the *Meno* as mythical, and the *Phaedo* version as dialectical, for reasons already discussed in chapter 3.[8] It would be rash indeed to be too certain of the question either from his point of view or mine, even apart from the disagreement that he rejects it as a myth in the *Phaedo* because it is an axiom, while I regard it as a myth for that very reason. It would be utterly artificial to attempt the kind of formal analysis that would seek to establish whether recollection is an independent axiom; that is, whether certain propositions deduced as theorems by Plato require its presence as an axiom, or whether recollection is itself a theorem deducible from the theory of forms (or even from the arguments for the immortality of the soul), which would deny it the status of an independent axiom. I do not believe that anyone has ever tried to formalize Plato's thought, and doubt that such an attempt could succeed, or that much would be gained if it did.

I propose to review the two principal passages in which recollection is discussed at some length, as well as the surprisingly small number of references to it elsewhere in the dialogues, and then to consider its relationship to the theory of forms and to the eschatological doctrines. I shall also want to show that because of the necessary role of sense experience as a sort of 'trigger' for recollection it also offers a partial solution to the problem of participation, the relation between sensed particulars and the forms.

The *Phaedo* version forms part of a series of arguments concerning the immortality of the soul. Some of them are persuasive, but in a way the pathos of the situation – it is Socrates' last day on earth – inhibits expression of the doubts his interlocutors undoubtedly feel about whether immortality has really been 'proved'. The doctrine of recollection is introduced as one that Socrates has 'often described' (72E), though there are only three or four other references to it in the dialogues. It is related to memory in the sense that for something to be remembered or recollected it must have been experienced before, but is distinguished from memory because of the quality of what is recalled. We have memory of objects and events experienced by the senses, and these experiences tell us, in the examples cited, if things are similar or dissimilar, or equal or not (74A). But we somehow infer from the imperfect and often unreliable perceptions of sense, which yield only approximations of similarity or equality, a notion of absolute equality (74D). Now that notion cannot be given by the senses, and so it must have some other origin, one prior to its being experienced by the senses (75A). And it is that prior knowledge that acts as a corrective and measure by which we validate the sense perception (75B).

We are hardly in a position at birth to be able to apply this knowledge, and may be said to have forgotten it, but later we are reminded by the particulars of sense (75E), and thus the process we call 'learning' is simply recollection of what we knew before (cf. *Theaetetus* 198E). That it is not memory is repeated at *Phaedrus* 275A and *Philebus* 34B; memory is the recalling of particulars – a friend's face or an article of clothing – whereas recollection is of the forms, those absolute ideas, real universals, that can be entertained only by the mind or soul. *Phaedrus* 250A puts the argument very succinctly, in the middle of the eschatological myth: '. . . every human soul has . . . had contemplation of true being; . . . but to be put in mind thereof by things here is not easy for every soul.' And *Meno* 98A expressly links memory at best to true opinion, but recollection is linked to knowledge. This qualitative distinction is, of course, what we have noted often enough before: an accumulation of particulars will generate an empirical concept, the validity of which is, strictly speaking, limited to the class of objects perceived (after allowing for misperceptions and other sources of error); such a concept can be applied only with some degree of probability (often a very high degree, approaching but not equal to certainty) to other objects believed to be members of the class. The form (e.g. of absolute equality or similarity) is not such an empirical concept; far from being corrigible by future experience it illuminates and corrects it.

The myth closes with the further argument that the soul, to have acquired this a priori knowledge, must have had a previous existence

(76CE) in which it gained its grasp of these and other absolutes, such as beauty and goodness; it is these which serve as patterns with which we can compare the imperfect copies encountered in physical experience. Having established the *prior* existence of the soul, Socrates ingeniously draws on a cyclical argument used earlier in the dialogue (70C–72A) which refers indirectly, but clearly enough, to the Pythagorean doctrine of the transmigration of souls, to show that before birth and after death are the same thing; it is in the period between incarnations that the soul acquires its knowledge of the forms. One last word on this: we have seen in the eschatological myths how Plato argues from the immortality of the soul to the immortality of the knowledge it possesses; here he argues the converse: from the knowledge to the immortality. It does not disturb me that the reasoning is apparently circular (tautological is the kinder word). What is troublesome, and leads to Frutiger's decision to treat this version of the myth as dialectic, is a question I must for the moment leave to the reader to puzzle out: which of these stories is the axiom (myth) and which the theorem (dialectic)?

Meno is bothered by what he calls a 'trick argument' (*Meno* 80E): no one would inquire into anything, because either he knows it or not. If he knows it he need not inquire, and if he doesn't he won't know what to look for. Socrates proposes to resolve this dilemma by showing that we already know the forms, but need to be reminded of them. They call a slave boy, presumably innocent of geometry, and Socrates invites Meno to listen carefully to be sure that the boy is only being reminded, not being taught by him (82B). By a process that a sterner judge might frown on, Socrates leads his witness through a demonstration of the incommensurability of the diagonal of a square with its side; and the further demonstration that the square on the diagonal is twice the area of the original square (82B–85B). Meno is certain that the boy has never been taught geometry (85E), and so he must have known it before his present existence. The answer to Meno's puzzle is that we do know, but also need to inquire in order to recover knowledge that we have forgotten. In much abbreviated form the same argument for immortality is repeated (86B) as we found in the *Phaedo*.

I think it is clear from these two accounts of recollection that without the perceptions of sense to stimulate recall of the forms there would be no such recollection.[9] There is no animus in Plato against the senses as such. In the *Republic* at VII, 523B ff., there is an interesting passage which distinguishes among sense perceptions some that 'do not provoke thought to reconsideration because the judgment of them by sensation seems adequate.' Others cannot be trusted because they give contradictory reports (the sort of phenomenon Socrates has in mind, apart from optical illusions, is, for example, if the hands are placed in containers of hot and cold water and then placed simultaneously into the same container of tepid water, the hand that was in hot water will feel cold and the other will feel hot, yet both are in water of the same temperature; cf. also the long discussion at *Theaetetus* 154B ff.). Somewhere between unproblematic reports of straightforward sense perception (this is my friend Flicka) and illusory reports that are unproblematic because they are obviously erroneous, are others that 'invite the intellect to reflection.' These are the perceptions that require interpretation; the issue is not what one is seeing – there is little doubt about that – but what does it mean? It is the stimulation of sense perceptions on thought that leads to recollection.

Phaedo 75E reiterates this: ' . . . by the exercise of our senses upon sensible objects [we] recover the knowledge which we had once before . . .' It is worth stressing this point as a corrective to the view, as much held by Plato's friends as by his enemies, that his mistrust of the senses is so profound, that the dichotomy between intellect and sense is unbridgeable. No wonder, then, that the problem seems insoluble of showing what the relationship is between particulars and forms. In the last analysis it is insoluble, I agree, but I would distinguish two kinds of insolubility: the one I reject says that because it is insoluble we are free to speculate about the reality of the forms uninhibited by the facts of sensory experience, because these are irrelevant – the forms are somehow discontinuous with the physical objects that are copies of them. That fathers on Plato the mysticism and intuitionism belonging to those interpreters. The kind of insolubility I prefer says instead that while we cannot specify in any definitive way what the connection is between forms and particulars, yet there *is* one such that we may not speculate in such a way as to run counter to the facts of experience. The divided line is after all a line, a continuous function; if Plato had not meant that image he could easily have invented a dotted or broken line, or a pair of isomorphic mountain ranges with an abyss between, or some other image – he is as good at imagery as anyone.

In the *Novum Organum* Francis Bacon has an elegant image that is apposite. Do not be an ant, he says, for ants heap up heterogeneous accumulations of fact, falsely imagining that coherence and order will of itself appear. Do not be a spider, he continues, for spiders weave a gossamer web out of their own substance, speculations without foundation in fact. Be a bee, he concludes, for bees gather from every flower in the world and, by a marvellous internal process, distil what they have gathered from the world into honey. Bacon, alas, did not follow his own advice, and remained a most indefatigable ant. That is something no one would ever mistake Plato for, but he is often taken to be a spider, full of baseless speculation. In fact he is a bee.

The doctrine of recollection is a myth invented as a possible solution to the problem posed by our apparently having the kind of knowledge that transcends the empirical.[10] It is possible to solve it without immediate involvement in metaphysical commitment either by treating universals nominalistically, or by treating axioms as conventions or theoretical constructs. Both doctrines, albeit in much less sophisticated versions than are now available, were considered and rejected by Plato, not so much on epistemological grounds, but, as I have tried to show in connection with the discussion of forms, because of the void that is left in moral and religious discourse. He is not prepared to separate facts from values.

III

The image of the sun (*Republic* VI, 508A–509D), the divided line (509D–511E), and the Cave (VII, 514A–517A) form a unity which I propose to treat in this section along with certain aspects of the theory of the tripartite soul (*Republic* IV, 434E–441C). Method and content are not easily separated in Plato, and so I shall be obliged to move across the somewhat artificial line that might be thought to distinguish them. Thus, while I have discussed the theory of soul in chapter 4, I return to it here once more because of the intimate connection, most clear in the divided line, between two of the three parts, the appetitive (sensuous) and the rational, and the dual realms of appearance and reality to which they correspond. The third part of the soul, the spirited part that is the source of courage, plays no part in these images; this is simply a matter of a different metaphor, not an inconsistency.

Between visibility, the capacity for being seen, and vision, the ability to see, there is a link, we are told (508A), and that is the light that illuminates the visible. The greatest such light is the sun, and it stands to the physical world of sensible objects as the good stands to reason and the intelligible world (508B). Without the light of the sun the eyes could not see, and things visible in principle, as it were, could not be seen. So, too, when the soul is fixed on 'the domain where truth and reality shine resplendent' (508D), it is capable of grasping that truth. Each of the forms is, of course, the truth and reality of the things subsumed beneath it, but what makes that truth accessible to reason and gives the knower the power to know, is the highest form, the good. And just as the sun is the source of the growth and nurture of physical things, so is the good the form of the forms, so to speak: '. . . the good itself is not essence [form] but still transcends essence in dignity and surpassing power' (509B). Lest Socrates be too carried away, Glaucon exclaims 'Heaven save us, hyperbole can go no further' (509C), another of the many warnings against being too literal in acceptance of speculations that outrun demonstrability.

Before we move to the divided line to which this image directly leads, it is worth noting the hierarchical structure of the forms foreshadowed here and made somewhat clearer in the divided line and in the later possible doctrine of elements, which stand to the forms as the forms stand to things. That doctrine of elements (*stoicheia*), while clearly traceable in the later dialogues between the *Theaetetus* and *Philebus*, is not identified as such by Plato.[11] As in the case of the theory of forms, it is to Aristotle, with his knowledge of the inner workings and debates of the Academy, that we must look. In the *Physics* (203a) he tells us of these higher-order elements by which the forms themselves are organized. Some of them are the great and small, the One and Being (*ousia*), similarity and dissimilarity, and others we have already encountered. There is no reason to doubt the accuracy of Aristotle's account, for we can infer from Plato's text the need of such higher-order principles. There is a minor problem of terminology to be noted in passing: it is not attributable to the practices of different translators into English who render *eide* and its derivatives into 'form', 'idea', or 'essence' indifferently, or even the overlapping translations whereby *stoicheia*, *archai*, and *eide* may be translated in ways that do not bring out connotations of rank order such as we are now addressing. The fault, if it is one, lies with Plato's unwillingness, already noted in other contexts, to fix upon a technical terminology. If the Greek were consistent in its usage, and if the terms were defined so as to be keyed to distinctly different meanings, it would be legitimate to expect the translators to take their clue from those specifics. But the text is deliberately vague because Plato is doubtful about the ability of language to convey this kind of meaning.

Nonetheless we can infer that something of this sort lurks in the language of the middle and later dialogues because it is demanded by the theory of knowledge emerging in that period. Here, in the image of the sun, we have only a hint in the brief passage cited above from 509B. I have discussed the hierarchy of forms of objects in the physical world in chapter 2: at the lowest level, to recall one example used there, we can easily see how from separate forms of tables and chairs, we can infer a form of furniture, and can go on from there to increasingly comprehensive forms finally encompassing forms of all physical objects. All of that is substantive in the sense I have applied to the myths in chapters 4 and 5: those increasingly comprehensive forms, like the eschatological and political myths, have a specific doctrinal content. But transcending them, as in these methodological myths, are principles of structure and organization that are to the substantive content of lower-level myths and ideas as algebra is to arithmetic. They are quite abstract principles to which nothing physical could possibly correspond. They are, to fall back on Bacon's image, the spider's work performed by the bee. This becomes easier to see in the divided line.

At 509D we are invited to envisage a line divided into two unequal portions, with each of the portions further divided into two sections in the same proportions. (The specification of those proportions has the mathematical consequence that the two middle sections are of the same length; this is probably fortuitous, but leaves the way open for arcane speculation by some commentators which I propose to ignore.) The upper and lower portions of the line correspond to the intelligible world presided over and illumined by the good, and to the visible world illuminated by the sun. The two parts into which the visible world is divided are, the lower (*eikasia*) which is perception of shadows or images, mere reflections of the objects of perception to be found in the upper section and the opinion or belief (*pistis*) we entertain about them. Those objects are plainly more real than their images or shadows.[12] The whole visible world stands in the same relation of image and reality to the intelligible world which, for its part, is likewise divided into first, higher-order images (*dianoia*, probable knowledge based on hypothesis) and second, the uppermost section, which is ultimate reality (*noesis*), the structure of reason in the realm of forms.

We are primarily interested in the upper half of the line. In its lower division, the third in the whole, Plato refers to mathematics which claims to be no longer concerned with any square or triangle which it can draw and look at, but with the abstract perfect square or triangle. But the hypotheses derive nonetheless from the visible figures; the hypothesis is a synthesis of particulars incapable of rising above itself:

This then is the class that I described as intelligible, it is true, but with the reservation first that the soul is compelled to employ assumptions in the investigation of it, not proceeding to a first principle because of its inability to extricate itself from and rise above its assumptions, and second, that it uses as images or likenesses the very objects that are themselves copied and adumbrated by the class below them . . . (511A).

The higher dialectic appears in the fourth or uppermost division. By its aid we are to rise above hypothesis and reach to the first principle itself:

. . . by the other section of the intelligible I mean that which the reason itself lays hold of by the power of dialectic, treating its assumptions not as absolute beginnings but literally as hypotheses, underpinnings, footings, and springboards so to speak, to enable it to rise to that which requires no assumption and is the starting point of all, and after attaining to that again taking hold of the first dependencies from it, so to proceed downward to the conclusion, making no use whatever of any object of sense but only of pure ideas moving on through ideas to ideas and ending with ideas (511B).

Dialectic is here reaffirmed as the science of reaching certain knowledge, if indeed we can satisfy its conditions, whereas geometry and, *a fortiori*, physics, being bound essentially to the visible world, remain in the third division. Physics, we know from the *Timaeus*, can be at best only a likely story, but it is a little surprising to find mathematics excluded from the highest division, which presently (511D) is called the correlate of reason in the list of faculties of the human mind which corresponds to this division. A tremendous dispute rages in the literature about this question, but I can find nothing in the text to support the view that Plato expected a programme of 'mathematiciz-ation' to solve the problems posed here about the foundations of mathematics. What mathematics offers is a model or metaphor of a process such that, *if* the hypothetical status of its presuppositions could be removed by being derived from logically prior and indisputable axioms, then mathematics would overcome the shortcomings signalled here. But the same is true of the higher dialectic of which mathematics is the metaphor. That is why I treat the whole account of dialectic, especially as it is embodied in these three images of sun, line, and cave, as a methodological myth. It would only be demonstrably true if it were demonstrated to be true. That this is not done, and cannot be done, has been shown in chapter 2. And in the final chapter I will contrast

Plato's myth of dialectic with rival myths that abandon truth in the Platonic sense as an aim of scientific method.

Plato's discussion does not tell us whether the human mind can in practice venture into the fourth division of the line at all. It is not unreasonable to conclude from the account of the soul and the necessarily imperfect union it forms with the body that the achievement of such knowledge is impossible. The jump from the third to the fourth division can never be made with certainty, or if made by one of those rare insights available to the saint, can surely not be explained by him to himself or to another, at least not by means of dialectic. It is open to myth to offer an attenuated form of explanation, and this is what Plato is doing here. It points the way, as I shall argue later, to a vindication of suprarational forms of art: while at its worst art is at the bottom of the lowest division of the line, mere image of an image, at its best it is at the top of the third division, an inspired hypothesis, unable to give an account of itself, such as, following the *Theaetetus*, would constitute true knowledge. But no epistemological doctrine, no matter how austere and rigorous, would be without its element of myth.

Immediately following the divided line, at the beginning of Book VII we have the myth of the Cave. We are to suppose men to sit fettered in a cave unable to look in any direction save at a wall on which are cast the shadows of objects moving between them and a fire behind them. As captives of sense they would be bound to take reality to be the shadows which is all they can see. If offered the opportunity of release most, being blinded by the brightness of direct vision of the light, would prefer the only reality they can tolerate.[13] Those whose eyes become accustomed to the light will see things as they are, but will be at a disadvantage if and when they return to the cave. First they will have again to become accustomed to the penumbra of reality in which their former associates dwell, and second, they will never again see things as they once did and so will be unable to comport themselves as the others do. They will not be able to defend themselves in law courts or argue about the shadow of justice when they have seen the reality. Men will be angered by the different perspectives of anyone who tries to impress a profounder knowledge on them, and if they can only catch him, they would put him to death (517A), a clear reference, one of several in the dialogues, to the fate of Socrates.

Even if we were to treat the divided line as an exercise in dialectic, this would be one of its mythic counterparts. There is a clear correlation between the parts of the line and the stages of the prisoner's liberation from the shadows of the lowest division. Unlike the ladder of beauty, which is another, and more rapturous, version of the myth of dialectic, the story of the cave contains some bitter observations, besides the poignant reference to Socrates, of the unwillingness of most men to search for the truth, and of the ease with which they may be swayed by demagogues. The philosopher who returned from the upper world, 'his imagined message articulate', as T. E. Lawrence said of the 40 000 prophets who wandered in the Arabian wilderness, would be mocked by his fellows. He would be no match for sophists skilled at explicating and naming the shadows (516CD); like Baudelaire's poet, the albatross sublime in flight but clumsy on the solid ground, he must be disaffected from common concerns, and sensing this, his associates' derision must soon turn to hatred. That only such a person is fit to rule, and that force will have to be exercised on the philosopher to make him return to the cave (520AD) is a tragicomic oxymoron of which only a great poet is capable. The image is laughable, but the mirth is Olympian, at our expense: at one level of irony it is wildly improbable, but at another it mocks the impotence of man to do the right thing because of the self-deception of denying part of his nature.

It is this, I think, that restores the place of the missing part of the soul to this section, and brings me back to *Republic* IV, 434E–441C. That passage, to which reference was made in chapter 4, is dense with methodological observations, most of which are reiterations of points already discussed in connection with the powers and limitations of dialectic. At 439E *thumos*, the spirited part of the soul, is enlisted on the side of reason (cf. 440E) as a kind of righteous anger directed to the curbing of appetite and its baser satisfactions. Here once more something like the charioteer of the *Phaedrus* (246 f.) appears; there he seemed somewhat ambiguous in his striving to balance reason against appetite, as though lowering the horizons of reason were the price of raising those of appetite. But here, at 440AB ff. we see the proper place of emotion in Plato's scheme: *thumos* is moral courage, apt to be likened to the auxiliaries and to true opinion that senses where the right lies and, even if it cannot be attained, maintains that faith in reason that perhaps in the last analysis represents the best we can do.

That is the noblest of myths, the conviction which is our principal heritage from the Greeks: however elusive *logos* might prove to be, the world is coherent, governed by rational principles sufficiently akin to those we find within ourselves that the quest for knowledge is intrinsically worthwhile. Its success is by no means assured; there is no foolish optimism such as animated later rationalists with the expectation that all problems, moral as well as epistemological, would presently be solved. Nor does this recognition of the limitations of reason fall on the side of scepticism, for all the critique of the foundations of knowledge we have examined. A middle position, closer to true opinion than to *episteme*, closer to *thumos* than to *logos*, is what we must accept. For beyond the best approximations we can attain is a vision of a perfection which, however unattainable in practice, shapes and directs our inquiry, and is a proper object of intellectual passion.

IV

It is that vision which the ladder of beauty (*Symposium* 210A–212A) expresses. We must accept at face value, I think, the sexual and homosexual imagery that lies on the surface of the text: the 'prescribed devotion to boyish beauties' (211B) means what it says, though it means a great deal besides.[14] Two things are being explained here: an epitome of the methods of acquiring knowledge of great abstraction such as appear in almost all the dialogues, and a passion founded in and kin to appetite that is ennobled as its object becomes more elevated.

The special role of beauty and its relation to the sense of sight lie in the background of the discussion. We have earlier noted as a commonplace of Greek literature, not confined to Plato, the privileged status of those senses that operate at a distance: sight and hearing. The latter is still inferior to sight (cf. *Republic* VI 507CD, and numerous other references) in part because, like the lower senses, hearing was thought to involve some contact with the source of sound through the medium of air. But the eye was thought of as the window of the soul, the bridge between sense and reason. To the Greeks 'I see' meant 'I understand' just as it does to us; the very word *theoria* is derived from vision. Of the objects of sight those that give the greatest insight are the beautiful ones. The beauty is one of the highest forms, a predicate of the One itself. All the forms are beautiful, we are repeatedly told, for their perfection, for being essences without admixture of the accidental, for being timeless and unchanging. Like goodness and truth, beauty converges on the One. But we must not rush up the ladder.

Not every sight is beautiful in that lofty meaning. We begin as we must, with that passion that seeks possession of its object. Spurred by the desire for generation, that passion is sexual in its origins, looking to sexual intercourse first merely to allay appetite, but then as a mode of acquiring immortality (as we have been told at 208E, a little before the myth, in one of many references to this theme). It is possible, of course, to remain fixated at these lower levels, to adopt a Freudian idiom, and those no doubt have their own satisfactions; but a sublimation lies before. Just as we have been told that there are other modes of assuring immortality, through one's works and public reputation, so there are levels of desire for beauty that transcend the sexual. Indeed, if we are to understand this passage, we must first see that the sexual imagery is a trope for the life of sense generally, so that desire for possession at thóse levels comprehends love of money and love of power as well: attachment to whatever rivets the soul to the body. And we must also note that our nature is such that we cannot rise to other levels without passing through these earlier and carnally rooted stages, even though these 'are only at the bottom of the true scale of perfection' (210A). I think we must understand the insistence on early 'devotion to the beauties of the body' (210A) which are 'prescribed' (211B), as being very much in line with what has been said earlier about the part played by empirical observation in the acquisition and development of knowledge. For better or worse our souls are incarnate, and we cannot rise to the higher forms of knowledge without the physical perception that, as we saw earlier, 'triggers' recollection.

That endowment of physical sense and desire, though an intrinsic part of our nature and not to be belied, does not exhaust it. For we may be led from the perception of the beauty of one person or thing to that of two or more (210B, 211C), and already the beauty becomes separable, as it were, no longer necessarily attached to the object. At the very least it first becomes an empirical concept, moving out of the second division of the line into the third, so that if one can take that step up the ladder, 'universal beauty dawns upon his inward sight' (211B). A further stage carries the initiate to the recognition, first of other forms of beauty not attached to persons or things, but to 'laws and institutions and learning' (210C, 211C), and finally to beauty's 'very self' (211D). By this time the attractions of the flesh have paled by comparison with a vision of beauty so austere in its perfection that we are brought close to what Spinoza called the intellectual love of God. For beauty is now seen to comprehend and unify the divine attributes of truth and goodness; and '*if* [my italics] it is given to man to put on immortality, it shall be given to him' (212A).[15]

This most ravishing of Platonic images feel into the hands of the neo-Platonists. Plotinus adopted it in the *Enneads* (I, vi, 3) and may be held responsible for what became of it, first among his direct followers, and finally in romantic versions. If one loses sight of the grounding of knowledge in perception, if only as a corrective to empty and uncontrolled speculation, then it follows by stages traceable in the subsequent history of this idea that empirical experience is irrelevant and that the limitations of rationality will breed irrationality. What I have called the epitome of the methods of dialectic, while plainly present in this myth, is so succinct that it is often overlooked, and it is taken instead by those intoxicated by its exquisite language as a mandate for irrationalism. For to those reading it in this light it would appear that discursive reasoning can at best bring us close to the goal, but ecstatic intuition, Plotinus' 'flight of the Alone to the Alone', can bring us closer, and so we can dispense with the tedious inhibitions of intellectual discipline. It has been a cruel misunderstanding that lays such a view at Plato's door: he offers no shortcut to instant insight, such as most of his friends and enemies impute to him.

He is as fallibist in his approach to the methods by which we seek knowledge as in the specific doctrines advanced. I have drawn together in this chapter many of the passages in which the methods of dialectic are surveyed with that aura of uncertainty that, together with the language in which they are couched, alerts us to their mythic status. For we can be no more certain that the structure of our knowledge, including the logic we employ, precisely corresponds with the structure of reality, than we can be sure that any particular proposition is true.

In dealing with the methodological myths I have tried to avoid the contentious areas that have given rise to a formidable literature. My concern is to find a middle ground, indicating only broadly where I disagree with the main lines of those disputes, so as to concentrate on the main thesis. It is enough for me to show that the forms and the other myths considered here are necessarily presupposed by Plato for his epistemological and other purposes, not whether he is right or wrong from some other perspective.

Thus I conclude with a speculation about Plato's doctrines that can only hesitantly be ascribed to him. If I am correct about his fallibilism as a tragic view of the incorrigible flaw in human knowledge, it surely follows that we must always return for such confirmation of our loftier insights as experience can provide. Where this confirmation is impossible (and *because* it is ultimately impossible), we must guard against the irrationality of reifying our metaphors. Kant was certain that Newton had settled physics once for all; Lord Kelvin would not countenance any physical theory that could not be displayed as a mechanical model; Einstein could not accept the notion that God might play dice with the world. Plato did not have before him a history of the shattering of such powerful images to reinforce the caution that is nonetheless implicit in his position. But it is only implicit. Surely these methodological myths show that observation of the physical world is indispensable as a point of departure. Do they not also show that we must return to that world to disconfirm those of our hypotheses that will not survive? I think so, and believe that to be the meaning of the lines quoted from *Symposium* 212A a page or two above.

7   The Defence

The very term 'myth' has become so settled in the text and discussion of Plato that it would be artificial in the extreme to displace it if only to avoid misunderstanding. Yet, for Plato, 'myth' is neither what it meant in his own day or earlier, nor what it has come to mean in our own. I am as reluctant as Plato is to dignify the purely semantic question of what name to give to those features of his dialogues commonly known as the myths, as if finding some other term would solve the problems the use of myths addresses. All that it might do, and that would not be entirely useless, I admit, is to distinguish his usage from earlier and later meanings by assigning some other word to perform this complex task. It is clearly more important to analyze the usage than to coin the word, and coining words is notoriously easier than solving problems, and so I have been content throughout this essay to follow Plato's example by using the term 'myth', along with a number of related terms, as he does. Those terms are made to refer to those passages in which he writes moral fables in elliptical language to reinforce some point otherwise made more formally, or in which he embeds fundamental presuppositions which cannot be asserted as true because they are the indemonstrable axioms of his system. These two reasons for the presence of myths in his works are the basis for what I have been calling the weak and the strong defences of poetry respectively.[1]

The aim of this chapter, then, will be to show in what ways Platonic myth varies from those other usages, and what constitutes the two defences of poetry. It will not hurt to remind the reader in these preliminary remarks that Plato himself is not wedded to the word 'myth'. As shown earlier, he uses it more or less interchangeably among a dozen or more words, including the approximate Greek equivalents of story, fiction, fable, lie, tale, narrative, hypothesis, and so on. These are all homely words, without esoteric or technical meanings; the stories they refer to are introduced so diffidently, and in so marked a departure from the style and manner of the more rigorously structured dialectic, that criticism should have been disarmed. Instead it has been sharpened, mostly because the critics have grafted onto Plato's use of 'myth' meanings utterly alien to his usage and purposes. If we can clear that up it will be seen that a very coherent picture emerges, one not to be confused with the aims of much of the criticism directed against the myths. I hope also that it will not seem odd to display why there is a range of myths as wide as the entire spectrum of philosophical problems to which Plato attends.

The idea of religious, cosmological, and moral myths is so familiar from its counterpart in the Bible and other wisdom literature that it is not surprising that the scholars who see the Platonic myths in those areas do not see the political and methodological myths. And those who do see the political myths tend to see them as examples of a more recent and sinister tradition of myth-making stretching from Machiavelli to Rosenberg; they dismiss the religious myths as evidence of pre-philosophic and 'unscientific' modes of thought, and they do not notice the methodological myths. But for Plato there are irresoluble problems about the foundations of all these areas, including the foundations of the very logic and modes of discourse by which we address them.

I

In the section in chapter 2 on philosophy and literature I have tried to draw some distinctions showing how the content of expressive literature has been related to the more rigorous language of philosophy in several ways. Of these only the first involves myth in a sense still familiar and generally acceptable without any special problems. At that early, pre-philosophic stage, myth might be said to be innocent: it tells stories of the creation and governance of the universe, locates man's place in it, and recounts exemplary deeds of gods and heroes. Its origins are dim in antiquity, transmitted by a mostly oral tradition, and surrounded by religious rites and beliefs that place it beyond question. No distinction is made among historical fact, legend, fantasy, science, morality, or chronology. What makes it innocent is that early myth is not consciously contrived; it seems oblivious to the random juxtaposition of great wisdom and equally great ignorance.

When myth departs from this state of innocence, and especially if it is made subordinate to some ideology, usually religious or political and often for a sinister purpose; if it should take on the aims of propaganda; if it 'manages' the news by selecting, suppressing, or investing the facts to correspond to some predetermined programme; if its appeal is emotional rather than rational, which is inevitable, or reinforces some impulse to irrationality, which is worse – under all these circumstances myth is rightly suspect. There are, of course, two suspicions lurking in what has just been said, and they give rise to different sorts of objection. It is not just outright lies that are suspect, though that is the easy part of the argument. Conscious contrivance is almost equally suspect, and here our misgivings are somewhat different from the objections that Plato raised against the Sophists, for not every product of contrivance is necessarily deceptive or self-serving.

We still have not resolved in our own minds the problem that Schiller addressed in his celebrated essay 'On Naive and Sentimental Poetry'. He traced his early intuitive hostility to Goethe to recognition that they were poets of two different types. Goethe was a 'natural phenomenon', the naive poet whose thoughts come to him with the spontaneous and inexhaustible flow of the tides, or perhaps in Goethe's case, of Niagara Falls. The sheer prodigality of his output, which seemed to pass directly from imagination to paper without conscious thought, offended an artist of the other type. Schiller identified himself as a sentimental poet, one whose labours to shape and polish his thoughts cost him tremendous effort; he worked, he said, 'with the critic looking over his shoulder', conscious of the effects he wished to produce and nicely calculating whether the intractable material of language had finally yielded the meaning he sought to impose on it. The story must be abbreviated here how Schiller gained the insight that led him to validate the mode of composition of both types. It was when Goethe was talking to him about the *Urpflanze* (primeval plant) that the epiphany occurred. Among Goethe's manifold interests were some pre-Darwinian notions of the differentiation of species from early prototypes, and he had sketched a plant the morphology of which was such that variations of one or other of its key features might lead to species apparently unrelated to each other, but derivable from the prototype. 'That is no plant, 'Schiller exclaimed, 'that is an idea!'

From this he corrected his analysis of the naive poet. The genius that permits the production of each to be of high quality is independent of the mode of composition, since there can be good and bad poets of each type; thus the doubts he had of his own poetic vocation attributable to his self-consciousness could be resolved. He goes on to see the poetic typology as a special case of a broader psychological typology,[2] in which realists (naive) see the world differently from idealists (sentimental), and so generate radically opposed philosophical perspectives. We may wonder why these poets make an unexpected appearance as paleo-botanists, and perhaps also challenge the validity of any analogy between the creativity of poets and that of scientists and philosophers, and we shall return to those questions in due course. For the moment, however, we must stay with the poets.

The objections that Plato directs against them are, in large measure, similar to Schiller's discomfort with the naive poets. It would go too far to attempt some sort of psychological analysis of Plato and so, without certifying a diagnosis, we can at least identify some of the symptoms. When Plato complains about the poets he is addressing two features: the process and the product of their efforts. The process, in a word, is the poets' 'madness'. So strong a term reflects the misunderstanding and even hostility that we find as much in Plato as in Schiller as a result of the substantially different processes by which naive and sentimental poets produce their works.

Naive poets are adherents of what might be called the 'magical' theory of creativity which seems to rely on intuition and inspiration. They are oblivious to whatever extraordinary inner transformations of experience unfold in their work, and are as astonished as any other observer at the product. Sometimes they will not even acknowledge a link between antecedent experience and their work, but are convinced that it transcends experience and has some source beyond themselves, divine or supernatural, but in any case impenetrable. Nor do they wish to explore how or whence inspiration comes, for fear that the bloom will be off and inspiration dry up. They prefer the spontaneity and passion of their own work to the calculation and coldness of their rivals'. And they are convinced that their work implies more than it says, and in any case much more than they consciously intend.

What the sentimental poet thinks of his deuteragonist we can gauge from Plato's criticism, and it is a rather more ambiguous judgement than would emerge from a simple inversion of the misunderstandings. The familiar part we need hardly repeat at length: the irrationality of the process, its disclaimer of authorship, as it were – I referred earlier to the poet who sees himself as 'amanuensis to the Muse'; the willingness to allow that the work might bear *any* meaning ascribed to it; the casual admixture of beliefs to be condemned as immoral – 'casual', because we cannot yet see in this either the justification of those beliefs, or a doctrine of art for art's sake.

But the evidence does not all run against the poets in the dialogues. Among the more foolish things done in the course of this study was to count and appraise the actual references to the poets. There are, for example, 142 quotations from Homer, 32 from Hesiod, and seven from Pindar. Further references to the poets increase those numbers, but it would be too boring to pursue these numbers in detail, so I choose Pindar as representative and manageable. Of the 13 references to him, four are critical (one because Asclepius, son of Apollo, could be bribed; three because Pindar vests justice in the powerful as a law of nature); the others are either favourable ('Pindar and many another of the poets who are divinely inspired' – *Meno* 81B) or neutral, tags added to lend colour and allusiveness to an argument. Hesiod does not fare so well by a small margin, and Homer slightly worse. In all cases, the majority of references are used, much as we might quote Shakespeare, as part of the way any cultivated person draws on literary allusions to illustrate a point: it refers to the argument and not to the author.

When he is not rebutting explicitly offensive doctrines, Plato is on the whole respectful of the role of inspiration. He himself elaborates no theory of poetic creativity such as first begins with Aristotle, and so we can only infer what he thinks. The poets are mad, ecstatic, possessed, oracular, and the like, and the source of their utterance is possibly divine; what they say cannot be rejected out of hand for that reason, and because Plato had his own uses, consonant with the religious practices of his day, for the mysterious interventions of the gods. But when the poets say things that are immoral, especially about the gods, they report falsely. Where their utterances are cryptic, as so often, the real burden is interpretation, just as it is of the oracles. I take this to mean, as earlier suggested, that Plato was aware, surely from his own experience, of how mysterious the process is that prompts the juxtaposition of images, the organization of elements of experience into new structures, and the formulation of explanatory hypotheses to make sense of discrete data. His work is full of imagery of all kinds: similes, metaphors, analogies, isomorphisms. That we all think in similar ways is plain; But the gift is unequally distributed. Aristotle said of it: 'It is the one thing that cannot be learnt from others; and it is also a sign of genius, since a good metaphor implies an intuitive perception of the similarity in dis-similars.'[3] There can be no question of Plato's genius by this or any other definition but one can only lament that he wrote no poetics of his own.

The gift, of course, is not confined to poetry, but extends to all fields in which imagination and creativity are needed in order to make experience coherent. We shall need to return to this theme later; for the moment I leave it with the observation that for Plato inspiration may propose, but reason disposes; it is the naive poet's uncritical and undifferentiated acceptance of his inspiration that is offensive, not the fact of inspiration itself.

Unlike the baffling process, the product of the poets' efforts is publicly inspectable, and so is easier to deal with; here, in a word, is the locus of Plato's charge of irresponsibility. Works of art (in which I shall want to include hypotheses of all kinds) may or may not have some intention or purpose, but they certainly have an effect, which may be moral, political, religious, or epistemological. To the extent that the earlier myths are the spontaneous overflowing of the collective unconscious, as Jung would have it, we should be very hard put indeed to ascribe a purpose; what we generally do is to infer one from the predominant effects. Much of the evidence for what I want to say now is in chapter 2, and so here I shall mostly confine myself to what I conclude from it.

One point that must be repeated, however, because it contrasts sharply with the much deflated esteem of poets in modern times, is the extraordinary role played by the poets in Plato's day. But we can correct for that if, in recognizing that the ancient poets were the physicists, cosmologists, moralists, legislators, politicians, religious leaders, and patriots of antiquity, we ask ourselves whether, despite our diminished interest in what poets have to say, we do not display as lively an interest as Plato's in the sayings and their consequences of this parade of worthies. We acknowledge the impact on the shaping of the popular sensibility, including moral attitudes, expectations, and public morale (confidence in self and in the effective and just ordering of society), of these publicists just as much in our day as Plato did in his. If we set to one side for the moment what action we might want to take against the propagation of beliefs we are sure are false or pernicious (action ranging from censorship to nothing at all), we surely keep open the notion that debate on their merits is proper.

What Plato is saying of these poets, and especially of the early myths, is that they have bad effects. They promote ignorance, stultify philosophic inquiry by surrounding falsehood with an aura of piety, and reinforce poor morality by exhibiting the gods as exemplars of the worst sort of misconduct. The imitation theory is of uneven importance: if artists produce copies at a third remove from reality, as he says, one can only hope that he meant only to castigate a failure to pierce the surface of appearance;[4] that he does not like men playing the parts of women is partly a matter of the theatrical conventions of his day (a convention abandoned in England only since the Restoration, and still maintained in many cultures, of which the Japanese Noh drama first comes to mind); but chiefly it is part of the tribute Plato pays to art in acknowledging its impact on the general public. It is the moral, religious, and political arguments that are the most important.

So long as the modern reader understands the attack on the poets in the narrower sense we give to that term, Plato is bound to appear reactionary and to be associated with the dreary history of censorship since his time, together with the distortions and propagandistic lies that ensue on the inevitable abuse of the authority vested in the censors. It might be unkind but not cynical, I hope, to suggest that the poets have so little influence in modern times compared with that exercised by Plato's targets, that they hardly seem a worthy target. Outside of the socialist people's republics and to a lesser degree in a number of other tyrannies nobody much minds what the poets say, and thus few hammers are flourished to crush those hermetic butterflies and hardly any sickles to crop the heads of a thousand flowers. But if we broaden the target to include a fair approximation to the groups Plato was attacking we find that our own institutions are not so far removed as at first appears in placing constraints on unlimited freedom of utterance. A strict comparison is impossible because of the substantially different institutions that have developed, but some of those institutions have their present shape largely in response to the issues that Plato has addressed.

Let us be as specific as possible. The modern rhetors are lawyers, journalists, politicians, admen, and other publicists, including lobbyists for various interests. Their task is to make their cause appear the better and, sometimes at least, it is indeed the better cause. But even good causes are undone for precisely the reasons Plato gives: the cynicism promoted when it is widely assumed, as it in fact is, that the publicist is indifferent to truth, but is charged to make the best case he or she can, regardless of the objective facts, where there are any. In certain cases we have developed laws, of which some of Plato's proposals are crude anticipations, to restrain the more obvious abuses of rhetoric. He was appalled by the ease with which juries can be swayed by practices we prohibit under the penalties for contempt of court; depending on the jurisdiction, one could cite a variety of provisions, with a common thread running through them, to limit freedom of speech concerning matters *sub judice*. Plato proposes some modest and unspecific constraints on malicious attacks on private individuals; this is a first move on something altogether novel in his day, but we have elaborate and often confusing laws of libel to limit or forbid the kind of utterance that led, among other things, to the death of Socrates.

The balance that Plato sought in preventing the interests of one class from destroying the rights of others is reflected in his concern for due process and the governance of laws rather than the tyrant's whim. We translate this into a variety of constitutional provisions – limited monarchy or sovereignty, bills of rights, the separation of powers (especially the independence of the judiciary), and the right of the individual to sue the Crown or State (only in some countries, and a novelty of this century). We require in some jurisdictions the registration of lobbyists, and the public declaration of private interests where a conflict might arise; and judges frequently recuse themselves. Since advertisers would tell any lie to promote adulterated and shoddy goods, considerable limits are set to their freedom of speech; and lawyers and other professionals are held to slightly higher standards by the canons of ethics almost universally adopted. Laws against blasphemy hardly exist now, save in the Soviet sphere, where almost any divergence from the party line is a crime; but in most other advanced jurisdictions, even where there is an established church, what is now prohibited is language tending to incite hatred or contempt of other religions or races, divisiveness in pluralistic societies having become a major problem that Plato could hardly have anticipated in the more homogeneous societies he knew.

My point in raising these matters is not to prove that Plato was or would have been a democratic centralist and civil libertarian, rather than the totalitarian he is made out to be by some of his critics. For all I know he might have developed into an extreme right- or left-winger, or into Bertrand Russell or Karl Popper in a later incarnation. What I do think it reasonable to argue on the available evidence in the dialogues is that his attack on the poets (which obviously includes the various publicists mentioned) is a critique of the effects they have on the public, and that no modern society, including the most temperate, has hesitated to place constraints where those effects are seen to impair the rights of others and, more broadly, the public interest.

I turn now to some ideological problems, which will bring us closer to the myths. The shaping of public opinion, which plainly underlies much of Plato's concern with the arts of persuasion, does not involve matters of fact as such. It reaches in a rather more amorphous way to questions of morale. By this, as indicated above, I mean whether a society is on the whole satisfied that its institutions function effectively, whether the inevitable discrepancy between its ideals and the perceived degree of their actualization is bearable or, to put it another way, whether expectations founded on those ideals are reasonably fulfilled. To the extent that there is an unbearable discrepancy, or disaffection in a society, we find a primary source of instability. One example close to ourselves and to Plato springs from what observers ancient and modern might agree to call the acquisitive society. It measures its goods by the material standard of living, which in itself is not necessarily a bad thing, but it often goes sour in ways not far from Plato's analysis of appetite. Among the arguments are some very straightforward and contemporary-sounding ones: that appetite is insatiable, that today's luxuries are tomorrow's necessities, that desire for further acquisition is the easiest of all appetites to whet, and especially if coupled with inequalities in society, is corrosive for the envy and hatred it excites. The sublime Parkinson has written that 'Expenditure rises to surpass income', and from this it may be argued that the myth that material expectations can be satisfied is on the whole more pernicious than that they cannot, or that they are unimportant. It is a myth deliciously parodied in Huxley's *Brave New World.*

Another myth that Plato addresses is that of equality. Not equality before the law, which of all legal fictions is hardly contested by anyone, though nearly everyone recognizes the defects in practice ('That's a most interesting case you have, Mr Simpkins. How much justice can you afford?'). Even the idea that society has an obligation to compensate for such inequalities as arise naturally or beyond the power of society to prevent, leads to expectations unlikely to be realized in practice, and so to a destabilizing disaffection. Plato rather ingeniously displaces, in the myth of the metals, responsibility for those inequalities away from society to the gods. On the other hand, he takes a fresh and for his time startling view of the equality of women, chiefly for genetic reasons, but with a lively sense of the waste of human talent attributable to the rival and current myth of their inequality.[5] It is perfectly plain that people are not equal in their natural endowments, whether in strength and manual dexterity, intelligence, shrewdness, or psychological stability, as well as in even more obviously measurable attributes. A society committed to compensating those who fall short is more likely to suffer from a drain on its resources that it cannot afford, or to place suicidal limits on the rewards of superior performance. If it does not want to level down, it will call the rewards 'socialist incentive', manage the news so that nobody knows about the privileges of the new class, and soon pay an even heavier price of cynicism and malcontent when the news gets out anyway. I have in mind the special stores, carefully graduated according to the rank of the beneficiaries, available in all so-called people's democracies to party functionaries, ballet dancers, and sportspersons.

One more myth, and that will be enough of examples to illustrate this part of my thesis. It is the myth of progress, coupled with the notion that all human problems are in principle soluble by human means. The best argument in favour of the myth is the inhibition of inquiry and experimentation with change, some of which is demonstrably desirable, that is the consequence of rival myths defending received opinion and the conviction that the cure is worse than the disease. I do not want to repeat the rebuttal in chapter 3 of Popper's charge of Plato's hidebound hostility to change; it is quite clear that Plato is a radical reformer, and that charge is merely absurd. The part of the myth I want to pursue here is the elusive problem of the extent and limits of human capacity to solve human problems. There has been a noticeable shift in the popular acceptance of the myth, so that in recent years there is much talk of finite resources, lowered expectations, the impossibility of raising the standard of living of the Third World to that of the Los Angeles suburbs (or what passes for it in the movies). The ecologists and population explosion people have begun to capture the popular ear, and we may soon see the end of a myth that has held sway for over a century. For all his talk in the *Critias* and elsewhere about stable population and soil erosion, Plato does not really consider these questions in terms recognizable in a modern context.

The myth that chills is the tragic view of life, a position closely related to Marx' characterization of religion as the opiate of the people. I have noted Plato's opposition to it in some earlier remarks about the 'destiny-spinning' of Aeschylus and Sophocles, those Attic Augustinians, with their often bleak vision of man's subordinate role in a cosmic order dominated by gods progressing towards rationality at the pace of a mental defective. Plato speeded that process overnight, as it were, but the price of the new perfection of the gods was to heighten, if possible, the imperfection of man. All the great tragic figures commanding the heights of world literature confirm that judgement, from Job to Lucifer, that other lightbearer, the Christian Prometheus, from Faust to Ahab, Hamlet to Lear. Plato's attitude on this matter is very ambivalent. To the extent that such myths vitiate personal responsibility he is opposed to them; but he is often ready to transfer blame to the gods where he sees no societal solution of a problem.[6]

I have selected these examples more or less arbitrarily from the many that might have been discussed in order to illustrate two principal points. The first is that I am using the term myth as Plato uses it, not in its modern connotation of superstitious adherence to beliefs exploded by positive knowledge, but to refer to postulations of doctrines immune to demonstration or rebuttal by which we develop explanations of insoluble (if that is too strong, then 'unsolved') problems. It will not do to argue, as some of the scholars earlier cited have claimed, that the myths represent primitive solutions or hypotheses concerning problems that Plato either lacked the philosophical means to solve, or which he, or more usually they (I think especially of Hegelians like Zeller) have by now solved, or shortly will. If I have a *parti pris* on this question, and I am afraid I do and had better confess it at once, it is that these problems are indeed insoluble and we shall probably vacillate between rival myths as devotion to one swing of the pendulum leads to an imbalance to be corrected by adoption for the nonce of the other extreme. I cannot say too often that such myths are not lies (there is only one lie in Plato, the rigging of the marriage lotteries), but postulations of indemonstrable axioms; Plato never advances as truths propositions incapable of demonstration, nor does he fall back on 'self-evidence' as sufficient ground for belief, since he is systematically suspicious of propositions claiming to be self-evident.[7] I shall pursue this issue in greater detail in discussing the 'strong defence'.

The second principal point I would like to bring out is the very difficult one on which, I am bound to agree with many of his critics, Plato does not fare so well. To what extent is public opinion malleable, and who should control the instrumentalities by which it is shaped? Those who argue, Plato among them, that public opinion is substantially influenced by what the public hears, will obviously want some degree of control over public utterances, and will equally obviously want to exercise that control in the interest of their own views. The question is not clearly decidable, though Plato's views are clear. Everybody would agree that children are influenceable, hence the concern to make secular education non-doctrinaire. As concerns adults we have the testimony of movie and television producers that in order to maximize audience size they aim at the intelligence level of 11-year-olds; viewing the rubbish that constitutes the bulk of popular entertainment, this is not a joke, and not intended to be. Advertisers and political campaigners are convinced that they can affect popular judgement, though they like to temper their more extravagant claims by admitting that you can't fool all the people all the time, and so in the last analysis it is the quality of the product that sells it, not the advertising – that doctrine has the added advantage of permitting credit to be claimed and blame disclaimed at need. Overselling the product is a phenomenon allowed for, so that a relentless diet of propaganda may prove self-defeating – hence 'institutional' advertising which keeps the company's name before the public without any explicit message beyond that; mere 'exposure' or 'image-building' that improves the politician's 'recognition' is its counterpart, and in this respect baby-kissing is better than taking a stand on the issues because the one is sure to win votes and the other to lose them. On a broader plane the same issues are presented by psychological theories of conditioning, including its latest version, behaviourism.

Fortunately we do not base our institutions on the factual resolution of such questions. To the extent that the facts are unequivocal we place constraints on unlimited freedom of speech to protect ourselves against fraud and misrepresentation. In the political arena we try to neutralize the effects of undue influence by provisions for equal time and the like. But that is only the negative side of the argument. What do we do about the positive side, to assure a monopoly of the promotion of the truth? In the western democracies we do nothing, chiefly because we have institutionalized fallibilism and deny that anyone has a monopoly of the truth. The rival fallibilist myth that we adopt speaks of the free marketplace of ideas; if all views are freely heard, the true ones, or at least the better ones, will drive the false ones out. The repugnance that is felt for any form of censorship by fallibilists on that ground alone is, furthermore, reinforced by the actual history of censorship with its almost infallible record of suppressing the wrong things. So egregious has that record been that we are prepared to put up with any amount of bath water in order to save the baby.

Totalitarianisms of various persuasions pursue an opposite myth. It rests either on an assumption that someone, the Führer perhaps, or the Politburo, has the truth or the best approximation to it, or on the assumption that the vice of democratic institutions is the very fallibilism which undermines the will to action. On the whole Nazism has few intellectual pretensions and exploded itself, though at hideous cost to the rest of the world. Its apologists did argue against intellect and the endless debate that delays action under democracy, with arguments so nicely balanced that inaction or pallid compromise is all that ensues. Marxism, however, does make serious intellectual claims, at least as a theory, and of these the most important is that correct reading of the facts of history dictates the correct course of action. 'Scientific' Marxism therefore assures the determination not only of which forms of utterance are socially damaging (which may or may not be empirically determinable), but also which are socially desirable. Hence the enormous importance attached to control of the media, since the combination of knowing what is best for the people, together with the doctrine of conditioning, makes irresistible the conclusion that it is critical to have total control of what the people should hear. Left-wingers in the western democracies who complain that the media are under the control of the right wing are usually correct: it costs so much risk capital to float and maintain popular newspapers, magazines, TV and radio stations, that only the very rich can do so, and inevitably they tilt in favour of their own interests, restrained only by fear of losing a profitable audience if they are too tendentious. No such consideration seems to restrain the left wing when they have a monopoly of media control. Nothing can be more boring and uninformative than the controlled press – I am thinking in particular of the East German press.

These observations are more apposite to an appraisal of Plato's views than may at first sight be apparent. He is notorious for his ejection of the poets because they tell lies about the gods, which is a fair approximation of Nazi reasons for book-burning and of Soviet reasons for suppression of dissident or deviationist artists. And since he includes among the 'poets' others who affect public opinion, especially sophists, rhetors, and so on, whom we may take as the equivalent of the modern politicians and publicists I have been talking about, we face some of the problems just addressed. There seems to be a profound anomaly in his position if the interpretation I have proposed of his myths is correct.

In practice there is commonly an association between the two doctrines of malleability of public opinion and possession of the truth. Certainly where both are held it follows necessarily that control of public opinion in accordance with truth must be a political objective, and it is this that is held against Plato by Popper and Crossman, among others. But it is an equally familiar political phenomenon that control of public opinion may be sought by interests indifferent to the truth, but with a lively sense of what serves their own selfish purposes, and that is held against the sophists and demagogues by Plato, among others. These alternatives may indeed be the most familiar, but they are far from exhausting the possibilities. We must look at some of the intermediate positions if we are to understand Plato.

First, as to the control and manipulation of public opinion, the soundest doctrine is probably Abraham Lincoln's about fooling some of the people all of the time, and so forth. This can be reduced to the dreary aphorism that Honesty is the best policy, but he and I have something more moral in mind, and that is not to want to manipulate public opinion even if and to the extent that it can be done. Second, as to knowing the truth, it is possible to deny, as fallibilists do, that anybody knows the truth, without falling into total scepticism. A middle position is available: we do not know the truth, but we do know of some things that are false. At the level of simple fact ('this coin weighs three grams') we hardly have a problem, and can pronounce such propositions true without serious risk. But more complex statements give endless trouble: trying to say whether two things are alike or different preoccupies Plato because such terms depend on the theoretical context and purpose for which the question is framed and on what kind of explanation is sought.

That difficulty is most acute in just those areas I have identified as involving myths, presupposed as axioms are in order to render classes of discrete propositions coherent. The curse of these axioms, notably in ethics and politics, but also in epistemology, is that it is entirely possible to generate two or more equally coherent theories, inconsistent with each other no doubt, but more or less internally consistent, and correspondent with the available facts, or with some of them. That is exactly where we are with the beliefs I have called myths, and much of the public debate we engage in is simply about the adequacy and appeal of those rival myths. They can be partly tested by observation of their adequacy in experience, and some may disappear, though most of those I have cited seem to go on for ever.

Now if we combine any degree of belief that public opinion can be educated (or manipulated, depending on whether we approve or not) with the belief that some myths are false, then we shall want to limit public access to the proponents of false myths. That, I think, is the extent of Plato's dismissal of the poets who invent these myths, but he will have to let back in those poets, including himself,[8] who invent the desirable ones, that is those not false, or leading to unacceptable conclusions. That last clause is not as question-begging as it seems, since it can always be debated; I put it in because Plato is not a sceptic, and is sure, perhaps too sure, about many things that are undesirable or unacceptable in society. Readers must decide for themselves how good it is to shout 'Fire!' in a crowded theatre, to incite racial or religious hatred, or in wartime to spread alarm and despondency. Plato looked for certainty in such questions, as we do, but he did not find it.

II

It is time to draw together the many threads of the argument that will lead us to the defence of poetry, both weak and strong. Let me first repeat that 'poetry' must be understood very broadly to cover certain aspects of the whole range of Platonic concerns, just as 'myth' must be understood to extend over the connotations of the many words he uses more or less synonymously with it. Thus poetry will include, but certainly cannot be confined to, expressive, often lyrical, utterances in verse, rhymed and metrical or not. Even within that more familiar usage we shall need to stress the etymological origins of the word, that 'making' or 'shaping' which is close enough to *poiesis* to trace in English what is intended by the Greek. For what we can readily see is that the poetic impulse is a special case of the wider faculty of bringing a heightened sensibility to bear on common experience grown contemptible through familiarity, so that new light is cast on the banal, old things are seen in new ways, fresh structures displace habitual modes of explanation. That is what Rimbaud meant by his 'illuminations', and what Joyce meant by an 'epiphany'. There is no significant difference in the process that gives rise to such restructuring of the facts of experience by poets, moralists, scientists, and philosophers, if we are to credit the accounts given of the sources of their insights and inspiration by innovators in the most diverse fields.[9] There are undoubtedly differences of weight given to fact, emotion, mode of utterance, in the several fields; but these are relatively unimportant compared with the major difference between, say, poetry and the mathematical sciences. That difference is largely defined by the process of verification that must ensue to test the validity and truth of the insight, a process manifestly more rigorous in the case of mathematics than of poetry. But that *follows* inspiration and, as I have earlier indicated, reason is to dispose where inspiration has proposed. I shall no more neglect than Plato does the indispensable requirement of rational scrutiny of every possible scheme advanced by imagination, including, along with those of demonstrable value, the wildly emotive, those subjective to the point of insanity, and the flatly erroneous. But we are here first concerned with the origins of inspiration.

Its first characteristic is imagination. In one of the few passages in Plato that speaks directly to the question we find that the recalling and juxtaposition of images is firmly rooted in experience. When imagination produces mythical animals (*Republic* IX, 588C) it may take the head of a lion, the wings of an eagle, and so on, to imagine a creature to which nothing corresponds in reality, though each of its elements has been experienced. This distinction between what is directly experienced and the ability of the mind to arrange and structure that experience is at the heart of the problem of knowledge that Plato repeatedly addresses. If we hold in abeyance those ways in which imagination may lead us astray, by ascribing reality to those creations of imagination, we are still left with the array of discrete experiences perceived which have no meaning or coherence unless they are ordered.[10] The critique of misperceptions, such as we find in the *Theaetetus* and elsewhere, should not mislead us, as it has so many commentators, into supposing that Plato believes that knowledge is independent of empirical experience or, as Professor Havelock rightly puts it, that abstract ideas 'come gliding into consciousness on clouds of illumination.'[11] I have already argued, and do not need to repeat here, that Plato has little quarrel with the elementary facts of experience; they are the necessary but not the sufficient conditions for knowledge.

Here I need to emphasize what the mind makes of those facts; how it goes about its business, and how it seeks to verify its hypotheses. The standard of verification, as it appears consistently throughout the dialogues, is the effective functioning of a craft or skill. We believe that carpenters, flute players, and shipbuilders know what they are doing because we cannot long be deceived by their products; either their ships sink and their houses fall down or they do not, and Plato constantly uses these examples to contrast with the spurious claims of poets, sophists, moralists, and the rest, to know something comparable with what the craftsman knows. It is, perhaps, an unreasonable demand, because once we move from the fairly primitive levels of fact and function it becomes increasingly more difficult and finally impossible to find an objective correlate at the level of factual experience that would correspond in the realm of abstract ideas to the functioning house or ship.

But even more problematic than that is the difficulty of prescribing a rule for the structuring of knowledge. In the discussion in chapter 2 of the formal methods of dialectic I have argued for their indispensability as well as for their necessary inconclusiveness. Now I need to turn to less formal methods by which the mind makes its uncertain way to the patterns and regularities of coherence. Plato's writings are singularly rich in metaphors, analogies, models, and other tropes which seek to capture whatever simulacrum of reality they can. Analogy is of particular interest because of the explicit, if limited, resemblance claimed usually between something the structure of which is familiar and something else, less well understood, the structure of which is held to be the same or similar. At a certain level analogies cannot mislead because they are understood, even by the pupil when the analogy is used for pedagogical purposes, to be mere semblances. No actual one-to-one correspondence between the elements of analogue and subject matter analogized need be implied or understood; only, say, that there is similarity of structure in specified ways. We can certainly help a newcomer to the study of electricity by making the comparison with water pressure, the diameter of pipes, the volume passing a given point, and so on; provided that we stay away from finding electrical meanings for hot and cold water, and from watery meanings for diodes and condensers.

Perhaps another analogy will help to clarify what I mean by the weak and the strong defence of poetry. If one is trying to make clear what the relationship is among facts, laws, and theories in a way that is idiomatic for Plato's discussion, and showing the connection among the levels of abstraction and the decreasing degree of certainty as one rises in them, the following might prove helpful, first to illustrate the weak defence, but later to show something about the strong defence also.

In this impoverished-looking crossword puzzle:

Across	1. Point	Down	1. Embroider
	4. Oriental name		2. Labour org.
	5. Child		3. Vie

let the clues represent facts given about the world, and the answers represent laws, that is, explanations of the facts adequate to them. In the puzzle that will mean no more than that a synonym is to be supplied with a meaning near enough to the clue. In the world, what constitutes an 'explanation' will be much more complex, but that need not be pursued now, beyond the suggestion that I mean the relationship between fact and explanation to cover at least what is understood by 'correspondence' in the correspondence theory of truth: a proposition about the world ('there is a chair in the room') will be true if and only if there is in fact a chair in the room.

The clues are ambiguous, just as facts are in the world, and there may be several synonyms which 'correspond' in the required sense. If the clue to one across were 'headgear', then cap, hat, tam, fez, and no doubt others, would fit in the sense that they have three letters and are acceptably synonymous. All that can be said of these possibilities is that they are unconfirmed hypotheses, but there is a method for sifting them. What limits the choice is the further requirement that the answer selected must also supply letters that are parts of equally acceptable answers to the down clues in the puzzle. I mean this further requirement to represent the 'consistency' theory of truth – that is, a proposition will be true if it can be validly deduced from other propositions within a system. The correctly solved puzzle satisfying both requirements represents a theory that is internally consistent and correspondent with the facts.

Historically it has been the case that empiricists have generally been satisfied with the correspondence theory, and rationalists with the consistency theory. Kant fused these strains in his first *Critique*, his most succinct formulation of the shortcomings of each position being the celebrated 'Concepts without percepts are empty; percepts without concepts are blind.' His analysis of Plato near the end of the *Critique of Pure Reason* makes of him a rationalist, a charge accepted by Findlay, who apparently glories in it, and by Popper, whose own criticism of Plato it reinforces. Equally wrong, I think, is Stewart, who mingles the two systems so as to produce a fictional Kantian Plato, but that is by the way. What is to the point is that the conclusion has often been irresistible that if both sets of conditions are satisfied we are as close to truth as we can be, if we are not already in possession of it. Kant himself, for example, was quite confident that certain aspects of our knowledge – Aristotelian logic, Euclidian geometry, Copernican astronomy, and Newtonian mechanics – were in principle unimprovable; that all have had to be revised or abandoned bears some significant implications to which we shall have to return.

I shall have further uses for this crossword puzzle later on, when I reach the strong defence. For the moment, though, I employ it to argue that analogies of this sort have distinct utility at least as a mode of introducing someone first learning about theories to a mode of organizing concepts at several levels of abstraction into a coherent whole. What saves such analogies from being no more than invidious comparisons is that underlying them is a securer source of knowledge which disciplines and corrects the misapplication of the analogy, containing it within those limits beyond which it ceases to be useful or is even conducive to error.

It should be added that both similes and metaphors are low level analogies, usually confined to a single or a limited number of features held to be comparable. The formal difference between a simile (A is like B) and a metaphor (A is B) takes on importance only when the 'is' of a metaphor is permitted to assume ontological significance. Unfortunately philosophers are as prone to reifying their metaphors as non-philosophers, so that they are often seduced by the explanatory force of some particularly persuasive metaphor into supposing that it describes a literal truth. La Mettrie's *L'Homme Machine* exploited the sophistication of Newtonian mechanics to see man as a clockwork; Freud, in his early writings, had some sort of hydraulic theory reminiscent of Descartes' mental and physical fluids interchanging pressures in the pineal gland; and the current reifiers include those whose version of brain function is that of a complex computer. The modern use of the term 'model' has the advantage of alerting the user that only a metaphor is intended, keeping metaphysics out of it, the sort of thing that Professor Nagel means by 'logic without ontology'. It is a mistake I think it safe to say Plato never makes: his myths are always flagged as such; they are always surrounded, where such safeguards are needed, by such expressions as 'I am persuaded that the truth is something like this.'

Poetry is the making of metaphors, the structuring of knowledge. In Plato's methodology no distinction is drawn, as is commonly the case in modern times, between science and morality, religion and politics, metaphysics and art. All these converge at the last in a unitary scheme, a product of rationality as far as we can carry it. To the extent that the unifying principles can be established – and there is considerable doubt about this in Plato, as we shall soon see – the role of the myths is to act as a pedagogical device. Underlying metaphor in this sense is knowledge of a more formal kind such as dialectic is capable of expressing with great rigour.

In certain other ways, the weak defence of poetry is familiar enough. All it requires is recognition of the need to sugar the pill of unpalatable or difficult truth for those lacking in energy, intellect, or interest sufficient to master an available truth.[12] By straddling the realms of poetic and scientific discourse such stories take truth capable of precise expression and make them accessible to those unable to follow the rigours of strict proof.[13] Moreover, an element of emotional force is added, proper to poetry, but which is not wholly alien to the scientific enterprise. When we hear mathematicians speak of the elegance of a solution, or physicists of the awesomeness of some comprehensive theory, we are in the presence of an aesthetic experience that, to be sure, adds nothing to the proof, whatever it may add to subjective conviction. Such a defence remains weak, though, because poetry here must be subordinate to science, and one must always be on one's guard against the seductiveness of some elegant analogy or metaphor which appears to illuminate, but in fact misleads.[14] Not for nothing did William James alert us to the ugly facts that have slain many a beautiful theory. From a scientific viewpoint the poetry is at best superfluous, reminiscent of the 'confused knowledge' of which Leibniz and Baumgarten spoke: the first dim adumbrations of the poetic, succeeded and superseded by strict knowledge.[15]

The final pages of Miss Murdoch's essay (72 ff.) furnish an eloquent version of the weak defence. 'Art is a special discerning exercise of intelligence in relation to the real; . . .' she says (78). And again, 'But surely great art points in the direction of the good and is at least more valuable to the moralist as an auxiliary than dangerous as an enemy' (77). She is rare indeed among Platonic commentators by seeing that 'Plato himself supplies a good deal of the material for a complete aesthetic, a defence and reasonable critique of art' (72). Her eloquence is a reminder that although she confines herself to the weak defence, that defence is only relatively weak, compared with the claims I am making for the strong defence. Careful scrutiny of Plato's doctrine such as she has undertaken at least reveals what has not been plain to all readers: Plato's acknowledgement of the power of art in support of the highest ideals.

Nor does she neglect the fundamental distinction in all that Plato has to say about art. The great danger is to reify our metaphors, and allow ourselves to be so seduced by their 'aesthetic' qualities as to substitute them for the endlessly open inquiry that characterizes the scientific attitude, or for the committed faith that defines morality grounded in religion. She correctly cites Kierkegaard's distinction between the ethical and the aesthetic, and Tolstoy's narrower and all too well defined views on art in support of her interpretation of Plato. Thus she goes far to vindicate the notion that Plato himself supplies a defence of poetry, but not far enough, and as it seems to me, not quite in the right direction. For she presses on to the treacherous conclusion that 'A reading of Plato helps us to see how good art is truthful' (79). But this is too romantic to meet the austere standard Plato has set. It is not enough for us to be overcome by the conviction that in the presence of some supreme work of art, say the Mass in B minor, we are transported out of the realm of rational discourse into a realm of pure being. However convinced we may be privately of such an opinion, the requisite standard of proof can never be met. To hold otherwise is to lapse from Platonic rigour into Schopenhaurian *Ueberschwang*.

More generally, of course, the weak defence is not confined to the subordination of poetry to science, and indeed this issue is now more familiar in some of its other forms: the subordination of poetry to religious or political ideology. The *Index Librorum Prohibitorum* was fairly close to the spirit of Plato's moral strictures, a spirit that has hardly disappeared with the *Index*. Where matters of faith and morals are involved, a standard external to the work of art is available against which it can be tested. The censor can certify to his bishop that there is no doctrinal objection, and the bishop can in turn let the book be printed. Leaving to one side works of theology to which such tests are unobjectionable, it is their application to works of art that is part of the weak defence. There is a parallel argument in St Thomas,[16] in the questions concerning the relationship of faith and reason, that restates the essentially Platonic version: all sorts of matters will have to be maintained on faith that are demonstrable by reason, simply because many individuals lack the intelligence, energy, and opportunity to make those demonstrations their own intellectual property. For such people these truths are maintained on faith: intuitively, on higher authority, emotively, in any case non-rationally.[17] To the extent, then, that rationally demonstrable truths are available, and it is their authority that underlies the bishop's certification (not the other way about), we are in the presence of the weak defence. St Thomas goes further, however, and offers a version of the strong defence: since human reason necessarily falls short of the divine, even the most intelligent and diligent thinkers will have to maintain certain truths on faith alone; but that is something to be pursued later. This Thomistic version offers as valuable a model as can be found of all forms of the weak defence that claim a religious-moral foundation, if only because most others lack his sophistication.

Besides these, there are moral arguments of a naturalistic and non-religious persuasion, and there are those resting their claim on psychological interpretations of human nature relatively free of direct moral implications (including so-called 'value-free' ones). These echo Plato's concerns about the effect of art on conduct, and art will be bad if it violates what is taken to be matter of fact (or rationally demonstrable) about human behaviour. All the arguments concerning obscenity, blasphemy, and sedition depend on such claims and, where children are involved, even the most ardent civil libertarians soften their opposition to constraints on freedom of speech. Inevitably, Plato's arguments from imitation and the exemplary effects of art on the individual recur and, even when these claims are confined to the effects of bad art, the criterion of bad art will largely derive from observed or anticipated ill effects on conduct. But the claims are not always so limited and, notably in the political versions, positive benefits for society are supposed to accrue when art is shaped to a political end. The argument now shifts, as it does in Plato, from the limited pronouncement *nihil obstat* through several shadings all the way to outright propaganda.

Let me first eliminate from serious consideration here those forms of propaganda that depend on deliberate falsification of known facts. Nothing in Plato suggests that he contemplates anything of the kind,[18] and so that problem, serious as it is, does not concern us here. But we must address the notion of art as 'programmatic', that is, as embodying ideals and aims, representing these as something to be attained in the future, however short of them the present may fall. Several times in the *Republic* Socrates draws a distinction between the desirability and the feasibility of proposals under discussion, rejecting the argument that politically infeasible ideas should not be pursued, and holding the discussion instead to their desirability (e.g. *Republic* V, 472CD). In the *Poetics* Aristotle makes this approach much more explicit by asserting that art is not only the imitation of what is, but also[19] the imitation of what ought to be (the moral argument) and of what might be (a looser argument that covers imaginative speculations as well as the postulation of ideals). These are versions of Browning's 'A man's reach must exceed his grasp,/Else what's a Heaven for?'

Social attitudes do change, as much by the impact of works of art as by legislation or other forms of political discourse. What Plato and the many inheritors of this argument begin with is not just a critique of bad art. For that criticism, to the extent it is apt, reveals how powerful a weapon the arts furnish in shaping the sensibility of a people. Why should the Devil have all the good tunes? The arts can as well be enlisted in the service of politically desirable ends, as for example, in the myths of the metals and of the equality of women. Of course, not everybody is as good an artist as Plato, who offers his versions of the right sort of poetry in the myths, nor have they been as stunningly successful: Platonism passed almost intact into Christianity, which has had a long run, not altogether over yet. Of the attempts we might bear in mind, there are some notable failures. Those in opposition, whom I take to be assorted realists, have devoted themselves to a dreary *verismo*, miserable *tranches de vie* that assure us, sometimes quite successfully, of the pointlessness of existence and of all human endeavour. The ensuing depression constitutes a not particularly subtle defence of the status quo, whatever its intentions.

If there is anything even more depressing, however, it is the products of those who accept Plato's argument (or variants of it): boring morality plays, *drames à thèse*, and other works in which the screech of axe-grinding makes every other utterance inaudible. Socialist realism, with its positive hero and jejune upbeat aspirations, is a parody of Plato's expectations of art. But, in the abstract at least, it satisfies the requirements: in that long dawn before the dictatorship of the proletariat it falls to the Party, as holders of the most authoritative truth, to prescribe the norms to which an art work must conform if it is to embody correctly the ideals and aspirations of society. The results of this doctrine have been deadly,[20] as I venture to suggest all forms of the weak defence are likely to prove at the last.[21]

III

What I call the strong defence of poetry is quite another matter. Let us suppose that the poet's intuitions and epiphanies, whatever their source, have been subjected to the intense scrutiny exercised by Plato. Many of them must fail for reasons which include the grounds on which he condemns the poets: beyond the trivial and incoherent lie inspirations so embedded in idiosyncrasy or topicality as to founder for lack of wider application. And beyond those come visitations of the muse offensive because untrue to common experience, violative of some moral principle, or because inconsistency undermines some comprehensive goal within a system encompassing epistemology, politics, and religion. Most poetry will fail one or other of these formidable tests, but some will survive, and it is the status of this 'successful' poetry that remains to be examined.

It is successful, as any set of axioms is successful, not because it is true, but because it has explanatory power, is fruitful in generating consequences (theorems) that accord with experience and intuition, and forearms against experience not yet encountered. The difference in form between dialogue and the often lengthy passages mostly narrated by Socrates signals, in most cases, the transition from dialectic to myth[22] and therewith from a mode of argumentation and analysis that sets out to prove something as contrasted with passages aiming at persuasion by means of philosophical rhetoric. To the extent that persuasion is offered where proof is available we find only a recourse to the weak defence. But where no proof is available because axioms are to be advanced, Plato falls back on the oblique mode of poetic utterance which he variously calls myths, lies, fables, apologues, and the like. The common failing of philosophers, from which Plato must be exempted, I think, is not to draw this distinction at all. Often they are not even aware of the primitives in their systems, or treat them as self-evident, or appeal to commonsense, or otherwise bludgeon their readers into acquiescence. But Plato is clearly aware, painfully so at times, of the impossibility of advancing such propositions as though they enjoyed so secure a status.

The noble lie is not a lie at all, but a myth. A sort of fundamentalism in reverse leads writers like Popper to accept the stories at their literal meaning and to hate every word. Surely the fact that the myth is acknowledged as such should disarm criticism. Or at least, criticism should be brought to bear on what the story means, or why it is so curiously told. While the myths cover a wide range of subject matter and also incorporate methodological as well as substantive issues, those constituting the strong defence of poetry have something in common: they present the axioms of Plato's system.

His own methodology demands something of the kind. It is true, as I have argued in chapter 2, that Plato's dialectical methods attempt to demonstrate something positive in contrast with the tentative soundings of Socrates' negative dialectic.[23] The programme of the *Phaedo* (101D ff.) and *Republic* (VII, 533C ff.) hopes to remove the hypothetical character of principles of ever-greater generality, but at the last there must remain within any system of thought statements which are primitive, which cannot themselves be proven within that system.[24] Of course, it is not permissible to postulate any statement regardless of its implications. It must satisfy the logical criteria of consistency and empirical criteria by corresponding with the phenomena which it purports to explain. If it fails to do so, then it falls. If it does satisfy those criteria, it does not follow that the postulate is true. If it could be proven to be true, it would then become a theorem deducible from some logically prior statement which in turn might be axiomatic.

Let me return to the crossword puzzle analogy to illustrate these points. When both logical and empirical criteria have been satisfied, the temptation is strong to suppose that a given theory has hit upon the truth. But what would the consequences be of discovering that there is more than one set of answers that satisfies the criteria? Here, for example, are two solutions to the puzzle given earlier:

¹ N	² I	³ B
⁴ E	L	I
⁵ T	A	D

¹ T	² I	³ P
⁴ A	L	I
⁵ T	O	T

Dismal as they are, they are equally adequate to the clues and equally coherent in structure. There is no ground for preferring one to the other, or for saying that one is true. There might be other solutions, so far undiscovered, and there might be some ground for asserting one of them to be true; though from a methodological viewpoint this is improbable in the extreme. While the puzzle itself is trivial, it illustrates a situation current in science to this day. Among unresolved conflicts between rival theories are the wave and particle theories of light, the 'big bang' and 'steady state' cosmological theories, and, I am assured, certain contemporary theories in plasma physics. Apart from purely methodological problems like the formal undecidability of arithmetic

(Gödel's Theorem), the progress of science is vexed by empirical questions like Heisenberg's indeterminacy principle and the empirical interpretation of geometries. I do not wish to imply that Plato had any notion of these problems, but he certainly foresaw some of the questions concerning formal systems and their empirical interpretation that have meanwhile become much more complex.

The crossword analogy is useful to a point, but its limitations are even more useful. The pattern into which the answers are to fit is a plane (two-dimensional) figure of specified size. A more accurate analogy would refer to a diagramless puzzle, the size and number of dimensions of which are part of the puzzle to be solved. Most puzzles in English have a rule of symmetry such that, for example, a five-letter word in the top right-hand corner will have corresponding to it a five-letter word in the bottom left-hand corner if the axis of symmetry is a diagonal. But a more accurate analogy will recognize that, despite our fondness for symmetries, we cannot be sure that there is one or where in the pattern it falls. All the words in the answers given above are to be found in a dictionary, but when scientific theories are formulated new words may have to be coined (joule and farad are examples) because they arise from the internal consistency of a theory. It is a little like discovering that 'PRSKT' *must* be a Slovakian river island because that is the only word that fits: the logic of the 'must' is the logic of the theory, which will collapse either because no one in Slovakia has ever heard of such a thing, or because, like 'phlogiston' or 'orgone energy', not only can none be found, but their continued postulation serves no useful purpose.

Modern science is full of such fictions. Depending where in the logical structure of a theory they appear they may be conventions, theoretical postulates or constructs, or they may be inferred entities like pi-mesons, the evidence for which is either non-existent or highly circumstantial and ambiguous. What Plato could not have foreseen was that the life expectancy of scientific theories has become shorter not longer in the last few centuries, and even the most secure-looking parts of our knowledge have been shattered by the emergence of new theories to replace those collapsing under the strain of new data and experimental methods. What Thomas Kuhn calls a 'paradigm shift' is very close to Plato's thinking, except that the prodigious feats of imagination that lead to scientific revolutions extend in Plato to the restructuring of moral, religious, and political beliefs also.

It is very hazardous to speculate about what Plato would have made of the modern adaptations to the discovery that all systematic thought rests on indemonstrable presuppositions. He falls silent at the point where he made something very like that discovery for himself. His own programme, if we are to credit the strongly mathematical structure of his thought, aimed at modelling knowledge on geometry. He began with the conventional belief in self-evident axioms and was impressed by the astonishing coincidence between theorems deduced from them and the empirical state of affairs they predicted. So confident was he of the certainties of the geometrical method that he did not regard the empirical evidence as confirming the theory, but regarded the theory as a test and corrective of the empirical evidence. To the extent that the knowledge we seek in other areas could be so organized it, too, would become as certain as geometry. Hence the attachment to dialectic in the discussions of abstract terms in morality, politics, epistemology, and so forth. But this programme fails because geometry fails. He does not tell us so in much detail: beyond the passages around *Republic* 510/11 and 531/3, which deal with the hypothetical status of the foundations of geometry, we find almost nothing by way of exploration of the consequences. He falls back instead on hints of an esoteric doctrine which he will not commit to writing, and instead of mathematicizing ethics, he supplies the myths. We are no better off.

For there is no way out of the problem of the hypothetical status of first premisses, though there may be different ways of handling it, as indeed we find in a number of other philosophers. Somewhere in every such system the primitives are maintained on faith; they may be asserted dogmatically, or a cloud may be drawn over their status: they can be bracketed or adopted heuristically, with one degree or another of willingness to abandon them if something better shows up. What Plato does is to flag them in his myths, surrounded by many expressions of doubt and uncertainty, the doubt applying not to his own belief in them, but to the possibility of asserting them in any more affirmative way. They mark the transition between knowledge rationally demonstrable and true belief in Plato's system. They represent his version of Socrates' *daimon*, which stopped him when he was wrong, but gave no license for asserting the truth of indemonstrable propositions, even when he was not stopped. It may even be too much to claim that they qualify as true beliefs, because as Plato uses the term, true belief is only fortuitously true.

The strong defence of poetry lies just in the implication of these observations: every system proposed must contain some terms that are primitive, indemonstrable, asserted on faith; and because no rules can be given for their invention a touch of the poet is necessarily found in every such system. That Plato is 'a poet of the very first rank' Shelley has assured us in his own *Defence of Poetry* and, indeed, Plato has no peer for the richness of his insights, and certainly none for the spell he has exercised on every succeeding generation of thinkers. He knows that if the axioms are to carry conviction (beyond the tests of correspondence and consistency referred to above) it will be on grounds not themselves susceptible of proof. The difference between Plato and most other philosophers is the relative diffidence with which they are advanced. This undoes a lot of criticism predicated on Plato's alleged dogmatism. He is not beyond criticism, of course, but it had better be on other grounds.

Grote, for example, is sound when he charges that Plato's prohibition of dialectical debate with the young in *Republic* VII, 539B belongs 'to the case of Meletus and Anytus in their indictment against Sokrates before the Athenian dikastery. It is identical with their charge against him, of corrupting youth, and inducing them to fancy themselves superior to the authority of established customs and opinions heard from their elders.'[25] Grote's objection is valid because it points out an inconsistency within Plato's system; even if Plato changed his mind, he had no business placing words of self-condemnation in Socrates' mouth. But the broad charges of authoritarianism by Crossman, Popper, and others can only be taken seriously once the curious status of the myths is considered, as they do not. The basis for their disagreement is not the uncovering of an internal inconsistency, but the adoption of a rival myth, one preferring, for example, heterogeneity to homogeneity in society, speech and inquiry open to all, and the minimizing of distinctions of class or intellect in the exercise of citizenship. These are predilections I share, as it happens, but this is not the question here. Those who deny metaphysics are simply brother metaphysicians with a rival theory of first principles, as F. H. Bradley said.[26] And when Peirce sought to establish on what grounds he fixed his own belief in the scientific method, as opposed to authority, intuition, and the like, he acknowledged with an irony worthy of Socrates, that he loved science best and so took her for his bride.[27] Such candour is rare and apparently reserved to those with a sense of humour.

A more serious problem lies before. How are fundamental presuppositions to be justified? And what is their source? The history of philosophy is full of thinkers who have done a first-class job criticizing their predecessors,[28] but who then come forward with no less arbitrary versions of their own clear and distinct ideas for the reconstruction of philosophy in a new key. Occasionally, but only rarely so, is there some awareness of the essential arbitrariness of rival systems equally able to survive tests of internal coherence and adequacy to experience. I cannot do more here than mention some of the people who have not been dismayed by the existence of rival, but equally valid philosophies. Schiller moved from naive and sentimental poets to idealists and realists; Coleridge said that everyone is born either a little Platonist or a little Aristotelian; William James called these tender- or tough-minded, twice- or once-born; Jung relates them to his psychological types. Dilthey identifies three types of *Weltanschauung* and shows how different metaphysical systems are derived from them. Stephen Pepper traces the different philosophical systems to what he calls 'root metaphors', and Abraham Edel speaks of 'existential perspectives'. Not all of these thinkers believe that the differences among these types are unbridgeable, and we can guess that Plato would be among them.

He was brought to the brink of this question, and clearly saw some of the implications of the indemonstrability of axioms. He is unique among ancient philosophers in his acknowledgement of the problem of the status of axioms by placing them in the myths; and this makes all the more inexplicable the criticism directed against him on the grounds that myths are intended to deceive. As I have already pointed out before, 'myth' is a misnomer if understood in this sense. But it dies hard: a typical and in its context accurate definition is:

A myth is an account of some past event or process in a community, which is in some way a distortion of reality, and often based on irrational or even supernatural foundations, but which embodies in symbolic form valued norms or beliefs of that community.[29]

If Plato had used 'model' or 'simulation' instead of 'myth', perhaps he would have escaped some of that criticism; meanwhile he is punished for his candour, and for the conscious production of his myths, as though an unconscious myth, which is as likely to deceive its creator as anyone else, were preferable. Yet his candour has its limitations. He falls back on silence[30] as to the status of his ultimate beliefs. He shifts from dialectic to myth at the point where rational discourse yields to suprarational rhetoric, where theorem yields to axiom.

And this is where we can locate the core of the strong defence of poetry. If we could find evidence only of isolated myths serving an illustrative or anecdotal purpose (like the ring of Gyges, or the myth of the grasshoppers) then we could settle, as so many commentators have, for one version or another of the weak defence. But it is plain that we cannot explain the presence of the myths in such numbers and on such weighty topics in these terms. Plato does not have one myth for eschatology, another for epistemology, a third for ethics, and so on. What he has is a unified vision combining his deepest convictions in all these areas into a harmonious *Weltanschauung*. Underlying it is an explicit awareness that 'the highest things can be shown only by means of examples' (*Statesman* 277C) precisely because the principles they exemplify are insusceptible of demonstration. This is half of the argument, but not yet a defence of poetry.

What completes the argument are the two aspects of poetic creativity mentioned earlier: the source of the axioms, and the methods of scrutinizing them. The source is as much of a mystery to him as it is to us, consisting of a mixture of intuition and experience difficult to apportion between the two, though both are clearly involved. There is a reciprocal interplay between the two, such that speculation seeking to render the content of experience meaningful proceeds by a process of trial and error, not unlike the account of dialectic given in chapter 2. A mind steeped in the widest possible array of discrete experiences sees, or thinks it sees, possible connections among them that may or may not withstand comparison with other experiences that the hypothesis should include or exclude. Wider and wider applications of this process lead to explanations satisfying ever-increasing domains of experience. How does the mind do this? That is the mystery, one that Plato seems chiefly to associate with the poet's 'madness', toward which his earlier ambivalence has been recorded (*Phaedrus* 245A). This gift, or affliction, is attributed by him to the gods, which is one way of indicating our ignorance as to its source. But it is clear that it is variously distributed, so that while at one end of the spectrum the most prosaic of people simply do not see objects and events with the richness of detail and possible relationships to each other, at the other end the more gifted do. There is no intrinsic difference in the application of this gift in the subject matter on which the mind dwells; the results will vary, but the process seems to be the same whether what is sought falls under poetry, science, or morality.

It is not surprising, therefore, that the attack on the poets is not launched from this direction; Plato speaks respectfully, if sometimes dubiously, of inspiration, the source of which may be divine. Neither he, nor anybody else, could get very far in explaining anything without it; and his is the sort of superlative genius whose mind teems with images of the possible connections and interrelationships among things. The attack is on the results of the process: these are publicly inspectable and can be scrutinized for their consistency and truth to experience, and above all for their consequences. His concerns are still our own, as I have tried to show by reference to the problems of censorship and freedom of utterance. If we had clear evidence of a direct connection, say, between the amount of violence shown on TV, the degree of exposure to it of the young and impressionable, and the rise in crimes of violence, we should not hesitate to regulate the showing of violence in the public interest, much the way we restrict access to toxic substances. In the absence of such evidence we do not permit, in the western democracies at least, mere intuitions that there may well be such a connection to warrant such restrictions, chiefly because we mistrust the censors for even stronger reasons.

What Herbert Read called 'the innocent eye' and Paul Klee called 'the child's eye' also plays a role in the strong defence of poetry. What they attribute to the child, perhaps out of misplaced sentimentality, is a freshness of vision free of all preconceptions. It is contrasted with the banality of adult perspectives on the world in which new experience is dulled by being all too readily assimilated to antecedent modes of explanation. Imagination is blunted, if it was ever keen, by the absence of any disposition to view objects and events in a way open to new structures. Rather, what passes usually for the literal-mindedness of such adults is the mistaken assumption that the explanatory metaphors they have absorbed are literally true, and new metaphors are false and unsettling. This has almost nothing whatever to do with children – all the great geniuses in almost every field have been adults. The exceptions in music, chess, and mathematics are generally attributed to the fact that a special gift for the grasp and manipulation of purely abstract relationships is independent of the need to encounter and absorb an enormous amount of concrete experience in every other field. The gifted adult has the requisite combination of that depth of experience, skill in abstract relationships, and openness to innovation. To these one may also add the willingness to suspend disbelief, to entertain alternatives for the sake of seeing where the argument leads, as well as the resolution to abandon exploded hypotheses (cf. *Republic* IV, 437A) however seductively attractive they may otherwise appear.

In these terms Plato's system survives unmatched in subtlety and plasticity. All the great inventors, whether of philosophies, religions, the arts and sciences, display the same rigorous devotion to the facts of experience and the same qualities of imagination to devise a structure in which those facts can be accommodated. So long as the facts can sustain rival hypotheses, and so long as we lack univocal methods for the definitive confirmation (as opposed to the disconfirmation) of any one hypothesis, the status of those hypotheses will be that of inventions not discoveries of reality. Only a poet can do these things, and they cannot be done at all without the poetic drive. Plato is among the greatest of such poets, and in his myths is found his own defence of poetry. We should not be surprised that he supplied one for, as he says, 'We ourselves are very conscious of her spell' (Rep. X, 607C).

Notes

CHAPTER 1: THE ATTACK

1. George Santayana, *Reason in Art* (New York, 1934), 100.
2. Cf. *Laws* XI, 935E–936A, forbidding the holding up of a citizen to ridicule. No doubt Plato here had in mind the treatment of Socrates by Aristophanes in *The Clouds*. See also *Apol.* 18B–19C and *Phaed.* 70C.
3. *Laws* II, 654B: A man can sing and dance well only 'if he sings *good* songs and dances good dances.'
4. This shapes much of Iris Murdoch's argument in *The Fire and the Sun* (Oxford, 1977), to which I will return later; in this context, see 64–5.
5. Compare the discussion of *poiein* at *Charm.* 163.
6. Indeed, Plato says as much of Socrates (*Lach.* 188D): 'the true musician . . . a harmony of words and deeds
7. This is much like the 'infectious' theory advanced by Tolstoy in *What is Art?*
8. John N. Findlay, *Plato: The Written and Unwritten Doctrines* (New York, 1974), 109. Unless explicitly cited from some other work, references to Findlay, with page number, are to this important book.
9. H. S. Thayer, 'Plato's Quarrel with Poetry: Simonides', *Journal of the History of Ideas*, 36 (1975), 3–26.
10. M. H. Partee, 'Plato on the Rhetoric of Poetry', *Journal of Aesthetics and Art Criticism*, 33 (1974), 203–12. H. S. Thayer, 'Plato on the Morality of Imagination', *Review of Metaphysics*, 30 (1977), 594–618.
11. Cf. I. M. Linforth, 'Telestic Madness in Plato, Phaedrus 244DE', *Univ. of California Publications in Classical Philogy*, XIII (1944–50), 163–72.
12. Karl Popper, *The Open Society and Its Enemies* (London, 1945). Later references, abbreviated OS, will be to the 4th, revised, edition (Princeton, 1962).
13. If the arts are despised for imitating nature we must first say nature imitates too. And further we must recognize that the arts do not only copy the visible world, but ascend to the principles on which nature is built up; and further, that many of their creations are original. For they make good the faults of things, as having the source of beauty in themselves.

    This beautiful passage expresses one of the seminal ideas of the Romanticism that has led so much Platonic scholarship astray.
14. 'If [the sculptors] were to reproduce the true proportions of a well-made figure, do you know, the upper parts would look too small, and the lower parts too large, because we see the one at a distance, the other close at hand.' (*Soph.* 235E–236A)
15. Jane E. Harrison, *Themis* (1912; reprinted Gloucester, Mass., 1974), 328.

16. M. P. Nilsson, *History of Greek Religion* (2nd edn, Oxford, 1949), 3.
17. Jane E. Harrison, loc. cit.
18. Curt Sachs, *Die Musik der Antike* (New York, 1929), *passim*.
19. See also *Rep.* VIII, 561D: 'abandoning himself to the lascivious pleasure of the flute.'
20. A. E. Taylor, *Plato: The Man and his Work* (London, 1926; 6th edn, 1949), 110.
21. Taylor, op. cit., 29.

CHAPTER 2: THE INCONCLUSIVENESS OF DIALECTIC

1. No attempt will be made in what follows to enter the question of chronology. Rather, the broad agreement in the findings of Lutoslawski, Ritter, Campbell, and Robin will be taken as a point of departure. The Table given in W. D. Ross, *Plato's Theory of Forms* (Oxford, 1951), 2, shows both the agreements and the divergencies.
2. Popper, *OS*, Vol. I. See 34, 194, 309, and *passim*, as well as the valuable note on the Socratic problem, 306–13.
3. For an interesting variation on this theme, cf. Gregory Vlastos, 'Socratic knowledge and Platonic "Pessimism"', *Philosophical Review*, 66 (1957), 226–38.
4. J. Burnet, *Greek Philosophy from Thales to Plato* (London, 1914), 168–70. A. E. Taylor, *Plato. The Man and his Work*, (4th edn, London, 1937), 287, and *Socrates. The Man and his Thought* (New York, 1953), 26.
5. Julius Stenzel, *Plato's Method of Dialectic*, trans. D. J. Allan (Oxford, 1940), 16.
6. Richard Robinson, *Plato's Earlier Dialectic* (2nd edn, Oxford, 1953).
7. A. K. Rogers, *The Socratic Problem* (New Haven, 1933), 96. But a little later (108) Rogers does contrast 'Socratic ignorance' with the Platonic 'quest for "definition" [that] no longer meets defeat', a view on the whole shared by R. B. Levinson, *In Defense of Plato* (Cambridge, Mass., 1953), 633.
8. Perhaps we should not overlook 6) the sheer joy of dispute as a means of sharpening the wits of a young respondent. Cf. *Euthydemus* 275E, where Dionysodorus says: 'Now look here, Socrates, I prophesy that whichever the lad answers, he will be refuted.'
9. There is a curious revival in the *Parmenides* of a form of dialectic very like that attributed here to Socrates in the early dialogues, but quite unlike the 'Platonic' dialectic in the probably contemporaneous *Sophist*. In the case of the *Parmenides*, however, the method seems closer to Zeno's antinomies; at 128D Zeno is made to say that he does not try to prove the Eleatic position, but only to show that denial of the presupposition that reality is one, leads to even greater difficulties than its assertion. John Burnet, *Early Greek Philosophy* (4th edn, London, 1930), 313–14, uses this passage to prove the pre-Socratic origin of 'Platonic' dialectic!
10. G. Grote, *Plato and the other Companions of Sokrates* (London, 1865), I, 543.

11. Paul Friedländer, *Plato: The Dialogues, First Period* (New York 1958), 99.
12. Cf. R. Robinson, 'Plato's Consciousness of Fallacy', *Mind*, N. S., 51 (1942), 97–114.
13. I have in mind here the 'reversal' in *Protagoras* 361AC, and perhaps also the 'rout' of Socrates in the first part of the *Parmenides*.
14. There is no internal evidence in the dialogues; nor is there anything in Xenophon's *Memorabilia*, despite the wealth of detail, much of it quite trivial, about Socrates' life and habits.
15. Levinson, op. cit., lends some support for this view. Cf. 64, 66.
16. Popper, *OS*, Vol. I, 311, makes Antisthenes, the founder of the Cynics and a defender of democracy, the 'only descendant of Socrates', despite the contrary opinion of others whom he cites, 277. Léon Robin, *La Pensée grecque* (Paris, 1923), 183, on the whole agrees with this view.
17. For example, the sum of $\sqrt{2}$ and $\sqrt{3}$ is sufficiently close to π for the difference to be attributable to error of measurement.
18. Cf. Anders Wedberg, *Plato's Philosophy of Mathematics* (Stockholm, 1955), 48–9.
19. Unless, of course, 'truth' is redefined to reflect this change of status.
20. See the discussion of Findlay in Chapter 3.
21. Findlay, 178.
22. It is worth noting in this context that Kant was convinced of the finality of Aristotelian logic, Euclidian geometry, Copernican astronomy, and Newtonian physics. Cf. *Critique of Pure Reason*, B viii.
23. At 530B the uselessness of astronomical observation is stressed in favour of a 'genuine study' of the a priori logic of heavenly motions. 531B derides students of harmonics who 'prefer their ears to their understanding'.
24. This is bitterly illustrated in the Cave allegory in the reluctance of the philosopher who has made the upward journey to return, and his probable fate if he does so.
25. Cf. in this context, *Statesman* 277C: 'It is difficult, my dear Socrates, to demonstrate anything of real importance without the use of examples.' Compare the translation of this sentence, here by Skemp, with Cornford's freer rendering: 'The highest things can be demonstrated only by means of example.' Neither version is false to the Greek; Cornford's translation serves my argument better, while Skemp's is a warning against reading too much into the text.
26. R. G. Collingwood, *An Essay on Metaphysics* (Oxford, 1940), 155–61, denies this view strenuously, calling it 'a positivistic misinterpretation of Plato.' It is, at all events, a misinterpretation shared by Jowett and Campbell, Bosanquet, and Nettleship. The support claimed by Collingwood from James Adam in his edition of the *Republic* (Cambridge, 1902), II, 192, is limited to the meaning of *anairein*, and does not really extend to Collingwood's whole position. This is designed to show that 'removing hypotheses' does not aim at establishing true first principles, but that the purpose of dialectic is to aim at a *reductio*, whereby any and all hypotheses can ultimately be 'unsupposed' by showing that they lead to contradictions. This would tend to assimilate these passages to 'Socratic' dialectic; but Collingwood attempts no argument along these lines. He appears to be quite isolated in interpreting these crucial passages in this way.

27. The best account is given in W. Lutoslawski, *The Origin and Growth of Plato's Logic* (2nd edn, London, 1905).
28. Cf. *Letters* VII, 342A.
29. Compare *Phaedrus* 275DE with *Laws* VII, 811CE and X, 890E–891A.
30. *Gorgias* 522E–527E; *Phaedo* 107D–115A; *Republic* X, 614A–621D; *Phaedrus* 246A–249D. These are discussed in chapter 4.
31. Cf. *Laws* IX, 870DE, X, 904D, XII, 959B.
32. The point is even clearer at *Timaeus* 29C: 'But when [words] express only the copy or likeness and not the eternal things themselves, they need only be likely and analogous . . . '
33. Prodicus appears and speaks in the *Protagoras*.
34. Cf.Jowett and Campbell, *Plato's Republic*, II, 292: 'In Plato, at all events, philosophical terminology is incipient, tentative, transitional.'

CHAPTER 3:   HOW THE MYTHS HAVE FARED

1. Since this was written Robert Zaslavsky's *Platonic Myth and Platonic Writing* (Washington, 1981) has appeared. While valuable for what it does say, it suffers from the unusual contraints imposed by the author's insistence on limiting his treatment to passages that Plato himself refers to as *mythoi* (or derivatives of *mythos*). His reasons for doing this (11–15) are not persuasive and run counter to every other approach to the question I have seen.
2. John N. Findlay, 'The Myths of Plato', *Dionysius* 2 (December 1978), 19–34. The passage cited is on 19.
3. Francis Bacon, *Works*, ed. Spedding and Ellis (London, 1870), VI, 698.
4. Vico, *Nova Scienza*, 4th Dissertation.
5. Cf. *Gorgias* 523A: 'Give ear then, as they say, to a very fine story, which you, I suppose, will consider fiction (*mython*), but I consider fact (*logon*), for what I am going to tell you I shall recount as the actual truth.'
6. Among many references in Hegel, one must suffice: ' . . . the supreme merit of Plato's philosophy has sometimes been held to consist in his myths which are scientifically valueless, . . .' *Phenomenology of Mind*, trans. Baillie (London, 1931), 129. Paul Friedländer sums up this view, tirelessly repeated by Hegel's followers: 'Hegel interpreted Plato's myths as representing a necessary stage in the education of the human race, which conceptual knowledge can discard as soon as it has grown up.' (*Plato: An Introduction*, trans. Meyerhoff (New York, 1958), 209.)
7. Ludwig Edelstein, 'The function of the myth in Plato's Philosophy', *Journal of the History of Ideas*, 10 (1949), 463–81.
8. *Summa theologica*, Part I, Q. 1, Art 8.
9. Frutiger (221) loses patience with Stewart at this point in the argument, and complains of the 'hodge-podge (*fatras*) with which he has cluttered his book.'
10. One of the most brilliant treatments of this question is found in John Livingston Lowes' *The Road to Xanadu* (Boston, 1927), in which he traces all the imagery of *Kubla Khan* to Coleridge's antecedent reading and to the

commonplaces of contemporary poetry, in opposition to Coleridge's claim that the poem was given to him as an inspired whole.

11. Otto Apelt, *Phaidon* (Leipzig, 1923).

12. Josef Pieper, *Ueber die platonischen Mythen* (Munich, 1965): '... die wirkliche Aneignung der mythischen Wahrheit notwendig das Zusammendenken des geglaubten und des Gewussten erzwingt.' (44)

13. Pieper: 'Wer den Kern der von Platon erzählten grossen Mythen als Wahrheit akzeptiert, vermag das jedenfalls, nicht anders als Sokrates, nur zu tun *ex akoes*, auf Grund des Hörens auf jene gleiche Stimme, die auch das Ohr Platons selbst erreicht haben muss.' (33–4).

14. Paul Tillich, cited in *Religion in Geschichte und Gegenwart*, Vol. 4, 3rd edn, (Tübingen, 1957–62), 1267 ff: article on 'Myth'.

15. W. Willi, *Versuch einer Grundlegung der platonischen Mythopoiie* (Zurich, 1925), 13.

16. My own generalization is a little sweeping: Deuschle and Teichmüller treat the entire theory of the soul as mythical; and while a case can be made for considering the *Timaeus* mythical in its totality, this is increasingly implausible when applied to the *Phaedo, Republic,* and *Laws*, as Couturat does in *De Plat. mythis.*

17. On the other hand Zeller, as already noted, tends to treat the myths as a shortcoming of Plato's philosophical ability, and so he identifies as little as possible as myth. Brochard (*Les mythes dans la philosophie de Platon,* 18) takes a similar tack for reasons not so easily classifiable.

18. The best known such attempt, apart from Lewis Campbell's stylometry, is W. Lutoslawski's *The Origin and Growth of Plato's Logic.*

19. It is worth reproducing Couturat's list here, though not for the reasons that he established it. *Paidia* (childish game); *paizein* (to play); *humnos* (festive song); *humnein* (to celebrate); *dithurambos* (lyric poem); *enkomion* (eulogy); *onar* (dream); *enupnion* (vision); *eikon* (likeness, image); *plasma* (image, imitation); *plattein* (to shape); *epadein* (to sing an incantation); *chresmodein* (to prophesy); *enthousiazein* (to be inspired); *peithein* (to persuade); *pepeisthai* (to be persuaded); *pisteuein* (to believe). The English approximations I have supplied, like their Greek counterparts, may be used in many meanings, depending on the context.

20. As earlier noted, Zaslavsky uses a similar, but opposite criterion, in confining his consideration only to those passages in which Plato has used the word *muthos* and its derivatives. So intent is he on this excessively narrow criterion that he supplies an exhaustive concordance of these occurrences (dutifully arranged by person, number, case, mood, voice, etc!) to supplement Ast and des Places (*Platonic Myth and Platonic Writing*, 224–9). However, he has overlooked an occurrence of *mython* (genitive plural) at *Laws* X, 903B2.

21. L. Couturat, *De Platonicis Mythis* (Paris, 1896), 59. A. Döring, 'Die eschatologischen Mythen Platons', *Archiv für Geschichte der Philosophie*, 6 (1893), 475.

22. I am of course fully aware that what I here describe as a 'better model' is precisely the sort of circular tautology that Plato was hoping to overcome by rising to the 'best of the higher hypotheses', and will return to this point again, notably in connection with Findlay's argument. Here, however, I am

concerned, not with Plato's programme (which remained necessarily unrealized), but with the actual state of the text. Frutiger has gone astray by employing the linear model when it is a cluster that he needs, and that is in fact inferrable from the text.

23. Popper several times quotes or refers to this passage. On 37, having quoted it in full, even repeating Plato's emphasis 'except for what is evil', Popper continues with the non sequitur: 'In brief, Plato teaches *that change is evil, and that rest is divine.*' (Popper's italics.)

24. See his note 15 (8) to ch. 3 and text, p. 212; note 3 to ch. 4, p. 217; and note 7 to ch. 4, p. 219.

25. *Dialogues of Plato*, III, cxxvi.

26. Popper has overlooked *Timaeus* 19A, in the brief recapitulation of the *Republic*, which explicitly repeats the notion of upward and downward mobility, depending on merit.

27. K. von Fritz, 'Zur Frage der esoterischen Philosophie Platons', *Archiv für Geschichte der Philosophie*, XLIX (1967), 255–68.

28. Konrad Gaiser, *Platons ungeschriebene Lehre* (Stuttgart, 1963). H. J. Krämer, *Arete bei Platon und Aristoteles* (Heidelberg, 1959).

29. J. N. Findlay, 'The Myths of Plato', *Dionysius*, 2 (Dec. 1978), 19–34.

CHAPTER 4: ESCHATOLOGICAL AND RELATED MYTHS

1. *Phaedo* 107D–115A; *Phaedrus* 248A–257B; *Gorgias* 522E–527E; *Republic* X, 614A–621B.

2. K. Reinhardt, *Platons Mythen* (Bonn, 1927) says 'There is hardly one among his dialogues in which the realm of death is not mentioned.' (27)

3. B. Jowett, *The Dialogues of Plato* (3rd edn, Oxford, 1892); J. A. Stewart, *The Myths of Plato* (London, 1905), who, as noted in chapter 3, gratuitously adds a Kantian idiom.

4. Josef Pieper, *Ueber die platonischen Mythen* (Munich, 1965), writes from a Christian perspective. He cites (85) Walter Willi, *Versuch einer Grundlegung der platonischen Mythopiie* (Zurich, 1925) 13, who says that 'almost all that is mythical in Plato is somehow otherworldly', and Paul Tillich, *Religion in Geschichte und Gegenwart*, Vol. 4 (3rd edn), 363 ff. (article on 'Myth'): 'Myth is divine history. That is *the* definition of the word that cannot be abandoned'; moreover, 'it is not a literary, but a religious category.'

5. Karl Popper, *OS*, *passim*.

6. Popper, *OS*, I, 184.

7. E. Frank, *Platon und die sogenannten Pythagoräer* (Halle, 1923), 194–8, shows the extent to which Plato modified the eschatological myths to be consonant with the newly available discoveries in astronomy and mathematics, rather than simply following the classical versions.

8. *Laws* IV, 721C; *Symposium* 207D, etc.

9. *Symposium* 208D ff.

10. *Odyssey* 11, 489 ff., quoted at *Republic* III, 386CD.

11. Frutiger has relatively little to say on the content and philosophical objectives of the eschatological myths. But cf. 212–15 and 249–65. The latter passage is a painstaking review of the parallels between the imagery of Plato's treatment and his sources in Empedocles, Pindar, and the Orphic tablets.

12. Cf. *Phaedo* 107C. See also Pieper, op. cit., 39: 'Evil-doing does not end with the deed.'

13. St Augustine is more cunning than Plato, and promises resurrection in the flesh, but in prime condition, whereas Plato has the dead remain more or less as they were in life, even 'if limbs were broken or distorted' (*Gorgias* 524 BC).

14. Frutiger (213) denounces the attempts at 'harmonization' of the contents of the four myths as 'childish'. He has Couturat (*De Plat. mythis*, 111–18) in mind. The temptation to treat them as so many synoptic Gospels should not even arise. The most that it is proper to say is that they are not inconsistent with one another.

15. The remark is, of course, ironical, but so is Euripides. What validates my observation in the text is that although Euripides, along with the other tragedians, is to be expelled for singing the praises of tyranny, 'the subtle minds among them will pardon us' (568C). Plato knows what Euripides means, but is fearful that the audience will not.

16. Cf. *Laws* X, 904C, which offers a rare example of a mixture of free will and predestination.

17. Cf. *Gorgias* 525C, where those beyond redemption suffer 'throughout eternity the greatest and most excruciating and terrifying tortures . . . suspended as examples there in the prison house in Hades.'

18. Op. cit., 30, n. 2.

19. Ficino also thought so, and made this a commonplace of Renaissance interpretation.

20. Cf. the speech of Aeschines against Timarchus. Also, Pausanius' speech in the *Symposium* (180C–185C).

21. On the Socratic *daimon*, see chapter 2.

22. Taylor (*Plato*, 305) suggests 'founders of religion', but there is no warrant for such an interpretation of this difficult passage. There is a valuable, if inconclusive, article by Ivan M. Linforth: 'Telestic Madness in Plato, *Phaedrus* 244DE', *University of California Publications in Classical Philology*, XIII (1944–50), 163–72. Linforth rejects Taylor, Pfister, Delatte, and refers to Wilamowitz' bafflement. He also rejects the house of Atreus among others (Orchomenus, Proetides) which suffered such divine wrath, as well as Thompson's suggestion that the inclusion of a phrase from Euripides' *Phoenisse* (*palaion ek menimaton*) in this passage might be an allusion to this play. He points out that madness does play a role in the play, but it brings no relief. Instead he suggests that Socrates was here creating a myth with a specifically Hellenic background that, without reference to any known case, would ring a bell in the Greek mind.

23. Cf. Laws 719CD; 801BC.

24. Stanley Rosen, *Plato's* Symposium (New Haven, 1968), 169–73, quite correctly sees in Agathon's egoistical substitution of the product of his own imagination for an objective reality a powerful threat to Socrates' position.

This is indeed an anticipation of Nietzschean creativity, the kind of aestheticism to which Plato is most bitterly opposed.
25. Note the explicit reference to Aristophanes' 'halves'. That should have disposed of some quite unnecessary speculation in the literature as to whether Diotima (there are several possible candidates) really told Socrates the story. She would have had to know that Aristophanes' story would be told before Socrates' narration – a wise woman indeed! It is safe to take her to be a Socratic/Platonic invention.
26. Cf. *Enneads*, I, vi, 3.
27. P. B. Shelley, *A Defence of Poetry*. Note also that the famous remark that the 'poets are the unacknowledged legislators of the world', from the same essay, is likewise offered in direct answer to the distinction made by Plato.
28. Most recently reconsidered by Phyllis Young Forsyth in *Atlantis* (Croom Helm, 1980). This includes some review of the Platonic versions, chiefly from the perspective cited above (*Timaeus* 22E), but also argues that the *Critias* version of Atlantis is modelled on Syracuse and was a thinly disguised warning by Plato to Dionysius of what might happen to him. Let me also mention, with some regret, a recent (1981) television movie in which Captain Nemo, revived after a hundred years of suspended animation, goes in quest of the Atlanteans, who turn out not to have been revived at all.
29. Or at any rate a member of the Academy.
30. Cf. *Plato's Cosmology*, 230–9. Findlay's explanation is keyed to *Phaedo* 110B where the earth is compared to a ball made of twelve skins: The Dodecahedron 'was reserved for the shape of the Cosmos as a whole, or some many-faceted, many-coloured jewel set in the crystalline round of the Cosmos . . . ' (326). Where are the animals? That much we can answer: they are such further worlds, construed as living organisms, as the Demi-urge might have made.
31. Friedländer, op. cit., (204 ff.) treats this as a political myth, for example.
32. *Republic* II, 379; III, 391D; also II, 364 ff., where the poets are denounced for attributing evil deeds to the gods; similarly *Laws* II, 672B.
33. Compare this story with the discussion in the *Protagoras* 320C ff.

CHAPTER 5: POLITICAL MYTHS

1. Plato's dilemma, to which I shall return, is how to make the good for society acceptable to those who, in principle, cannot know what that is. Sometimes the imagery is medical: 'For if we were right in what we were just saying and falsehood is in very deed useless to gods, but to men useful as a remedy or form of medicine, it is obvious that such a thing must be assigned to physicians, and laymen should have nothing to do with it.' (*Republic* III, 398B; cf. also 382D).
2. In *Plato Today* Crossman comes close to combining both charges by associating Plato's position with those totalitarianisms in which, inevitably in his opinion, the élite is both convinced of the rightness of its dogmas and contemptuous of the ease with which ordinary people can be fooled.
3. For two very different opinions of this phenomenon, compare Karl Mannheim's *Ideology and Utopia* with Ernst Cassirer's *Myth of the State*.

4. Much of the criticism of this passage in the *Republic* is made to depend on the commentator's views of individualism, mostly as its history has emerged in the last 200 years. For more balanced treatments among the very large literature on this topic alone, two may serve to complement what is said here: Gregory Vlastos, 'Justice and Happiness in the *Republic*', in *Plato II: Ethics, Politics, and Philosophy*, ed. Vlastos (New York, 1971), 66–95; and Rudolph Weingartner, 'Vulgar Justice and Platonic Justice', *Philosophy and Phenomenological Research*, 25 (1964–65), 248–52.

5. 'The structure of the *Republic* rests entirely upon the homology between soul and state. And it must be a reading in Plato's sense when we see the final myth as the fulfillment of the entire construction: human soul, state, and cosmos conceived as three forms symmetrically placed around the same center . . . ' Friedländer, op. cit., 189.

6. Only one of the many references to heavenly conflicts is apparently favourable. In the surely ironical *Menexenus* Socrates says that Athens must be dear to the gods: 'This is proved by the strife and contention of the gods respecting her.' (237C)

7. Those reluctant to allow any 'democratic' leanings to Plato make Protagoras the originator of this myth. To those mentioned in the text we may add Nestle and Vlastos for Protagoras, and Friedländer and Cherniss against. I would supplement Friedländer's reasons (op. cit., 176) with reference to the passage in the *Phaedrus* (249B) which makes the soul's passage into human form conditional on some recollection of the Ideas.

8. For an ingenious examination of certain aspects of the *Protagoras* myth, treated as an inexact analogy to be closely analyzed for its aptness, see Renford Bambrough, 'Plato's Political Analogies', in *Philosophy, Politics, and Society*, ed. Laslett (Oxford, 1956), 98–115, esp. 101 ff.

9. Among the soberer examinations of this contested passage, see John Wild, *Plato's Modern Enemies and the Theory of Natural Law* (Chicago, 1953), 51–3. Wild ably defends Plato on the 'noble lie' as a mode of advancing the 'underlying sense of unity and a feeling of devotion to the common purpose' (52).

10. Levinson, *In Defense of Plato* (538 text and n. 96, 540) concedes too much to Popper by discounting *Timaeus* 19A as inapplicable 'to prove or disprove Plato's intention of elevating children of workers.' Yet the Greek is clear enough, and a random review of some translations (Jowett, Cornford, Bury, and in German, Kiefer) confirms that unworthy children of good parents go down, and worthy children of bad parents rise.

11. Among several recent articles, two are of particular interest. Christine Allen Garside, 'Plato and Women', *Feminist Studies* 2 (1975), 131–8, argues that sexual differences, while relevant to bodies, are irrelevant to souls, the education of which leads to release from the body. From this, she concludes, equal education follows. Julia Annas, 'Plato's *Republic* and Feminism', *Philosophy* 51 (1976), 307–21, is less persuaded of Plato's benignity, since he is not guided by any concern for women as such, but rather by the service each person renders the state. These are rival views about feminism rather than about Plato, in whose text both positions are soundly grounded.

12. Sir Ernest Barker, *The Political Thought of Plato and Aristotle* (London, 1918) takes the view most commonly repeated since. He recognizes the

analogy with animal husbandry (148) and finds it 'one of the most repulsive things in the *Republic* . . . that Plato should make his State a breeding establishment for the production of fine animals' (148–9). In a brief note on method (67), he finds the analogy inapt.

13. The appeal of Lysenkoism to Stalin, which ruined Soviet biology for several decades, may be explained in analogous terms, though human beings were not directly involved. If characteristics acquired by conditioning in one generation (e.g. frost-resistance in winter wheat) could be transmitted genetically to subsequent generations, might one not consider that having conditioned the first generation of young Communists, the rest could be bred?

14. Barker, op. cit., 176–8, while acknowledging that some commentators (e.g. Nettleship) see a philosophy of history in Book VIII, generally supports the view I am arguing here.

15. Friedländer links these stories not just to a broad Utopia such as the *Republic* might be, but to an interpretation of the *Menexenus* (and other passages) as Plato's 'reconciliation' with Athens, by postulation of its immemorial origins (202–3, 208).

CHAPTER 6:   METHODOLOGICAL MYTHS

1. Cf. the very similar argument at *Philebus* 15C.
2. Cf. *Republic* VII, 525B.
3. This is only one of the interpretations of an obscurely phrased doctrine. See G. S. Kirk and J. E. Raven, *The Presocratic Philosophers* (Cambridge, 1957), 367 ff.
4. Cf. *Cratylus* 440C.
5. See, for example, *Sophist* 246AC.
6. Cf. *Sophist* 259E.
7. See *Sophist* 247C, which agrees that some materialists in fact move in this direction.
8. There is a valuable discussion in J. H. Randall, Jr, *Plato: Dramatist of the Life of Reason* (New York, 1970), 191–2. Both versions are treated as mythical.
9. This claim is much debated. A. E. Taylor, *Plato: The Man and his Work* (4th edn, London, 1937), 136, 187, combines the stimulus of 'an arresting sense-experience' with an almost Humean notion of association.
10. 'This myth [*Meno* 85 etc.] is called on to safeguard the possibility of knowledge.' Paul Friedländer, *Plato: An Introduction*, trans. Meyerhoff (New York, 1958), 182.
11. Findlay's chapters VI and VII treat some middle and late writings as 'Stoicheiological Dialogues'. He of course acknowledges Aristotle's part in this terminology, but does not warn the reader how much is being imported into Plato that is not to be found there directly, even though it is logically needed and abundantly hinted at.
12. For a very clear account of the Line, see Thomas Gould, *Platonic Love* (New York and London, 1963), 94–8.
13. Compare the very similar image at *Phaedo* 82D–83C.

14. Gould's discussion in chapter 2 of *Platonic Love* is most direct and balanced.
15. For a different, but most ingenious approach, see Gould, op. cit., which builds up to a veritable *Liebestod* by the end of chapter 3 on Diotima. Iris Murdoch similarly argues that 'it is the whole Eros that concerns [Plato], and not just some passionless distillation.' (*The Fire and the Sun*, Oxford, 1977, 33.)

CHAPTER 7: THE DEFENCE

1. In contrasting the inchoate mystical leanings of Kephalos in Book I of the *Republic* with the eschatological myth of Book X, Friedländer says: 'On the first level, the myth is preparation for the dialectical path; on the second, it is a view beyond the limits to which dialectics can lead.' (Op. cit., 184.)
2. One, by the way, that is the basis of Jung's *Psychological Types* (London, 1930). The most familiar of these, quite close to Schiller's analysis, as Jung acknowledges, are introverts and extraverts.
3. *Poetics* 22, 1459a, 5.
4. Here and there Iris Murdoch acknowledges that Plato allows the artists to emerge from the fire into the sun: 'In a magnificent myth he at last frankly embraces the image and sanctifies the artist, while giving to the Forms a final radiant though mysterious role. There is only one true artist, God, and only one true work of art, the Cosmos' (op. cit., 49). She is speaking of the *Timaeus* as a myth in its entirety, 'wherein moral imagery and scientific speculation are remarkably blended' (50).
5. This theme is not confined to the 'digression' in the *Republic*, but persists in essentially the same terms as late as *Laws* VII, 804E ff.
6 He does this in the myth of the metals, and in several references to the drawing of lots, some of which have been cited in chapter 4. I do not have space here to document this more fully, but a very useful paper could be devoted to this point, which has been overlooked in the literature.
7. The ever-wise Friedländer comes to my aid again here: 'Since his myths are never to be understood *literaliter*, they are constantly ready to bring such 'mystical' interpretations back to the original concrete image. Thus Plato escapes the danger of a metaphysical dogmatism . . . ' (op. cit., 210).
8. Any number of commentators, including Grote and Findlay, conclude, correctly I think, that Plato would have to expel himself along with the other poets if no defence can be offered.
9. From the very large literature on this topic I cite only the following for the wealth of examples they include: Arthur Koestler, *The Act of Creation* (London, 1964): Jacques Hadamard, *The Psychology of Invention in the Mathematical Field* (Princeton, 1949); Brewster Ghiselin, ed., *The Creative Process* (Berkeley, 1952).
10. I do not want to import here, there being no foundation for it in the Platonic text, the rival claims of Gestaltists and some empiricists as to whether whole configurations are perceived, or discrete fragments. The Gestalt is to epistemology what deep structure is to linguistics: both imply some ontological claims of enormous interest and controversy; but one can stretch the Platonic text only so far.

11. Eric. A. Havelock, *A Preface to Plato* (Cambridge, Mass., 1963).
12. E. Zeller, *Philosophie der Griechen* (5th edn, Leipzig, 1922), allows that 'The myths appear where something is to be represented which the philosopher regards as true indeed, but the scientific demonstration of which surpasses his means' (II, 1, 581). Frutiger (op. cit., 219–20) correctly, I believe, rejects this approach (also adopted by Stewart, op. cit., 42–76, and by others, including Willi) as too narrow: it does not allow for those passages in which Plato chooses a mythical form for matters capable of dialectical demonstration. Zeller himself has acknowledged this (II, 1, 582, note 1) in commentary on the *Symposium* myth: 'the undertaking is only a description of Eros, a definition of the term that could just as well have been given in purely dialectical form, if artistic considerations had not led the philosopher to clothe his thoughts in a thin and transparent sheath.' Teichmüller (*Die platonische Frage*, Gotha, 1876, 91) attacks Zeller for this inconsistency. Little has changed since, with commentators placing what I call the weak defence (myth where dialectic is possible) in opposition to the strong defence (myth beyond dialectical limitations).
13. P.-M. Schuhl, *La fabulation platonicienne* (Paris, 1968, 21) offers a succinct version: 'The myths express in concrete terms abstract reasoning inaccessible to the vulgar.' L. Edelstein, 'The function of the Myth in Plato's philosophy', *Journal of the History of Ideas*, 10 (1949) 463–81, is similarly confined to the weak defence.
14. Popper, *OS, passim*. I cannot resist citing Hegel in this note on the same side of the question as Popper. 'The only form in which truth exists is in a scientific system' (*Phänomenologie des Geistes*, Hamburg, 1952, 12). Elsewhere (*Sämtliche Werke, Jubiläumsausgabe*, Stuttgart, 1927–40, XVIII, 179) Hegel complains that all that Plato gives us is the dialogue instead of 'a purely philosophical work, truly didactic.' Zeller, op. cit., 580, speaks for a whole school of rationalist philosophers: 'The Platonic myths almost always point to a defect in scientific knowledge', a defect they believe they have remedied.
15. 'The Platonic myth is . . . his first essay toward a new truth, the shaping of his first groupings . . . but in philosophical-conceptual terms it is still unformed.' So P. Stöcklein, *Ueber die philosophische Bedeutung von Platons Mythen, Philologus*, Suppl. 30, 3 (Leipzig, 1937), 3. On page 5 it is a 'preliminary stage of logos' ('*eine Vorstufe des Logos*'). At the other extreme is Findlay in his 1978 article previously cited – the myths are not mythic at all, 'but sober accounts of the geography of Being.'
16. St Thomas Aquinas, *Summa Contra Gentiles*, I, 4.
17. R. B. Levinson, *In Defense of Plato* (Cambridge, Mass., 1953, 64), affirms much the same thing: 'To the defense and reinforcement of these spiritual divinations, logical proofs are required to contribute as best they can. Reason and faith are thus enlisted in a common cause, and Plato does not always mark their precise mutual frontiers, something of "myth" creeping at times into his "logos," to balance the rational element that pervades so many of his avowed myths.'
18. Except, as previously noted, the passage at *Republic* V, 460A, which provides for the rigging of the mating lotteries so as to improve the breed of Guardians.

19. *Poetics*, 1451a, 36; 1460b, 10.
20. Zhdanov's words at the 1934 congress of writers aim at the 'historically specific depiction of reality in its revolutionary development. This authenticity and historical specificity in the depiction of reality should be combined with the task of ideologically reshaping and educating the toilers in the spirit of socialism.' (*Russkaya sovetskaya literatura*, Moscow, 1963, 316). For the theory, see C. Vaughan James, *Soviet Socialist Realism: Origins and Theory*, London, 1973. For recent practice see the moderately sympathetic *Beyond Socialist Realism* by Geoffrey Hosking, London, 1980.
21. In *Plato's Thought* (London, 1935) G. M. A. Grube limits himself to the weak defence: 'Only when [the nature of justice] is fully established does Plato go on to the myth of the day of judgment. The myth is not the main argument, it is only a story with a merely corroborative force for those who believe in immortality.' (157) There is just one hint of the strong defence: '. . . do not his myths represent, however dimly, truth which the human intellect . . . cannot reach scientifically' (204).
22. This should not be understood mechanically, as Frutiger has pointed out (op. cit., 19 ff.) Passages of narrative as long as a whole book (e.g. *Laws* V) are dialectical, not mythical; and some passages of dialogue are mythical.
23. G. Grote, *Plato and the other Companions of Sokrates* (London, 1865), was the first I think to speak of 'negative dialectic' (III, 240).
24. Cf. Norman Gulley, *Plato's Theory of Knowledge* (London, 1962), 43: 'Plato recognizes, moreover, the limitations of the method of hypothesis, and of human argument in general, as a means of establishing with certainty the truth of *any* postulate.' This claim, which I am convinced is correct, has often been rejected, most recently by J. T. Bedu-Addo, 'The Role of the Hypothetical Method in the *Phaedo*', *Phronesis* 24 (1979), 111–32.
25. G. Grote, op. cit., III, 239.
26. *Appearance and Reality* (Oxford, 1893), 1.
27. *Collected Papers of C. S. Peirce* (Cambridge, Mass., 1934) V, 247.
28. Plato is himself not above alluding to the doctrines of Empedocles, Parmenides, etc., as treating 'us as children to whom we tell a story' (*Sophist* 242C).
29. G. K. Roberts, *A Dictionary of Political Analysis* (London, 1971), 131.
30. Hence the famous remarks at *Letters* II, 341C and VII, 341C; these in turn have encouraged the speculations of Gaiser and Findlay, among others.

Bibliography

A. TEXTS

Plato: The Collected Dialogues, Edith Hamilton and Huntington Cairns, eds., New York, 1961. This is the best one-volume edition in English, translated by several hands. It is used throughout, save where otherwise indicated.

B. BIBLIOGRAPHIES

H. F. Cherniss, 'Plato (1950–1957)', *Lustrum* IV (1959), 5–308; V (1960), 323–648.

J. B. Skemp, *Plato* (Oxford, 1976).

R. D. McKirahan, *Plato and Socrates. A Comprehensive Bibliography, 1958–1973* (New York and London, 1978).

C. STUDIES OF THE MYTHS (Adapted from Frutiger, 287)

C. Crome, *De mythis Platonicis imprimis de necyiis* (1835).

A. Jahn, *Dissertatio Platonica* (1839).

G. Schwanitz, *Die Mythen des Plato* (1852).

J. Deuschle, *Die platonischen Mythen* (1854).

A. Fisher, *De mythis Platonicis* (1865).

B. F. Westcott, 'The myths of Plato', *Contemporary Review* II (1866), 199–211, 469–81.

R. Hirzel, *Ueber das Rhetorische und seine Bedeutung bei Plato (1871)*.

Volquardsen, *Platons Theorie vom Mythus und seine Mythen* (1871).

E. Forster, *Die platonischen Mythen* (1873).

P. Gregoriades, *Peri ton muthon para Platoni* (1879).

K. Thiemann, *Die platonische Eschatologie* (1892).

A. Döring, 'Die eschatologischen Mythen Platons', *Archiv für Geschichte der Philosophie*, 6 (1893), 475–90.

L. Couturat, *De Platonicis mythis* (1896).

V. Brochard, 'Les mythes dans la philosophie de Platon', *Année philosophique* XI (1900), 1–13. Reprinted in *Études de philosophie ancienne et de philosophie moderne*, 46–59 (1912).

J. A. Stewart, *The Myths of Plato* (1905).

W. Willi, *Versuch einer Grundlegung der platonischen Mythopoiie* (1925).

K. Reinhardt, *Platons Mythen* (1927).

P. Frutiger, *Les mythes de Platon* (1930).

P. Stöcklein, *Ueber die philosophische Bedeutung von Platons Mythen*, *Philologus*, Suppl. 30, 3 (1937).

L. Edelstein, 'The function of the myth in Plato's philosophy', *Journal of the History of Ideas*, 10 (1949), 463–81.
J. Pieper, *Ueber die platonischen Mythen* (1965).
P.-M. Schuhl, *La fabulation platonicienne* (1968).
M. J. Gregory, 'Myth and transcendence in Plato', *Thought* 43 (1968), 273–96.
V. Sease, 'The myth in Plato's theory of ideas', *South-West Journal of Philosophy* V (1970), 186–97.
S. Gaffney, 'Dialectic, the myths of Plato, and the transcendent in the world', Proc. of the Catholic Philosophical Assn. XLV (1971), 77–85.
G. Stormer, 'Plato's theory of myth', *Personalist* 55 (1974), 216–43.
J. N. Findlay, 'The Myths of Plato', *Dionysius*, 2 (1978), 19–34.
R. Zaslavsky, *Platonic Myth and Platonic Writing* (1981).

OTHER WORKS

J. Annas, 'Plato's *Republic* and Feminism', *Philosophy* 51 (1976), 307–21.
——, *An Introduction to Plato's* Republic (Oxford, 1982).
O. Apelt, *Phaidon* (Leipzig, 1923).
R. Bambrough, 'Plato's Political Analogies', in *Philosophy, Politics, and Society*, ed. Laslett (Oxford, 1956), 98–115.
Sir E. Barker, *The Political Thought of Plato and Aristotle* (London, 1918).
J. Burnet, *Greek Philosophy from Thales to Plato* (London, 1914).
——, *Early Greek Philosophy* (4th edn, London, 1930).
E. Cassirer, *The Myth of the State* (New Haven, 1946).
C. Cavarnos, *Plato's Theory of Fine Art* (Athens, 1973).
R. G. Collingwood, *An Essay on Metaphysics* (Oxford, 1940).
F. M. Cornford, *Plato's Theory of Knowledge* (London, 1935).
——, *Plato's Cosmology* (London, 1937).
——, *Plato and Parmenides* (London, 1939).
R. H. S. Crossman, *Plato Today* (London, 1937).
J. Dewey, *Art as Experience* (New York, 1934).
E. R. Dodds, *The Greeks and the Irrational* (Berkeley, 1951).
J. A. Elias, ' "Socratic" vs. "Platonic" Dialectic', *Journal of the History of Philosophy*, 6 (1968), 205–16.
J. N. Findlay, *Plato: The Written and Unwritten Doctrines* (New York, 1974).
W. Fite, *The Platonic Legend* (New York, 1934).
E. Frank, *Platon und die sogenannten Pythagoräer* (Halle, 1923).
P. Friedländer, *Plato: An Introduction*, trans. Hans Meyerhoff (New York, 1958).
——, Plato: *The Dialogues, First Period* (New York, 1958).
K. von Fritz, 'Zur Frage der esoterischen Philosophie Platons', *Archiv für Geschichte der Philosophie*, XIIX (1967), 255–68.
K. Gaiser, *Platons ungeschriebene Lehre* (Stuttgart, 1963).
C. Allen Garside, 'Plato and Women', *Feminist Studies*, 2 (1975), 131–8.
T. Gould, *Platonic Love* (New York and London, 1963).
——, 'Plato's Hostility to Art', *Arion*, III (1964), 70–91.
G. Grote, *Plato and the other Companions of Sokrates* (London, 1865).
G. M. A. Grube, *Plato's Thought* (London, 1935).
N. Gulley, *Plato's Theory of Knowledge* (London, 1962).

J. E. Harrison, *Themis* (London, 1912).

E. A. Havelock, *A Preface to Plato* (Cambridge, Mass., 1963).

G. S. Kirk and J. E. Raven, *The Presocratic Philosophers* (Cambridge, 1957).

H. J. Krämer, *Arete bei Platon und Aristoteles* (Heidelberg, 1959).

R. B. Levinson, *In Defense of Plato* (Cambridge, Mass., 1953).

I. M. Linforth, 'Telestic Madness in Plato, *Phaedrus* 244DE', *University of California Publications in Classical Philology*, XIII (1944–50), 163–72.

J. Livingston Lowes, *The Road to Xanadu* (Boston, 1927).

W. Lutoslawski, *The Origin and Growth of Plato's Logic* (2nd edn, London, 1905).

I. Murdoch, *The Fire and the Sun: Why Plato Banished the Artists* (Oxford, 1977).

M. P. Nilsson, *A History of Greek Religion* (2nd edn, Oxford, 1949).

W. J. Oates, *Plato's View of Art* (New York, 1972).

M. H. Partee, 'Plato's Banishment of Beauty', *Journal of Aesthetics and Art Criticism*, XXVIII (1970), 209–22.

——, 'Plato on the Rhetoric of Poetry', *Journal of Aesthetics and Art Criticism*, XXXIII (1974), 203–12.

——, *Plato's Poetics: the Authority of Beauty* (Utah, 1982).

J. Pieper, *Enthusiasm and Divine Madness: The Platonic Dialogue Phaedrus*, trans. R. & C. Winston (New York, 1964).

K. Popper, *The Open Society and Its Enemies* (4th edn, Princeton, 1962).

J. H. Randall, Jr, *Plato: Dramatist of the Life of Reason* (New York, 1970).

L. Robin, *La Pensée grecque* (Paris, 1923).

R. Robinson, 'Plato's Consciousness of Fallacy', *Mind*, N. S. 51 (1942), 97–114.

——, *Plato's Earlier Dialectic* (2nd edn, Oxford, 1953).

A. K. Rogers, *The Socratic Problem* (New Haven, 1933).

S. Rosen, *Plato's* Symposium (New Haven, 1968).

W. D. Ross, *Plato's Theory of Forms* (Oxford, 1951).

G. Ryle, *Plato's Progress* (Cambridge, 1966).

G. Santayana, *Reason in Art* (New York, 1934).

P. Shorey, *What Plato Said* (6th edn, Chicago, 1965).

H. L. Sinaiko, *Love, Knowledge and Discourse in Plato: Dialogue and Dialectic in Phaedrus, Republic, Parmenides* (Chicago, 1965).

R. Kent Sprague, 'Socrates' Safest Answer, *Phaedo* 100d', *Hermes*, XCVI (1968–69), 632–5.

J. Stenzel, *Plato's Method of Dialectic*, trans. D. J. Allan (Oxford, 1940).

A. E. Taylor, *Plato: the Man and his Work* (4th edn, London, 1937).

——, *Socrates. The Man and his Thought* (New York, 1953).

H. S. Thayer, 'Plato's Quarrel with Poetry: Simonides', *Journal of the History of Ideas*, 36 (1975), 3–26.

——, 'Plato on the Morality of Imagination', *Review of Metaphysics*, 30 (1977), 594–618.

W. J. Verdenius, *Mimesis: Plato's Doctrine of Artistic Imitation and its Meaning for us* (Leiden, 1949).

L. Versenyi, 'The Quarrel between Poetry and Philosophy', *Philosophical Forum*, II (1970–71), 200–12.

G. Vlastos, 'Socratic Knowledge and Platonic "Pessimism"', *Philosophical Review*, 66 (1957), 226–38.

G. Vlastos, 'Justice and Happiness in the *Republic*', in *Plato II: Ethics, Politics, and Philosophy*, ed. Vlastos (New York, 1971).

——, ed., *Plato. A Collection of critical essays*. Vol. I: *Metaphysics and Epistemology*. Vol. II: *Ethics, Politics, and Philosophy of Art and Religion* (Princeton, 1973).

A. Wedberg, *Plato's Philosophy of Mathematics* (Stockholm, 1955).

R. Weingartner, 'Vulgar Justice and Platonic Justice', *Philosophy and Phenomenological Research*, 25 (1964–65), 248–52.

——, *The Unity of the Platonic Dialogue. The Cratylus, the Protagoras, the Parmenides* (Indianapolis, 1973).

N. P. White, *Plato on Knowledge and Reality* (New York, 1976).

J. Wild, *Plato's Modern Enemies and the Theory of Natural Law* (Chicago, 1953).

F. Yartz, 'Infinite Regress and the Sense World in Plato', *South-West Journal of Philosophy*, 6 (1975), 17–28.

Zeller, *Philosophie der Griechen* (5th edn, Leipzig, 1922).

Index Nominum

Index Locorum